HARAMBEE COUNTRY
A Guide to Kenya

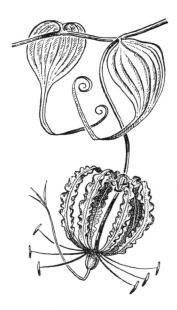

The Gloriosa Lily

Harambee Country

A Guide to Kenya

A completely revised and up-to-date
edition of *The Lion and the Lily*

by

KENNETH BOLTON

With specialist chapters by:
S. O. AYODO
D. R. M. STEWART
PEREZ OLINDO
JOHN G. WILLIAMS
H. F. STONEHAM
H. B. SHARPE
SYDNEY DOWNEY

Foreword by
MALCOLM MACDONALD O.M., P.C.

GEOFFREY BLES · LONDON

© 1970: KENNETH BOLTON (Section One)
© 1970: GEOFFREY BLES LTD. (Section Two)

SBN: 7138 0266 9

Printed in Great Britain
by Richard Clay (The Chaucer Press) Ltd
Bungay, Suffolk

Published by
GEOFFREY BLES LTD
52 Doughty Street, London, W.C.1
36–38 Clarence Street, Sydney 2000, N.S.W.
353 Elizabeth Street, Melbourne, C.1
246 Queen Street, Brisbane
CML Building, King William Street, Adelaide
Lake Road, Northcote, Auckland
100 Lesmill Road, Don Mills, Ontario
P.O. Box 8879, Johannesburg
P.O. Box 834, Cape Town
P.O. Box 2800, Salisbury, Rhodesia

Foreword

by MALCOLM MACDONALD, o.m., p.c.

Kenya is a beautiful, fascinating and important country. Its beauty springs partly from the unusual variety of landscapes contained within its comparatively small space. Its luscious tropical coasts bordering the Indian Ocean, its cooler yet generally sunny highlands climbing to the almost incredible phenomenon of perpetually snow-capped Mount Kenya rising alongside the Equator, its wide areas of cultivated farmlands (incidentally including more brilliantly flowering gardens than bloom in almost any other country), its austerely lovely, if rather arid, semi-desert, its string of lakes strewn along the floor of the fabulous Rift Valley and its untamed pastoral regions are just a few of its variations on the theme of Nature's divine beauty.

As for Kenya's fascination, I need mention only one feature. In its National Parks you can watch the everyday life of countless sorts of wild animals with extraordinary intimacy. In those splendid reserves one passes as close to herds of elephants, prides of lions, groups of giraffes, parties of ostriches, troupes of zebras, families of rhinoceroses, flocks of storks, mobs of flamingos, and multitudes of other species of birds and beasts as one can to crowds of human pedestrians in the city streets of Nairobi.

Under the leadership of the great President Mzee Jomo Kenyatta, black, white and brown peoples are living contentedly side by side in a not only multi-tribal but also multi-racial nation which—if it continues to prosper—can be a model of harmonious human friendship for all the rest of mankind.

I could write much more about that attractive country, its characterful peoples, and its significance. But no one is better qualified to expand on the subject than Kenneth Bolton, who has lived and worked in Kenya for many years, who as editor of its influential daily newspaper *The East African Standard* has made (and continues to make) a fine personal contribution to the peaceful, co-operative progress of its mixed population during difficult, historic and promising times, and who commands the

Foreword

trust and friendship of Africans, Europeans and Asians there alike. *Harambee Country* describes very well many varied aspects of Kenya and the Kenyans. It is an excellent account of them—an admirable guide for residents, visitors and students alike. I am happy to introduce to them this instructive and enjoyable book.

Preface

When it was decided to produce a revised and up-to-date version of *The Lion and the Lily*, it was scarcely realised how much amendment and enlargement would be needed.

Kenya attained independence a year after the original book was published. So much has happened in the succeeding eight years that the more my co-authors and I worked on the revision the more it became evident that very nearly a new book would be required, using the warp and weft of the old pattern.

While the country's scenic features, the lakes and mountains, have remained unaltered, as have the wildlife and other tourist attractions, the whole concept of living and the ordering of everyday affairs has been transformed.

Gone are the colonial Government and the colonial outlook, even though some legacies lurk around. Fresh ideas, political, economic, social, have started to work. The physical counterparts can be seen in the skyscraper hotels and office blocks rising among Nairobi's older buildings.

Two chapters—I and VII—have been added, while entire passages have been rewritten and enlarged in the others; for example the long account of Kenya's national economy, using the latest available statistics, and the new chapter on the Security Force. Also, there are extra illustrations.

The first chapter sets the scene of the Kenyatta Era, introducing some of the politicians who played parts in the drama before and after independence, but I have tried to keep the subject-matter non-political beyond the narrative of events.

The chapter on sport reviews the astonishing achievements of Kenya's Olympic stars; and describes other sports and pastimes; such as fishing in the trout streams and at the Coast, and playing golf with an inquisitive lion on the fairway. For almost any oddity can happen in this enchanting country and often does.

In the Specialist Section, there are contributions, replacing the old, from the ex-Minister for Tourism and Wildlife, Mr. "Sam" Ayodo, who writes on the policy of the Ministry; Dr. D. R. M.

Preface

Stewart, who is Head of the Game Department's research division and writes about wildlife and its conservation; and Mr. Perez Olindo, the Director of the National Parks, describes the parks he administers.

The ornithologist, Mr. John G. Williams, and the professional hunter Mr. Sydney Downey, have very kindly revised their own contributions.

Unhappily, since the original publication, Lt.-Col. Stoneham and Mr. Sharpe have died, so I have tried to bring theirs up to date with slight amendments.

Because every chapter ought to stand on its own, inevitably, and maybe to advantage, there is a degree of overlapping between the treatment of some topics in the two sections; but the intention has been to enable the specialists to develop their themes from their expert knowledge.

Harambee Country is a guide-book, though not the kind that lists hotels and tours by cost and classification. Instead, we want to interpret Kenya to Kenyans and describe its sunshine life, on the beaches, in the towns, on the mountain-tops, out in the bush and along the streams, to the tourists who are visiting in ever-increasing numbers as the jet-age draws the world closer together.

Detailed information about hotels should be sought from the East African Hotelkeepers' Association, P.O. Box 4365, Nairobi. Advice about travel facilities can be obtained from air and shipping lines mentioned in the list of Travel Addresses; and about entry permits, health and immigration regulations from the Kenya Embassies or High Commissions scattered around the world's capitals, in London at Kenya House, 172, The Strand, W.C.2.

Immigration inquiries inside Kenya should be addressed to the Principal Immigration Officer, Jogoo House, Harambee Avenue, P.O. Box 30191, Nairobi, or the Senior Immigration Officer, P.O. Box 84, Mombasa.

Publicity material is available from the Ministry of Information and Broadcasting, Jogoo House, Harambee Avenue, P.O. Box 30025, Nairobi; and Nairobi Publicity Association, Information Bureau, Kimathi Street, P.O. Box 2278, Nairobi; and the Tourist Board, a wing of the Ministry of Tourism and Wildlife, P.O. Box 30027, Nairobi, which also has a representative in the Kenya Office in London.

K.B.

Contents

Contents

Illustrations

List of Illustrations

Acknowledgements

[1] East African Railways Corporation
[2] East African Standard
[3] Len Young, A.I.B.P., A.R.P.S.
[4] R. Hutton
[5] S. Downey

Cover pictures by S. A. Azim (East African Standard): Mount Kenya and Sunset at the Coast

Travel Addresses

The following is a short list of air and shipping lines which may prove helpful to travellers

Air France

Kenya: Lugard House, Government Road, P.O. Box 3006, Nairobi.

France: 1, Square Max Hymas, Paris, 15.

Alitalia

Kenya: Kenyatta Avenue, P.O. Box 12651, Nairobi.

Italy: Piazzale Bell Post Office Arte, Rome.

British Overseas Airways Corporation

Kenya: Prudential Building, Wabera Street, P.O. Box 5050, Nairobi.

U.K.: Airways Terminus, Buckingham Palace Road, London, S.W.1.

U.S.A.: 530, Fifth Avenue, New York 36, N.Y.

British United Airways

Kenya: Mutual Building, Kimathi Street, P.O. Box 2474, Nairobi.

U.K.: 35, Piccadilly, London, W.1.

East African Airways Corporation

Kenya: Nairobi Airport, Embakasi, P.O. Box 19002, Nairobi; Airways Terminal, Koinange Street, P.O. Box 1010, Nairobi (passenger and freight bookings); and Mackinnon Building, Kenyatta Avenue, P.O. Box 30030, Nairobi (passenger bookings).

Note: East African Airways have pooling arrangements with B.O.A.C., B.U.A. and certain other airlines, also using B.O.A.C. office facilities in London and New York.

Travel Addresses

K.L.M. Royal Dutch Airlines
Kenya: Mansion House, Wabera Street, P.O. Box 9239, Nairobi.
Holland: Plesmanweg 1, P.O. Box 121, The Hague.

Lufthansa German Airlines
Kenya: I.P.S. Building, Kimathi Street, P.O. Box 30320, Nairobi.
W. Germany: Claudius Strasse 1, Cologne.

Pan-American World Airways
Kenya: Pan-Am, Commerce House, Government Road, P.O.
Box 30544, Nairobi.
U.S.A.: Pan-Am Building, 80, East 42nd Street, New York, N.Y.

Sabena Belgian Airlines
Kenya: Corner House, Queensway, P.O. Box 3708, Nairobi.
Belgium: 35, Rue Cardinale Mercier, Air Terminus, Brussels.

Scandinavian Airlines System
Kenya: Kenyatta Avenue, P.O. Box 20200, Nairobi.
Sweden: Bronna Airport, Stockholm.

Swissair
Kenya: Pearl Assurance House, Queensway, P.O. Box 4549,
Nairobi.
Switzerland: Bahnhofstrasse 27, Zurich, and Hotel Inter-
Continental, Chemin du Petit-Sacinnex 7-9, Geneva.

Trans-World Airways
Kenya: I.P.S. Building, Kimathi Street, P.O. Box 20117, Nairobi.
U.S.A.: 605, Third Avenue, New York, N.Y.

INTERNAL AIR SERVICES

East African Airways
As above.

Autair Helicopters (E.A.) Ltd.
Wilson Airport, Langata Road, P.O. Box 20447, Nairobi.

Kenya Flying Safaris
Wilson Airport, Langata Road, P.O. Box 5646, Nairobi.

Safari Air Services Ltd.
Wilson Airport, Langata Road, P.O. Box 1951, Nairobi.

Wilkenair Ltd.
Wilson Airport, Langata Road, P.O. Box 4580, Nairobi.

Travel Addresses

SHIPPING LINES

British India Steam Navigation Co. Ltd.
Kenya: Mombasa agents, Dalgety Ltd., P.O. Box, 20 Mombasa.
U.K.: B.I. Steam Navigation Co. Ltd., 1, Old Gate, London,
E.C.3.

Union Castle Mail Steamship Co. Ltd.
Kenya: Kilindini Road, P.O. Box 86, Mombasa (there are also
many agents in Nairobi).
London: Head Office, Kayser House, 4, St. Mary Axe, E.C.3;
Chief Passenger Office, Rotherwick House, 19/21, Old Bond
Street, W.1.
New York: Cunard Steam Ship Co. Ltd., Cunard Buildings, 25,
Broadway, and 441, Park Avenue.

Lloyd Triestino
Trieste: Ufficio Passeggeri, Via dell'Orologio, 1.
Venice: Ufficio Passeggeri, Calle Larga XXII Marzo N. 2288.
Kenya agents: Mitchell Cotts and Co. (East Africa) Ltd., at Cotts
House, Wabera Street, P.O. Box 664, Nairobi, and Kilindini
Road, P.O. Box 141, Mombasa.

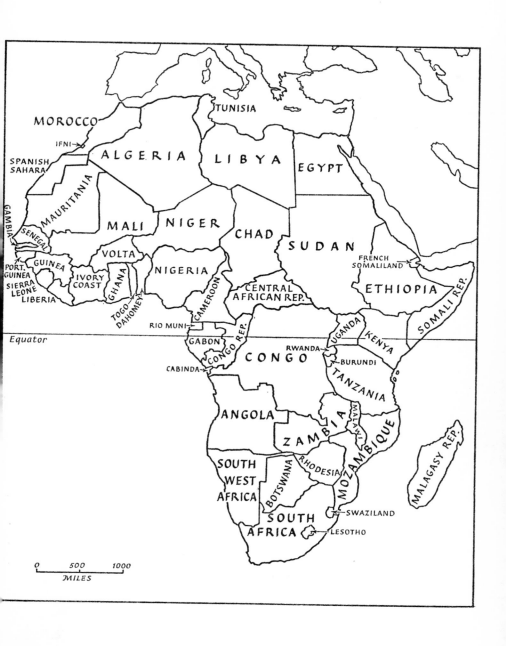

Section One

by

KENNETH BOLTON

CHAPTER I

The Kenyatta Era

There is a combination of three K's about this incomparable land we live in. K for Kenya, its name; K for Kenyatta, who will go down in history as the first Prime Minister and then first President, and who will be forever remembered as its "Founding Father"; and K for Keino, the fantastic runner among a bunch of world-renowned athletes.

Kenya gained independence from British colonial rule in 1963; but *uhuru* (the Swahili word meaning "freedom" in a political sense) was only the end of the beginning. What a surge of peaceful revolutionary changes the country has experienced since the ceremony at midnight on December 12, attended by H.R.H. the Duke of Edinburgh, who handed over authority formally on behalf of Queen Elizabeth II. The last of the colonial Governors, Mr. Malcolm MacDonald, was there too, next day to be translated into Governor-General; and Mr. Jomo Kenyatta, the President of the Kenya African National Union (Kanu) which had won the General Election early that year, so that he held the office of Prime Minister when Kenya attained *madaraka* (internal self-government) on June 1, 1963, a brief six months before full independence. Accompanying him was his wife, who has become popularly known as Mama Ngina, in unison with her husband as Father of the Nation.

Silence fell upon the throng in Uhuru Field, the dignitaries who had assembled from neighbouring African countries and most of the world's capitals to join Kenya's leaders in witnessing

I

the ceremonial, and the masses of jubilant Kenyans packed in the stands or waiting in dense crowds behind the crush barriers around the arena. At midnight the Union Jack came down and the Kenya Flag was broken up to a burst of wild cheering. It fluttered in the spotlight at the top of the mast, its colours black, red and green, divided by white stripes, with the shield and crossed spears of the national coat of arms in the centre.

There is a story, which may or may not be true, that as the little group waited in the centre of the arena for this solemn moment, the Duke of Edinburgh whispered to Mr. Kenyatta: "You have ten minutes to change your mind!" If he did, it was a typical jest in English humour at such a dramatic climax; but, if he did, Mr. Kenyatta could not have been amused. *Uhuru* was what he and his compatriots had striven for through many long years of political campaigning, through tribulation, the sacrifice of very many lives; the "suffering without bitterness" as he came to describe it all later, when he also pleaded with his countrymen "forgive and forget" and pleaded successfully.

It is difficult to put a precise time span to the years of Kenya's existence as a British colonial dependency. As we shall see presently in more detail, the country was first known as IBEA when the Imperial British East Africa Company began its administration in 1888. The British Government took over from the company in 1895, when Kenya came under the Foreign Office, to be transferred to the Colonial Office in 1905.

Some folk will tell you more happened in the first seven years of independence than in the whole of the previous 70-odd under British rule. Obviously, this is not factually accurate; manifestly, it is not true when you look at the physical creations, for Kenya was carved out of the bush and empty plainlands into a viable State, with its neat farms, network of roads and railways, and all the accoutrements of a sophisticated modern country, with Nairobi in the centre as its capital. This is the lovely "City in the Sun", as the Nairobi City Council's slogan goes. Yet even in Nairobi, many of the developments, including some of the sky-scraper buildings and international hotels, have taken place since independence.

Apart from things material, there is sound justification for the claim that Africans themselves have achieved more than the British in the relatively short period they have had the country under their own control. They have fundamentally changed its purpose and direction. Kenya has been fashioned into a land for Africans, being developed for their economic progress, education and social welfare, while they are adapting their tribal legacies to modern expectations and practising their own political institutions under the general style of "African Socialism", a political doctrine defined at some length in a Sessional Paper issued by the Government.

"Tribal", in the preceding paragraph, is not a very commendable word to use, since the basic principle of this Harambee Country is to mould the people of all tribes, Kikuyu, Luo, Kamba, Masai, Abaluhya, Giriama, Kalenjin and the others, together with Kenya citizens of Asian and European ethnic origins, into one cohesive nation.

For years before independence, Kenya was ravaged by political turbulence. Quite apart from the African struggle, intense rivalry existed almost from the very beginning between the Europeans, mainly of British stock, and the Asians (Indians and Pakistanis) and, as though all this was not difficult enough, the communities suffered their internecine rivalries for political domination, with a general Settler versus Official antagonism superimposed. "Blood pressure and politics" described the goings-on in Nairobi and the farming Highlands, with only "sea level and sanity" at the Coast, and even there they had their own brand, with the people of Arab extraction injecting another kind of salt into the broth.

The Kikuyu formed the spearhead of the Mau Mau revolt which pinned down the equivalent of a whole corps of British troops during the State of Emergency which lasted from October 12, 1952, until January 12, 1960. They lost many thousands of lives in the forest fighting and in the operations which swept through every village of the area in Central Kenya, densely inhabited by the Kikuyu, as farmers, mechanics, clerks and servants, for they were, and are, an industrious people.

The Mau Mau rising was the precursor to independence. When *uhuru* came, so soon after the State of Emergency had been lifted, the land was full of the prophets of gloom predicting disaster. They were to be proved false. This was the decade when the British Prime Minister, Mr. Harold Macmillan, let loose the "winds of change" and his vociferous opponents in Kenya had no

3

reservation about saying "how wrong could he be?" and crying havoc. "So rough a wind" Sir Michael Blundell wryly commented, adapting a Shakespearean quotation for the title of his reminiscences. He led the European delegations to the succession of constitutional conferences in Lancaster House and Marlborough House, London, during the three years beginning early in 1960. Sir Michael stayed on in Kenya when so many compatriot farmers left; but he forsook politics for the soil he loves, to run his farm at Subukia, work in the beautiful garden of his home there, and take part in business affairs in Nairobi. Others of his group, happily, stayed on—Sir Wilfred Havelock, busy with all manner of activities on the Coast including Lawford's hotel, where he makes his old friends and countless "package tour" German visitors feel very much at home. Mr. Reggie Alexander, too, who had a carry-over in politics as a Specially Elected M.P., but he, also, turned more and more to the travel business and his beloved Olympics as a member of the International Olympic Committee and for many years chairman of Kenya's Olympic and Commonwealth Committee. Another sporting personality, Sir Derek Erskine—horses and athletics in his case—had long been a liberal in politics, advocating support for the African cause. He and Lady Erskine were to find their convictions materialise in the new Kenya.

Mr. Jan Mohammed comes to mind from those conference wrangles. He was elected to a Kanu seat in Parliament and became an Assistant Minister for Tourism and Wildlife. Two of the politicians of pre-independence times went on in a distinguished partnership for the life of the first Parliament. Mr. Humphrey Slade and Dr. Fitz De Souza, both lawyers, became the Speaker and his Deputy, respectively, of the House of Representatives, which later merged with the Senate to become the National Assembly, and both were greatly respected by the Members. Mr. Speaker Slade dedicated himself to upholding the dignity of Parliamentary proceedings and safeguarding public confidence in Parliamentary institutions. Two other lawyers were to join the Bench—Mr. Justice Madan and Mr. Justice Chanan Singh—after having careers in politics.

Mr. Bruce McKenzie is another of the farming politicians. He had a brilliant and daring war career as a pilot and, it is said, wears his curling whiskers by royal authority, having been given permission to do so when he was perversely doing so anyway,

4

during a visit paid to his squadron by the late King George VI. Bruce I hold in special regard, for his unremitting service to farming in Kenya—he was Minister for Agriculture in both the pre- and post-*uhuru* governments—and to the interests of the expatriate people, some of whom attacked him as bitterly as illogically.

Both Bruce McKenzie and Michael Blundell, who were neighbours on their farms near Nakuru, were reviled and suffered great personal hardships; but time has justified their liberal beliefs and deeds. And, so help me, mine also I trust in the challenges and excitement of these changing years.

The constitutional conferences in London were at first a series of disputes between the ethnic groups, Asian, African and European, after the pattern of politics back home in Kenya, with the Asian delegates leaning more towards the African Elected Members than did the Europeans. Ultimately, European political domination and Asian influence were whittled away and Africans were out there in the front of the field.

So, at the last conference, they thrashed it out between themselves: the issue being how best to go into *uhuru*. The two main parties were Kanu, led by Mr. Kenyatta, who had been released from detention ensuing after completing his prison sentence imposed during the Emergency, and Kadu (Kenya African Democratic Union) led by Mr. Daniel arap Moi, Mr. Ronald Ngala and Mr. Musinde Muliro.

Their chief difference was that Kanu, which had a strong complement of Kikuyu leaders, though others were included, such as the late Mr. Tom Mboya (a Luo), wanted unity. They believed only a unified country, under a strong central Government, could have a hope of success when standing on its independent feet, and they were to be proved correct not only by events in Kenya itself but by the disintegrating fate of federations elsewhere. Kadu, an amalgam of other tribes, was intent on *majimbo*, a regional system dividing the country into administrative areas roughly corresponding to tribal groupings, having their own elected Regional Assemblies and retaining substantial authority over local affairs.

This is no political treatise; the purpose is to describe Kenya, as a country, and its people. But nobody can possibly understand the Kenya of today without knowing at least the bare outline of the prelude to independence. From that understanding dawns the

5

realisation of all that the man who was the then Kanu President has accomplished for the country of which he became President.

At the stage of internal self-government, he was Prime Minister. He remained in the same office when Kenya became a sovereign State and a member of the Commonwealth. A year later, on the first Jamhuri Day (Republic Day) December 12, 1964, he became His Excellency Jomo Kenyatta, President of the Republic, still a sturdy Commonwealth member, but constitutional changes were rapidly taking place. Universally in Kenya, the President is affectionately and respectfully known as The Mzee. There are many *mzees*, a term of respect for the wisdom of elders, but there is only one The Mzee.

Into a disputatious country he had infused the principle of nationhood, of working together, *harambee*, and wherever Kenyatta's country is known it is linked with his famous slogan of *harambee*. He did not coin the word, but it was seldom previously heard except when the Kikuyu were working together as a team, hauling a fallen tree out of the *bundu* (bush country) or shoulders to the wheel unditching a cart. Then they would have a kind of tug-o'-war team leader, shouting *har-am-bee*, meaning "all-together-heave".

The word was first publicly used by The Mzee during the elections in 1963 which preceded internal self-government. It was so little known generally that nobody quite knew how to spell the word—some favoured an Arabic Swahili version, *kharambee*, some *karambee*, until finally it settled down to *harambee*.

The first time it appeared in print was in the report of The Mzee's speech after the election results had been announced. Simultaneously, it was used as the heading to a leader written for the *East African Standard* of May 28—*Uhuru na Karambee*—commenting on the outcome. For some time, the Kanu slogan had been *uhuru na kazi* (freedom and work) and now the intention was to remark on the change the election had started. Mr. Kenyatta, the leader, and his party repeated they were resolved on a new task, of welding Kenya into a united nation.

"Mr. Kenyatta," the editorial went on, "has a Swahili word for it—*karambee*—which is preferable to the slogan *uhuru na kazi* since its meaning implies hard work and co-operation with an admixture of astronaut go-slang", to suit a new nation which had emerged suddenly into the space age.

6

The Kenyatta Era

It is fantastic to see the faces light up and hear the lusty voices joining in to respond to The Mzee when he raises his ornamental fly-whisk and leads the *harambee* chorus, at a mass rally or after some formal luncheon or other occasion. The final *"bay"* rises into a long-drawn-out tone of jubilation; and the chorus is generally followed by everybody singing the party song, *Kanu Yajenga Nchi* (Kanu builds the nation).

Under The Mzee's leadership, many people in all walks of life strove to unify a nation composed of Asians, Africans and Europeans, of different ethnic origins, tribes, creeds and religions, different stages of educational and economic progress. First, Kadu threw in its lot with Kanu and a voluntary one-party system resulted which did not have to be provided for by legislation. Then the Government set about dismantling the unwieldly apparatus of the *majimbo* constitution.

As explained earlier, the Senate and House of Representatives were amalgamated into one National Assembly. Legislation passed through the House to change the regions into Provinces and abolish the "little Parliaments" known as the Regional Assemblies, their functions devolving on the Central Government or the local authorities of county and municipal councils.

From the start, the Government pursued a policy of non-alignment in world affairs, which some call "positive non-alignment" inferring that neutrality between power blocs does not mean holding no opinions and doing nothing. On the contrary, Kenya's representatives have been extremely active, at the Organisation of African Unity, in the United Nations and at Commonwealth Conferences. They have been impelled by the principle of a non-racial rather than multi-racial society, implacably opposed to apartheid and determined to help remove the last vestiges of colonialism from Africa. That is why, for example, trade bans were imposed ahead of most other countries against South Africa and the U.D.I. régime in Rhodesia (known by its African name of Zimbabwe).

One after another of the constitutional changes directed by The Mzee and his Government were converted into legislation—for no reform was made illegally—by his untiring aide, the Attorney-General, Mr. Charles Njonjo, and the Law Officers working with him. Whether dressed in the formal pin-stripes of a lawyer, or wearing his brightly coloured pullover at a motor rally or football

7

match, Mr. Njonjo is one of those remarkable characters who always manages to appear immaculately attired. He is as shrewd as he is charming, a barrister of Gray's Inn who had his early education at the Alliance High School, Kikuyu, which has turned out so many Kenyans holding first-rank positions in the Government, the Administration and in education. Let me mention but three who will represent them all—Chief Justice Kitili Mwendwa; the ex-Finance Minister, Mr. James Gichuru, a colleague of Mr. Kenyatta's political campaigns over many years; and Mr. Duncan Ndegwa, who was at first head of the independent Civil Service and later the first Governor of the Central Bank of Kenya.

While Kenya was shooting the rapids of constitutional change, other political influences were at work of a different type. At the outset, Mr. Oginga Odinga—*Jaramogi*, the Luo leader from Nyanza—had been at Mr. Kenyatta's side in Kanu and became Kenya's first Vice-President. With a coterie of supporters, Jaramogi had campaigned during the colonial days for the release of Mr. Kenyatta, whom he dubbed "the Father of the Nation" long before the first Lancaster House conference. Mr. Kenyatta's appointment as Prime Minister justified Jaramogi's pledge that this would come about.

Imperceptibly at first, but in a slide gaining momentum, Mr. Odinga and his Luo followers began to slip away from Kanu over political differences, deriving support and inspiration from the policies of Communist countries. Though Jaramogi himself is not a Communist, he publicly avers he will accept aid from countries of the East, and why not, he asks. Talking with him, one feels he is deeply impressed by the Chinese revolution and Chinese methods of organising peasant labour. The Luo Mr. Mboya did not accompany Jaramogi into opposition, remaining as Secretary-General of Kanu and Minister for Economic Planning and Development, until his assassination (on July 5, 1969).

Ultimately, Mr. Odinga formed the Kenya People's Union (K.P.U.). Legislation forced those M.P.s who crossed the floor to seek re-election and, at the so-called Little General Election of June 1966, Kanu emerged victorious with a heavy majority of the contested seats. By now, Kanu controlled almost the entire National Assembly and presently there were several K.P.U. defections, so that even after the K.P.U. won the Gem by-election

8

in May 1969, caused by the death in a road accident of the Minister of State for External Affairs, Mr. Clem Argwings-Kodhek, K.P.U. had only eight seats out of 158 for Elected Members in Parliament.

Mr. Odinga was succeeded as Vice-President by Mr. "Joe" Murumbi, who had returned with his wife and a library of 3,000 books from political exile in England during the Emergency. Mr. Murumbi was one of the first African intellectuals to join Mr. Kenyatta's independence crusade years earlier, which had pursued the struggle where Harry Thuku left off. Mr. Murumbi wearied of active politics in office and soon resigned to enter business and be at home with his books. In turn, he was succeeded by Mr. Daniel arap Moi, the upstanding and energetic Tugen (one of the Kalenjin group of tribes) from the Rift Valley, who had remained on close terms of friendship with Mr. Kenyatta even while a staunch Kadu leader, and thus the marriage of Kadu and Kanu was completed.

Kenya entered the new decade of the 1970s with its second Parliament entirely composed of Kanu Members. In the elections at the close of 1969, the party won all 158 seats, though with considerable changes within its ranks. Five Ministers were among about 100 of the former M.P.s who were defeated. President Kenyatta was returned unopposed for a second tour of office, with Mr. Daniel arap Moi as his Vice-President; while Mr. Fred Mati, who had frequently deputised in the Chair in the past, became the first African Speaker.

The electoral form fell into two parts: first the primaries in every constituency, followed by the General Election. In the event, the latter was a formality. Polling was unnecessary as all the candidates—those who had won in the primaries—were from Kanu.

The K.P.U. had been prohibited some time previously on security grounds, while Mr. Oginga Odinga and other leaders were detained. This came about after the October rioting in Kisumu, when the President went there to open the Russian-sponsored hospital. A number of people were killed and injured when the escort opened fire to disperse the demonstrators.

At independence, many political problems were swept under the carpet by the British in their anxiety to withdraw and the African leaders eager to take over. One of these was the "Ten-

Mile Strip", a slice of land down the Coast leased by the old British Administration from the Sultan of Zanzibar. The Strip was incorporated in Kenya, for a sum of money paid in compensation to the Sultan, for the benefit of his people; but very soon afterwards the Sultan was swept away in the revolution which followed the island's independence.

Another related to the disputed frontier drawn in colonial times between Somalia and Kenya across the empty spaces of the North-Eastern Province (formerly called the Northern Frontier District). Many people of Somali origins lived their nomadic lives tending their livestock in this arid region, or in the tiny townships. The fact that explorations indicated the likelihood of oil under the desert added point to the claims.

An unhappy period of *shifta* activity set in, *shifta* being a word denoting a rebel fighter. The Kenya army and the para-military wing of the Police Force known as the General Service Units were deployed on active service for many months as the guerrilla fighting dragged on, and the loss of life seemed interminable until the scene was suddenly transformed. President Kenyatta and the Prime Minister of Somalia, Mr. Egal, on the authority of President Shermarke, met for negotiations. Under the chairmanship of President Kaunda from Zambia, they composed their countries' differences in the Arusha Agreement which restored peace and neighbourly relations.

All these changes and political movements, The Mzee piloted. "What a very wise Old Man Kenya has!" exclaimed Mr. Malcolm MacDonald, who was himself something of a wizard. He has been a man of many offices, plenipotentiary this and extraordinary that, but he arrived in Kenya as a colonial Governor. To be honest, he looked rather uneasy in his uniform and plumes, ceremonial sword buckled at his waist. All the diehards, indeed many other Europeans as well, regarded him with suspicion when he succeeded the late Sir Patrick Renison. Mr. MacDonald had a reputation for alacrity in giving away bits of the Empire and they thought he had arrived to give away Kenya. They were right, too; for this is what he did, yet he earned the gratitude and the affection of those very opponents, indeed of the men and women of all races living in Kenya.

Soon, he was affectionately being called "Mr. Mac" by the Africans, who warmed to his unconventional manner, his diminutive figure and sometimes quaint attire, his odd mixture of reticence and ebullience. In short, to his entire character. Kenya was fortunate, indeed, to have the conjunction of Mzee Kenyatta and Mzee MacDonald. After independence, Mr. MacDonald stayed on, to acquire the unique record of being Governor, Governor-General, High Commissioner (after Kenya became a Republic) and finally British Special Representative in Africa, with headquarters in Nairobi. Among all the complicated problems of State, he found time to loiter in the garden, make safaris into the bush, to write (for he began his career as a reporter on *Tit-bits*, or was it *Answers*?) and to produce a beautiful matcher for Kenya to his book on birds in India. The son of Britain's first Socialist Premier, for whom he retained the deepest affection, Malcolm MacDonald is one of the outstanding Britons of his age.

Under him and his successors, the British High Commission in Nairobi undertook immense tasks in the post-independence years, not always enjoying popularity with the expatriate population, as how could anybody having to handle such difficult and sometimes heart-rending human problems? Not only had they to cope with the personal troubles of British subjects, but with the technical, legal and financial questions of the revolution in land ownership.

Very many European settlers were bought out, their farms turned over to Africans, particularly on the Kinangop—erstwhile White Highlands—bordering the densely populated Kikuyu areas. These were almost entirely mixed farms of several hundred acres, which were split into smallholdings down to ten acres for the settlement of 33,131 African families within five years, a politico-socio-economic necessity of the times, though sad it was to see some of the lovely homes decaying into ruins.

Later, large farms were preserved in co-operative forms under central managament. On the Kenyan side, the transition into African ownership and agricultural methods was expertly guided by Mr. Bruce McKenzie, at the Ministry for Agriculture, in the various land settlement programmes, notably the "1,000,000-acre scheme". A proportion of European farmers remained elsewhere in the country, for example in the Mt. Elgon district, and so did the large plantations of coffee, tea and sisal, and the ranches. But the process of wholesale Africanisation (otherwise called Kenyanisation, since citizens of all ethnic origins have equality before the law) which began in the Administration and has transformed Kenya, spread first across the land, as is right, for Kenya is primarily an agricultural country.

Immediately before and after independence, many thousands of Asians applied for British citizenship and were granted British passports. This was the genesis of the demands they made for entry into Britain when the process of Africanisation in trade and commerce, and the system of entry permits controlling various types of jobs, later caused the waves of emigration collectively known as "the Asian exodus".

Bitterness with Britain was stoked because all the British-Asians were not admitted readily. As the exodus mounted, immigrants from Kenya swelling the numbers arriving from other Commonwealth countries, the voucher system was introduced in Britain, supposedly limiting the number to 1,500 in one year. This fell far below requirements in Kenya alone. The Indian and Pakistani High Commissions in Nairobi adopted the attitude that they had relatively few nationals on their hands, as so many others of their kith-and-kin held British passports and, therefore, were Britain's responsibility. Somewhat reluctantly, British-Asians were admitted to India and Pakistan, on condition that they would be entitled to eventual admission to Britain.

During the period when so many Asian residents took British nationality, the Kenya Government had opened the door to Kenya citizenship. Two years' grace was allowed, expiring on December 12, 1965, for people of all races, having the required birth or residential qualifications, to apply for registration. Processing the shoals of applications lasted from months into years as the thousands of new Kenya citizens were enrolled.

Besides the diplomatic missions which have been mentioned, scores of others were opened, until the total rose into the fifties. The U.S.A. converted its Consul-General into an Ambassador, heading a strong Embassy, for Americans began to arrive in large detachments, in trade, the airways and hotels, Peace Corps workers and Crossroaders, strengthening the American presence felt for years through visitors on safari and other tourists.

Countries from the East (both the Soviet Union and People's China included) and West hastened to open missions in Nairobi, and many have given Kenya valuable aid both material and technical. They celebrate their National Days with functions appropriate to their national characteristics. But their finest hour is when they sink whatever differences divide them—personal or political arising out of non-recognition by their respective governments— to play in the annual football match Ministers versus Diplomats. Then you can even see Arab and Israeli playing for the same side.

Politics and sport form abiding interests in Kenya, especially athletics among the Africans, who have made astonishing progress in the span of only four years, from the unknown to break through into the top world class. Kipchoge Keino is the brightest star of Kenya's world beaters. They come from high altitudes, 5,000–7,000 ft., which led to acrimony among some of the sea-level athletes and sports writers at the 1968 Olympics in Mexico City.

Kenya did better than any other country except the Soviet Union in the Olympic athletic events that year, taking three Gold, four Silver and two Bronze Medals. Later, the Kenya newspapers added two more awarded by the Olympic Press Committee in Mexico: a Silver for editorials in the *East African Standard* and a Bronze for a pictorial supplement published by the *Daily Nation*.

Keino, already the 3,000 metres world champion, beat the Olympic record in 3 mins. 34·9 secs. to win the 1,500 m. and the headlines were "Keino the Lion of Kenya". He had been unwell and failed in the earlier 10,000 but he took a Silver in the 5,000 m. Running in the 10,000 m. his team mate, Naftali Temu, glanced round and saw Keino stumble. As Temu said afterwards, he "thought he had better carry on". He did and won the race for his Gold; and later added a Bronze in the 5,000 m.

Young Amos Biwott, almost unheard of outside Kenya, had a runaway victory to win the Gold in the 3,000-m. steeplechase, with Benjamin Kogo second. Wilson Kiprugut, in the 800 m., and the Kenya team in the Relay, won Silvers. Philip Waruinge, who took a Bronze in the featherweight contest, was subsequently acclaimed the best boxer in the tournament by the International Amateur Boxing Association.

This, then, is modern Kenya on the move. The succeeding chapters will describe its scenic beauty, the sunshine and the sea, the people and how they live, the unrivalled wildlife and Game Parks which make this country a tourist's paradise.

CHAPTER II

Where—and Why—is Kenya?

In order to explain where Kenya is, at the beginning of *The Lion and the Lily* I recounted the (true) story of meeting a Scottish newspaper editor some years ago, by one of those quirks of cosmopolitan chance, in Birmingham. He was interested to discover I followed the same craft; to discover how my entirely Sassenach appearance could be reconciled with his notion of what the denizens of darkest Africa should really look like.

Possibly he thought news ought to be carried by cleft stick in Africa, which it sometimes is; or beaten out on throbbing tom-toms, which, again, it sometimes is; but never printed in quite normal-looking English language newspapers, which it very often is. To show sympathy with a fellow-scribbler, he confided that he had recently written an editorial article about Kenya, our life and problems, notably our politics. A powerful piece.

People who live in faraway places become used to strangers flitting through the land who, having spent three weeks in passage, go home to write books not only on the way of life, but the salvation of the national soul. Much of it is nonsense, but it can be entertaining if you have that kind of a sense of humour. Should we be surprised, then, that a Scottish editor should write about Kenya? Not at all. Though he had never been there, he knew it was a British Crown Colony going up for independence that very year. Also, he fixed its geographical position on the west coast of Africa, somewhere in the never-never regions between the Cameroons and Angola. He was wrong by about 2,500 miles and as different as East from West can be.

During the years since this illuminating conversation took place, Kenya has come out in the world, earning so much fame that there can be very few people who take an interest in international or sporting affairs who have never heard of the country, Kenyatta's and Keino's country, the land of the lion and the Gloriosa lily, and do not know more or less exactly where to

14

The President, Mr. Kenyatta, and the Chief of the Defence Staff, Maj-Gen J. M. L. Ndolo, watch a services' parade during Jamhuri anniversary celebrations

Kenya's Parliament Buildings with Harambee House

find it on the map. However, to make sure—just where is Kenya?

In Africa, on the East Coast, where the breakers and the surf of the Indian Ocean roll up the sandy beaches of an African Riviera, there is more sunshine in six months than the Côte d'Azur gets in twelve. In consequence of the June war between Israel and the surrounding Arab countries in 1967, the Suez Canal was closed to shipping, so the traditional Mediterranean route down the East Coast had to be abandoned for the far longer Atlantic sailing round the Cape of Good Hope. Though some visitors with the time to spare for cruising still take the sea route, by far the greater number travel by air. In this jet-age, Kenya is well within twelve hours of Europe, even allowing for the differences in times, and only a day by direct flight from the U.S.A.

But in the leisurely bygone days, and again after Suez is re-opened (for the Middle East crisis surely cannot keep the waterway closed for ever), sailing to Kenya by way of Suez and the Red Sea, you round Cape Guardafui, where your ship may wallow in a rough sea, and hugging the curving coastline of the under-belly of the Horn of Africa, cross the Equator before docking at Mombasa, three weeks out from London.

This is interesting in itself for, having crossed the Line and been suitably initiated, you would be handed a Proclamation, by the ship's Master *per Neptunus Oceani Rex*, admitting you to member-ship of the Ancient Order of the Deep, placing the strictest injunctions upon all sharks, dolphins, whales and mermaids to treat you with due respect, if by any chance you should fall over-board. The appeal to mermaids is not so far-fetched as you may think; for the waters off the Kenya coast are the home of the *dugong*, the ancient mariner's original mermaid.

Living in Kenya, you can cross and recross the Equator every day of your life if you wish, and many people have to do so if they farm up at 9,000 ft. in the Highlands, because the Equator runs right across their lands. Here and there the Line becomes visible where it is marked, as at the place called Equator on the road and the railway line to Uganda.

Near Nanyuki there is a hotel named The Silverbeck where, standing in the bar, you can place one foot in the Northern and the other in the Southern Hemisphere; close under the towering mass of Mt. Kenya, whose snow-capped peak and glaciers reflect

c   15 the sunshine, high in the wreathing clouds, white, golden, flaming in the sunset. Mr. William Holden, the American film star, and others who know what they like and can afford it, have a fabulous country club, the Mount Kenya Safari Club (plate p. 191), in this bewitching bit of Switzerland in the tropics.

Kenya straddles the Equator by about 5 degrees each side. One of the most curious features is that you are never so far down below that you lose the North Star for the Southern Cross. Why do we bring the stars into this? Because the blue velvet of the night and the stars that shine in unnumbered silver sparkles, the rustling of the gum trees, and the immense lonely sigh of the bush country in Kenya, are among some of the wonders of the world. Once having fallen under this spell, some uncanny magnetism draws you back to Africa, whether you go away to live in Surbiton or at the Golden Gate of San Francisco.

Economically by means of the East African Community (and there has been much abortive discussion over the years about forming a political federation) Kenya is part of the trilogy of states in East Africa. The others are Uganda in the west and the Union of Tanzania to the south, composed of mainland Tanganyika and the island group of Zanzibar and Pemba. These islands lie in the Indian Ocean, below Mombasa and just above Dar es Salaam, which is Tanzania's capital.

All this sprawling area of East Africa, whose frontiers were drawn without much regard to ethnic or ecological factors, lies between the Republic of Somalia, Ethiopia and the Sudan to the north, Malawi and Zambia to the south, stretching away to Rhodesia, Mozambique and South Africa.

When the maps of this part of Africa were blanker than cabbage leaves, the sort of wide open grid spaces the Eighth Army had to fight from in the Western Desert, the cartographers had it all their own way. They drew fine straight lines, permitting themselves a few wiggles here and there, to signify the frontiers. Occasionally they cut right through a people's or tribe's domain, as the Abaluhya who were partitioned into Kenya and Uganda, and the Masai, split into Kenya and Tanzania. If these tribespeople cannot recognise boundaries which artificially separate them, it is certain that wild animals know no frontiers, real or imaginary.

Did I say the cartographers had it all their own way? Not

quite, for there was one occasion when, Queen Victoria wishing to give Mt. Kilimanjaro, Africa's highest mountain, to Kaiser Wilhelm for a birthday present, the frontier had to be redrawn to slice that part of the country out of Kenya and include it in what was then German East Africa, later to become Tanganyika and now Tanzania.

Distance lends enchantment, and also narrows the gaps between places in East Africa which, further apart than London and Moscow, are often four times more inaccessible, though there is an ever-expanding network of main, tarmac roads, while the East African Airways Corporation's internal flights connect most of the main towns. Until quite recently, it was difficult and tedious to get from Nairobi to the Seychelles, another of the islands in the Indian Ocean, for there was no air service, a ship on the Bombay run from Mombasa called only once every three weeks, and no radio-telephone, only a cable line. Lately, American flying-boats have made the flight from Nairobi. The Seychelles is burgeoning; the construction of a runway to take the super-jets is going to "open-up" the haven for which so many civil servants and businessmen yearned in their retirement; and the trammels of civilisation will be festooned about its simple ways.

As the international airlines fly their giant jet-liners, Nairobi is 4,248 miles from London, 4,027 from Paris, 7,356 from New York, 9,596 from San Francisco and 1,826 from Johannesburg. Nairobi's main airport is Embakasi, opened by Queen Elizabeth the Queen Mother, and probably the most delightfully up to date in all Africa. Embakasi stands at an aerial crossroads. So there is a sign-post just outside the terminal building. These mileages were copied from the place-names and distances recorded on its fingerposts, though presumably they will have to be converted by the 6-10 rule to kilometres with the introduction of the metric system.

There is another signpost of a different kind in the centre of Nairobi, this one for landlubbers. It is called the Milliary Stone and stands just off Kenyatta (formerly Delamere) Avenue, a memorial to the country's first motorist, Galton-Fenzi, and it records overland distances, including "Mombasa 321 miles". Galton-Fenzi was the founder of the Automobile Association of East Africa, which has its headquarters in Nairobi and branches in Kampala and Dar es Salaam.

Flights arrive at and leave Embakasi all day long and most of the night, on the routes to the Middle East and Europe, north-south and east–west across Africa, direct to the U.S.A., or with connections in Rome, Paris and London, and to the Far East, to Bombay and Bangkok, Hong Kong and Tokyo.

Maybe it is trite nowadays to talk about countries shrinking into one world, a very small world. But to somebody like me, who woke up to travel in a pony-trap clip-clopping through the lanes of greenest Worcestershire, there is still something slightly bewildering about having dinner at Nairobi airport (*langouste* and a bottle of Montrachet) and, soon after breakfast next morning, to be unpacking in London, all inside 12 hours by the clock. There is a small complication here, when you come to do your time and distance sums, because Kenya is two hours ahead of British Summer and three of Greenwich Mean Time. Accordingly, you gain or lose, depending upon the direction you are flying.

If you want to visit Kenya, to make a life-long dream come true, like Teddy Roosevelt's fantastic shooting safari in 1909 after he had finished his term as President of the U.S.A., or like so many thousands of ordinary folk today, you can do so by aeroplane; or, if you can spare the time, by ship, with the greatest ease and comfort. The fares, especially for the increasingly popular package tours from the U.K. and the Continent, are coming within the capacity of the pockets of people who, in England, save up for their annual holidays at Clacton-on-Sea, or maybe, Spain or the Dalmatian Coast. Some discerning holiday travellers, making the best of both worlds, cross Europe by train or car to Trieste or Venice, where they board ship for the voyage, and the Italian cooking, to Africa.

Instead of climbing Snowdon, or an Alp at Chamonix, more and more tourists reach out to Nairobi which has the advantage of being in the sterling area from the point of view of overseas allowances in the U.K. In Kenya you can see the lion lie down with the zebra, the eternal equatorial snows on Mt. Kenya, the rolling bushland, the majestic—if, sometimes on a dull day, ominous—Great Rift Valley, that enormous geological fault which scars the earth from Central Africa to the Red Sea and is at its most extreme in Kenya, edged by extinct volcanoes including Longonot and Menengai. You can see tropical trees from the scraggy thorn bushes to the ethereal blue Jacaranda, the Flame Tree with miniature bursts of orange shellfire for its flowers, and many brooding giants of the immemorial forests.

You will see wild flowers in the hedgerows and the bush; the Gloriosa lily which is Kenya's unofficial national flower, a red and gold dragonfly prancing on its slender green stem; the primrose from England and the violet from Africa; rose gardens, azaleas, lilac upside down in the purple spikes of the Pride of India; cascades of heavy honeysuckle expressively called Golden Rain; the blue trumpets of Morning Glory; and smell the scent of Yesterday, Today and Tomorrow and the Tobacco Plant flowers heavy on the night air.

Every garden is full of birds and butterflies in the most beautiful hues. One of the unforgettable sights in all human experience is to stand on the shores of the lake, at Nakuru or Elmenteita, to watch a million flamingoes rising in pink clouds, to bank and wheel away across the pink horizon of the sunrise. As always when you live close to nature, there is cruelty and suffering, for God has given this lovely country its share of troubles, which mankind has too often improved upon.

Why is Kenya? This is the other problem you will want to have explained. Kenya is indivisible from the neighbouring territories, despite the arbitrary frontiers. Economic influences have fostered a common market in trade and Customs, common public services and, ultimately, one might anticipate the practicability of a political federation at the apex.

"How did the British ever get involved in Kenya at all?" you ask. Colonialism played a part though, in its classic sense, not a very significant part. Trade follows the flag, even if Victorian mercantile adventuring did not plant the Union Jack entirely with self-interest.

The evangelical Victorian conscience had been stirred by the discoveries of Livingstone and Speke in central Africa, by the reports from Bishop Hannington and others about the pagan savagery they had witnessed in Uganda, by the slave trade inland along the caravan routes from Mombasa. Those were the days of the Christian revivalists in Britain. "Benighted pagans" were waiting to be saved from their ignorance and sin in the dark interior of Africa, where no white man had penetrated until the close of the nineteenth century. Or so they thought. Latter-day science is brushing aside their historical assumptions, while social and political challenges are being made to the achievements of their crusading and those who came after them.

As the result of discoveries made by Dr. L. S. B. Leakey and his wife at the prehistoric site of Olduvai, across the frontier in Tanzania, and finds at Olorgesailie, which was first noted by the archaeologist J. W. Gregory in 1893, on Rusinga Island in Lake Victoria and at Fort Ternan, it seems that mankind may have been cradled here and the aborigines all have had white skins. Who knows? The scientists with their Geiger counters are not certain, but these are the theories some of them hold. At any rate, to the reforming Victorians, years before they knew that radioactive deposits in Mrima Hill, down the coast from Mombasa, were the cause of ships' compasses going wrong, and not some mermaidly prank, here was a land where missionary zeal could abolish the slave trade.

Arab slave-traders were still calling at Mombasa in their dhows, much the same as the craft their forefathers had sailed across the ocean since the eighth century, when Arab settlers arrived from Oman and the Persian Gulf. They were the first significant colonial arrivals and the routes their caravans took into the interior are frequently marked by the mango trees, or their descendants, which they were so fond of planting. Mombasa was known to seafaring adventurers in the first century A.D. when it was visited by an unknown Greek. He wrote of Mombasa as Tonike in the anonymous *Periplus*. Besides the dhows you can see bobbing around the waters of the port, traces of Arab civilisation remain in the Old Town of Mombasa.

You will find a drawing of a dhow on the wall of a house unearthed in the ancient city of Gedi, among many interesting relics, including Chinese pottery. Gedi was discovered in the 1920s, its mysterious ruins lying on a site in the forest between Mombasa and Malindi. Local people, who believed the dark, forbidding place to be haunted, would not venture anywhere near.

As the result of excavations carried out under Mr. John Kirkman, many of the buildings, shops and streets have been exposed and some of the places restored. It would now seem that Gedi has given up at least part of its secret history: it is mainly Arabic, flourished between the twelfth and seventeenth centuries, and was built on the site of a much older place which was probably

Persian. The people of Gedi, besides being subjects of the Sultan (his palace is still there to see), were devout Muslims, for there are five mosques, the Great Mosque having been completely cleared and partially restored.

Fort Jesus was the centre of the earliest European settlement. The Portuguese first appeared there under the intrepid Vasco da Gama in 1498. His ships and his men were welcomed by the people who then dwelt around Malindi, which is now a fashionable holiday place 76 miles north of Mombasa. From Malindi's shelving, sandy beach he sailed away to discover India. In 1960, the Presidency Minister of Portugal, Dr. Pedro Pereira, unveiled a Vasco da Gama memorial at Malindi, in the form of a pillar rising 20 ft. from a mosaic pool, the column set with a billowing sail emblazoned with the Cross of the Order of Christ. He also opened a museum at Fort Jesus, the Gulbenkian Foundation having given £30,000 for a home for historical research and the restoration of the fort. These ceremonies did not pass without demonstrations by those African political leaders who, sensitive to the commemoration of anything colonial, wished also to protest against Portuguese policy in other parts of Africa and Goa, the enclave at that time left behind in India, later integrated with Mother India.

If you think Kenya is a new and, perhaps, brash country despite its wildlife and wide open spaces, please refer to some of its ancient history. Why, the poet John Milton was our first Public Relations Officer, as Edward Rodwell once pointed out. "Roddy", who lives on the Coast and of whom more later, breathes legend and folklore. In one of his whimsical *Coast Causerie* articles, he claimed that "Milton was one of the first Information Officers for the Coast" because, when writing *Paradise Lost* in the seventeenth century, he "depicted the angel Michael showing a vision of the world to Adam". He quoted the passage about "the empire of Negus" in which this line occurs—*Mombasa and Quiloa and Melind*.

"Roddy" says he has an old map which shows the lands of Ethiopia, Tharshish and Sheba as occupying the African Coast, stretching from the Red Sea to Mozambique, and legend has it that Sheba was the Queen who ruled over these territories. There is another connection. After Sheba had visited King Solomon, as described in the Old Testament, she returned to

21

Ethiopia. Theirs was something of a love-match for she gave birth to a son who became King Menelik the First.

The story of his death may be woven from legend; but it goes that, advanced in years and a great *Mzee*, he was leading his last military expedition homewards from the south when his army passed Mt. Kilimanjaro. The old king looked up to its snow-sheathed table-top rising into the clouds. "There," he thought, "is a mountain fit to be my last resting-place and memorial." He had himself borne to a cave beyond the snow-line, wearing his royal robes and on his finger the ring his mother had given him— Solomon's Seal.

His bodyguard of officers laid him down in the cave, bade the old king farewell, and the army marched away across what is now Kenya, to their homeland in the north. No Kenya, or Tanganyika, or Tanzania existed in those faraway days.

Victorian crusading, or colonising, enterprise in East Africa was chiefly directed to Uganda, around the shores of Lake Victoria, the inland sea which the adventurers named after their queen. Kenya was an afterthought and created as a by-product. The crusade needed a railway so, with that matter-of-fact approach characteristic of the times, a railway was driven, all the way from Mombasa. If the track had to rise 8,000 or 9,000 ft. and down again, what did that matter? They drove across hundreds of miles of bush alive with marauding wild animals, swamps before anti-malarial medicines were available, the Great Rift Valley itself, to Lake Victoria, the source of the Nile, and on again. All this could be accomplished, and was.

The railroad reached the lake port of Kisumu in 1901, after unbelievable human endurance and engineering feats, and was then driven forward to Kampala, Uganda's present capital. Kampala lay in Buganda, which was the kingdom of the Kabaka until the last of the line, Sir Edward Mutesa, left for exile in Britain where, later, he died, and his former domain was integrated with the other kingdoms in a unified Uganda.

When the railroad reached the top of the Rift Valley escarpment, equipment and rolling-stock were lowered on pulleys to the bottom, a sheer drop of many hundreds of feet, where it started off again. You can still detect how this was done from the marks in the bluff overhanging the twisting escarpment road, just above the tiny Italian church by the side of the main road from Nairobi to Nakuru, a road built by Italian prisoner-of-war labour in the 1940s.

Down on the farm at the bottom of the cliffs is the site where the railway line started off again, travellers having descended from the heights in the years before the railroad was realigned to run the whole distance without a break from Mombasa to Kampala and, as a result of the extension in 1956, to Kasese, on the Congo border, a total distance of 1,081 miles.

Nairobi, the skyscraping city it is today, rose from a swamp ("swamp" is the literal translation of its name and another Nairobi, still only a papyrus swamp, exists at the northern end of Lake Rudolf to this day). The railroad halted while more supplies were brought up, before crossing the swamp, and a camp was made at railhead. One of the engineers, a Sapper sergeant named Ellis, must have lived the rôle of an African squire in the tent he pitched on a muddy track which is now Sgt. Ellis Avenue, and runs alongside the huge stone block of the City Hall.

The City Hall, with its Charter Hall for conferences, was built during the Emergency and dedicated "as an act of faith". Gatherings of world-wide organisations are held there, and it has even been nominated not only for the annual Olympic Games conference but for the United Nations if it should ever want to meet outside New York, in the new continent which is exciting such universal attention. Nairobi, indeed, has become an international conference city.

The Kenya–Uganda railway forms part of the East African network controlled by the E.A. Railway Corporation, with headquarters in Nairobi, which was split from the former E.A. Railways and Harbours Corporation soon after the E.A. Community was launched. The Harbours Corporation betook itself to Dar es Salaam and, under the same arrangement, the head offices of the Posts and Telecommunications Corporation moved to Kampala. These moves were part of the decentralisation programme for the East African Common Services.

To build the Uganda Railway, as it was called, thousands of coolies were taken over to Africa from India, where the British Raj was then in all its splendour. Many died along the route. Those who remained originated the considerable Asian population living in East Africa, their numbers increased by waves of immigrants to a land of promise compared with the poverty of their own lot.

Asians, of various "tribes" and religions became the *fundis* (mechanics and craftsmen), the *duka wallahs* (shopkeepers), the *keranis* (clerks) and the big businessmen in commerce. Their mosques and temples are to be seen in Nairobi and scattered all over the country.

This is how it comes about that there are three main racial groups in Kenya: the indigenous Africans with the immigrant Asians and Europeans, who have also bred their generations of indigenous Kenyans. A great many Europeans and Asians left in the immediate years after independence and of the total population of 10,209,000 recorded in 1968 9,941,000 were African, 182,000 Asian, 42,000 European, 40,000 Arab and 4,000 others.

Similar to India and the British East India Company, Kenya was at first a field for the operations of the Imperial British East Africa Company, formed in 1888 with a capital of just under £250,000. Capital of this order was woefully insufficient for such pioneering enterprise. Loss followed trading loss; the cost of military actions, especially in Uganda, drained the money away. Finally, the Congo Basin Treaty, concluded by Britain with the Sultan of Zanzibar, started the free trade zone of the common market, destroying the company's last hopes. In 1895, the British Government bought the company's assets and the Foreign Office took over responsibility for a territory known as IBEA, a name composed from the initials of the company's name—which shows this habit did not start during the Second World War, as might have been supposed.

It was not until 1905 that Kenya's adminstration was transferred to the Colonial Office. A year later, a Legislative Council was formed, originally with Nominated Members but, as the years advanced, with a combination of Colonial Service administrators, Nominated and Elected Members. The introduction of a Legislative Council, with the appointment of successive Colonial Governors living at Government House, Mombasa, and then at Government House, Nairobi (now changed into State Houses), when the seat of Government moved, with all the accoutrements of a Colonial Administration, were made necessary by the flights of European settlement.

In 1895, Britain had come to an agreement with the Sultan of Zanzibar to pay him an annual rent for a strip of land ten miles wide running down the extent of Kenya's coastline, which formed part of his Sultanate. Officially, this Strip was to be administered direct from London but, for administrative convenience, these functions were delegated to the Kenya Government, with an Arab Liwali for the Coast. Thus began a long controversy over the Coastal Strip, Arabs demanding autonomy from Kenya as the Colony approached sovereignty, while Africans sought to retain the Strip as part of their independent country.

The B.E.A. Company began farming experiments in the early 1880s, long before the railway was started. Missionaries joined in. One of them, the Rev. Stuart Watt, already had a decade of African experience, albeit his wanderlust had taken him off to Australia in between.

He returned, drawn by Africa's strange magnetism, and he settled at Machakos, where he started fruit farming. Machakos, now a market town on the main route to Nairobi from Mombasa, was then a lonely outpost, 250 miles across the arid bushland. There is a story of how the Rev. Watt, his wife and children, walked from the coast all the way to Fort Smith, a place in Kikuyuland a few miles beyond Nairobi. Mrs. Watt was, literally, the first white woman to set foot inside East Africa, if the scientists are not substantiated in their theories about millions of years ago!

Hundreds of immigrant pioneers followed in their footsteps. From another direction, and impelled by other motives, came Lord Delamere, the third Baron of his name. His interest lay in shooting wild game and he pentrated Kenya by a route from the Somalias. When, in 1897, he first saw the countryside that became known as the White Highlands, he must have felt something like Cortez who, you remember, fell silent upon a peak in Darien when he discovered Georgia.

Delamere found a lovely land of towering mountain ranges, downs nestling in the folds, forests and tinkling streams. His imagination was fired. Imagination of what could be done by agricultural development; here were wild animals of many species (excepting the tiger) roaming ready for the hunter. Kenya seemed to him to have everything. He returned, to lose a great deal of money, but to pioneer the settlement of a new country. His son continued farming the estates and, while President of the Kenya National Farmers' Union, saw the country rushing into self-government which his father, and his co-pioneers, would never have considered possible in this century.

Harambee Country

The wide thoroughfare in the centre of Nairobi was named Delamere Avenue, changed to Kenyatta Avenue after *uhuru* and Lord Delamere's statue was discreetly moved, with his son's prior agreement. Flowering shrubs were planted round the site but, with characteristic African courtesy, no other statue was erected there, the plinth being converted into a fountain. President Kenyatta's statue, an imposing piece of sculpture, stands outside Parliament Buildings.

To those early arrivals in the first two decades of the twentieth century, who were mainly of farming stock, Kenya seemed a piece of England set in the tropics, where even the equatorial sun was kind. Perhaps to the Afrikaaners who took part in the long trek from South Africa, across the then Rhodesias to settle around Eldoret, their plateau was part of Holland. Almost all, if not all of them and the families they had bred, trekked away after *uhuru*.

Newcomers in the early 1900s and in the soldier-settler schemes after the First World War, saw Kenya as they would, but always as a land where hardship had to be endured, to conquer the encroaching bush and bamboo forest, and the pests which afflicted crops and stock. Tsetse-fly, rinderpest, foot-and-mouth epidemics ravaged their stock; other diseases cankered their growing wheat. They laboured and many lost their money; but they loved the life. The memorial to what these farmers, aided by the scientific research workers of later years, have accomplished can be seen in the broad acres of cultivated lands, in the irrigation which enables cattle to be reared on ranches supporting perhaps only one head to four, six or ten acres, and in the schemes to prevent soil erosion by bench terracing.

On to the primitive way of life of the indigenous Africans, some pastoral, others nomadic, the European settlers grafted a modern civilisation slight at first, but ever widening; a friendly, fiery, disputatious mixture of communities which inevitably threw up racial, political and economic stresses. Ponder, and be astounded to think how Africans who, at the turn of the century, could not make a wheel, whose first contact with the white man occurred in the lives of their fathers or grandfathers, were projected into the age of nuclear fission, and are acquitting themselves so creditably in administration, farming, commerce, the arts and professions.

Seventy years is negligible in the vast evolution of the human race. Or would be if such miracles of agrarian and political revolution had not taken place, telescoping the evolution of 700 years elsewhere in the world. This is the country, which became so engrossed in politics in later years, which, for all its tropical situation, has a climate softened by the heights and is the last redoubt in the world for wild animals living in their natural surroundings. Heights? The people of Nairobi and the Highlands, who spend their lives at 5,000–9,000 ft., love to quote that sardonic saying against themselves: "Sea level and sanity".

CHAPTER III

People and their Religions

Ever and again, there is a burst of speculation and some informed antiquarian interest in the origins of the names attached to the East African countries. I recall one such round of suggestions and counter explanations started by a lady, living at Eldoret, who wrote to a newspaper asking how Tanganyika came to get its name. She had heard a cook say, in her kitchen, that the word *tanganyika* was the Swahili for "a mixture", and she complained she had never heard anybody use the word *mchanganyo*, which is correct by the textbook.

There have been many explanations, some erudite, others imaginative. The name Tanganyika, it was held, was fabricated in 1918 and applied to the whole country after the end of the German occupation, having originated in the name of Lake Tanganyika which is situated on its western borders. On the authority of one of the very earliest missionaries, E. Hore, who was stationed in the Ujiji area, the name of the lake does mean, literally, "a mixture", or "mingling", though not of ingredients for a pudding but of streams flowing from every direction down the slopes into the basin of the lake. The contemporary name of the country Tanzania, was adopted when Tanganyika formed a union with Zanzibar and is based on an abbreviated amalgam of the two.

Uganda and Kenya are straightforward enough. Uganda comes from the Bantu word *Buganda*, which was pronounced lazily as *Uganda* and taken into use as such by the early explorers. Uganda, under the British protectorate, consisted of five regions, the kingdom of Buganda being one, and the people of this kingdom were known as the Baganda, all kingdoms now having been closely knitted together in one country having one Government and President.

Kenya comes from the tribal name for Mt. Kenya—*Kilinyaa*, meaning "the white mountain". Somebody once told me the name Zanzibar was a mystery wrapped up in an enigma; but I believe it is correct to attribute the root of this onomatopoeic word, in whose lilt you can breathe the scent of the cloves and feel the violent beauty of the beaches by night, to the Persian compound of *Zang*—"black"—and *bar*—the suffix "land"— which put together mean "land of the black".

Swahili is the lingua franca on which you can get around pretty well throughout East Africa, even though there are wide linguistic differences between the tribal areas. Swahili originated in Zanzibar, spreading to the mainland. All those centuries ago, the people of Zanzibar thought the mainland a very big island indeed, and they were right by anybody's standards. *Siwa* means "a big island" and *hili* "this big" and so, together, *siwahili*, its people *wasiwahili* and their language *kisiwahili*, shortened into *swahili*.

How many people live in East Africa and what are the racial proportions of their polyglot society? According to the 1960 population statistics, Africans numbered about 22,000,000, with some 340,000 Asians, 102,000 Europeans, 66,000 Arabs and 13,000 others, all in round figures. It should be understood that population figures cannot be anything more conclusive than informed estimates, because there is still no effective East Africa-wide system of registration of births and taking regular censuses; but it can be justifiably assumed that the African population has increased substantially since then, while the numbers of Asians and Europeans have thinned out since the three countries attained independence.

To reduce this question to a Kenya context, the African population in 1960 was in the region of 7,000,000 increasing at a rate sufficient to double itself in 30 years. This figure put the Africans about 1,000,000 ahead of the previous estimate. By 1968, their numbers had risen to 9,941,000 and a great controversy was raging over the rights and wrongs of family planning. The advocates of birth control pointed to the risks of a "population explosion", as they do in all the developing countries, fearfully wondering how the masses of the future will be fed, housed and educated. Their opponents consider restriction unnatural and that, as the earth is capable of far greater food production, Nature will provide, a somewhat escapist argument of the permissive society.

Kenya's non-African population in 1960 was put at about 300,000, being then composed of 174,300 Asians, 67,700 Europeans 38,600 Arabs and 6,100 others. The Asian bracket included all people living in the country of Indian, Pakistani or Goan origins. Some notion of the "flight of population" that has taken place can be gauged from comparisons with the 1968 totals. Despite their natural increase in the size of families, Asians then totalled 182,000, showing a rise of only 7,700 though the exodus did not reach its peak until late that year and in 1969. The European population had fallen to 42,000, a drop of 25,700 in the eight years, and it must be remembered that, although a great proportion of civil servants, farmers and others had left, several thousands arrived annually as experts, volunteer workers and business people on short-term contracts of two or three years' duration. By 1968, the Arabs totalled 40,000, having increased by 1,400, and "others" were nationally down by 2,100.

European and Asian settlement having started in earnest during the early years of the twentieth century, it follows that the early settlers have descendants to the third and fourth generation; and these are indigenous Kenyans who have no other home but Kenya. They do not have one foot in Kenya and the other in Buckingham, as a former Governor, Lord Howick (then Sir Evelyn Baring) used to say. Many people in Britain made a grave mistake when they classified all the white folk of Kenya as colonial Britishers who emigrated from Britain or, more harshly, as remittance men. Apart from the pre-independence army of Civil Service officers, scientific or technical experts in the Colonial Service, most of the white people were born and bred in Kenya, or became legally "Ordinary Residents", having made their homes in the country. They were not birds of passage; and much the same goes for the vast majority of Asians, who had nowhere to go outside Kenya where their presence, in the very first instance, was at the behest of the British, as I explained earlier, to help build the Uganda railway.

The history of the so-called immigrant races, or expatriates, in Kenya is one of grafting the technologies and methods of modernity on to the existing order they discovered; on the European side, originally of administration, agricultural development, public services, the professions, trade and education; on the Asian side, administration in the junior ranks of the Civil Service, in trade, commerce, as artisans and craftsmen, builders, doctors, lawyers, teachers. Africans provided the labour for the vast undertakings which have transformed the country from the

Opening of a new National Assembly

The trunk of the wild fig tree at Thika, the subject of a prophecy

primitive to a land beautiful. Latterly, as they acquired more education, they have entered every branch of the country's life, though their numbers are necessarily few in medicine, the law and the sciences.

"Crash programmes" of education and practical training have been launched to speed up the ingress of Africans to the conduct of the economic, as well as political affairs of their country. There are, for example, Schools of Medicine and of Law besides several institutions for the sciences and technological instruction. Their combined efforts release increasing numbers of qualified Africans into the stream of life every year, diminishing the reliance on training in overseas universities, not always found successful because of the environmental differences.

Despite the magnet of the towns, to white collar or sophisticated jobs, the majority still live on the land, as farmers in co-operatives and on smallholdings—their numbers vastly increased by the settlement schemes in the wake of departed European farmers—or tending their herds in the distant grazing lands, as their ancestors did for countless generations. Because of the overcrowding in urban areas, with the unemployment created by people flocking into the towns seeking work, President Kenyatta initiated a determined campaign to put the process into reverse, under his call "go back to the land".

One of the most heartening characteristics of the post-independence Kenya has been the regard accorded those of the pioneering families, and others of expatriate origins, who stayed on to do what they could towards building the new nation. This is a regard shown by leaders and *wananchi* (ordinary people) which does not attract the glare of publicity turned on the deportation of some who did not "fit in" or were guilty of various offences. "Forgive and forget", President Kenyatta advised his people and the old bitterness of Emergency times was soon dissipated, for a myriad constructive tasks and purposes required full-time energies.

Every year, the Pioneers' Society holds an annual dinner. The words of Sir Ferdinand Cavendish-Bentinck, at the 1961 dinner which coincided with the Diamond Jubilee Royal Show of the (then) Royal Agricultural Society of Kenya, summarised pioneer achievement (the name has been changed to the Agricultural Society of Kenya). Although the early settlers may have played and lived hard, he said, they did a good job of work.

"It sometimes makes one a little sick to hear the point of view that anybody who is a settler or colonialist only came out here to avoid the 'terrible hardships of England' and to have a nice peaceful time at the expense of the wonderful African country, flowing with honey," Sir Ferdinand went on.

"Most of you know the honey took a great deal of extracting and the task was not as easy as it might seem to have been. We have lived at a time when we thought we were building up something and our aims and objectives have not been reached in the way we thought. Our sons will have to readjust themselves to this new type of country. I still believe that, in our generation, we did what we thought was right; that we did a good job; and that we have created and left behind something I believe to be absolutely worth while. It is a country we regard as home, where we have been living for a long time, but we have got to face changes."

His words are worth remembering, to be pondered deeply by those who have gone and those who remain living together in this land of opportunity. Sir Ferdinand is yet another of those who carried on from pre- to post-*uhuru*, but no longer in politics, turning to business and welfare work, including the Charity Sweepstakes regularly raising funds for national organisations and help for aged and destitute Europeans who had to be helped to be returned to Britain. As I write, he has become a very active octogenarian.

When he was Member (equivalent to Minister) in the old-style Legislative Council, he had been responsible for the settlement of numbers of farmers from Britain and he felt deeply grieved over their plight in the turn politics had taken. He became Speaker of the Legislative Council, but resigned after the results of Mr. Ian Macleod's first constitutional conference at Lancaster House were made known. This was the conference which charted the country's initial course to independence. Sir Ferdinand devoted himself to the European cause, becoming leader of the Kenya Coalition, but was defeated by Sir (then Mr.) Michael Blundell's huge African vote at the 1961 elections.

At the same dinner, the then Governor, the late Sir Patrick Renison, made a controversial speech which demonstrated great moral courage, for he was at the time conducting talks on constitutional progress between the various political groups which were constantly going on to the rocks.

"The way to help a country to find peace and prosperity is not to scuttle, run or disappear," he said. This had reference to the uncertainty which was causing some people to quit Kenya and many others to think about doing so even in those times when the general prediction for the date of independence was between five and fifteen years hence.

"People should hold fast," he continued, "carry on and let the quality of what you are doing prove its indispensability." He admitted, before that essentially critical audience, to carrying out policies of which many of them disapproved, policies which they felt threatened their life's work in the country. The Royal Show at Mitchell Park, Nairobi, was a "symbol of British achievement in one lifespan of which I am intensely proud," and he added:

"This is a land of many problems and this is an age of tensions, ill-discipline and over-publicity and over-adulation for the selfish, over-ambitious little man—particularly if he has the advantage of being an oppressed colonial.

"We want to complete our task here in a way so that it is accomplished in friendship and without damage to the immensely valuable institutions and economy which have been built up by you and people like you."

You can imagine he had a sympathetic hearing at the dinner but also see why his speech took great courage to deliver at a time of clamant African nationalism, in the wake of the release of President Kenyatta and his colleagues of the Kapenguria trial who had been imprisoned or detained for several years during the Emergency.

Sir Patrick it was who made the notorious "leader to darkness and death" speech in relation to Jomo Kenyatta, having been grossly ill-advised by his Civil Servant aides. The detainee who was later to become President bore the Governor no malice. Many who were "in the know" felt Sir Patrick was ill-used when he resigned the Governorship during Mr. Duncan Sandys' term at the Colonial Office. To show their regard, Mr. Kenyatta and the Cabinet, including all the African Ministers, turned out at the airport to bid him farewell.

Africans have ascended the ladder in all spheres of activity, in businesses, the banks and shops, schools, Government and municipal departments and as *fundis* (mechanics or craftsmen). Naturally, they still provide almost 100 per cent of the unskilled labour.

According to the report of the Royal Commission on Land and Population (1955), there is no problem of over-population and unemployment, but rather a superabundance of work for the labour available. This equation must be conditioned, of course, by the state of the economy, whether flourishing or depressed, and can only be true when the tempo of development is rising. Which, in turn, depends to a critical degree upon investment capital from overseas.

Before the immigrants appeared, wide tracts of land were unoccupied, though almost always looked upon as tribal domains by the pastoral and the nomadic peoples, even if they did not habitually move across considerable portions. In essence, this started the dispute between Africans and Europeans over the White Highlands which, the Europeans argued, they found empty and entered upon to develop into plantations, mixed farms, ranches; while the Africans counterclaimed the land as theirs by birthright, though outside their immediate needs they did not cultivate, clear the bush or tame the primeval forests until this century.

Possession of land by Europeans was by freehold purchase, or more often 999-year leases, from the British Crown; from which it will be noticed that farmers paid for the land they then set about developing and the purchase price went to the Government.

Since independence, the State having replaced the Crown, and the Kenya Government having taken over responsibility from the British, land purchase is controlled by the Central Government, through Ministries of Lands and Settlement and Agriculture, certain powers being delegated to the District Land Boards. Non-citizens can, and do, buy property and land in the urban areas but, in a general sense, ownership of agricultural land is reserved for citizens.

Though great stress is being laid on breaking down tribal barriers in order to mould one nation of Kenya people, it cannot pass unremarked that there are perhaps fifty tribes, or groups, some related and in perennial peace, others which were at enmity in bygone years and retain rivalries, though nowadays in different directions as do, shall we say, some of the Welsh, Scots and Irish towards the English.

They fall mainly into four great ethnic and linguistic groups, i.e. Hamitic, Nilo-Hamitic, Nilotic and Bantu. Every tribe has

34

lived within its own area for generations, with remarkably little intermingling until comparatively recent years when travel has become easier and the urban areas have attracted people from the Reserves, as those areas the colonial regime designated for African ownership are still known. Forays by one tribe against another, particularly between the Kikuyu and Masai, frequently occurred in those lawless times, but there is little or no written evidence and accounts of the tribal wars are the hearsay of stories handed down by word of mouth from father to son. This is one illustration of the absence of anything permanent—buildings, writing, implements and other articles—in the African heritage, which so puzzles archaeologists and anthropologists, making their researches extremely difficult, with the exception of discoveries concentrated in particular areas.

The first of the principal ethnic groups is the Hamitic, generally agreed to be of Arabic and Egyptian origins. Most of the other African races are believed to have evolved over the centuries from the Hamites, in conjunction with the Negroes and Bushmen. In this group, and its associated Nilo-Hamites and Nilotes (the two last geographically limited to the Nile Valley and its vicinity), are to be found the Masai, Somalis, the Nandi (comprising Nandi, Kipsigis, Suk, etc.) and the Luo and Teso groupings (Teso, Karamojong, Turkana, etc.).

The other main ethnic group is the Bantu, who are found throughout the continent. Bantu really means "people" but, in Kenya at any rate, the Bantu are a mixture of Hamitic and Negroid, including the Kikuyu, Embu and Meru and the Kamba. Scarcely anybody would quarrel with the assertion that the Kikuyu were from the beginning the most alert and politically active tribe in Kenya, which is saying something in a country where almost everybody loves arguing politics. In the Kenya African National Union, the Kikuyu became allied with their neighbours, the Luo, from Nyanza, a truly remarkable alliance made possible only by their leaders uniting against colonial rule; for these two tribes have a history of rivalry. The Kikuyu endured a period of internecine war during the Emergency, when they are reckoned to have lost more than 13,000 lives—11,500 listed as forest or other freedom fighters and the remainder as civilians or members of the Security Forces who were killed in the fighting.

Although the powers of witch doctors are receding slowly,

it would be a brave African indeed who would claim to have no fear of the supernatural and the spells intoned by the witch doctors, armed with their strange paraphernalia of gourds, bones, feathers and other objects. Witch doctors still inhabit the remoter areas and make their way into the towns. They take payment in coin or kind for their services—for casting spells on some, lifting them from others by more "powerful magic". The sophisticated Westerner should not lightly dismiss the influence wielded by witch doctors, for their spells have had the most uncanny results, even to predicted death, and if the mental state of the victim can be diagnosed by the realist as the prime cause, nevertheless the witch doctors and medicine men have performed some very strange deeds. Not all their spells are fatal, not all their magic bad. Gradually, their powers are being shaken loose by the *dawa* (medicine) of the qualified medical men with their injections, sprays and tablets. As an indication of the lingering respect for their powers, it is enough to say that, recently, one M.P. suggested in the National Assembly that, as honours went to Western doctors for their services and discoveries, the witch doctors should have their medals.

Altogether, I can list the following tribes (and there may be other subdivisions) beginning with the biggest: Kikuyu, with their relatives the Embu and Meru and their neighbours (also distant relatives in many cases) the Wakamba and Masai, the Luo, Abaluhya (numbering about 2,000,000 and a powerful force if they should ever be reunited, but at present split by the frontier between Uganda and Kenya), Kisii, Maragoli, Kipsigis, Nandi, Nyika, Turkana, Kamasai, Rendille, Warda, Samburu, Teso, Tiriki, Karamojong, Bagishu, Suk, Marakwet, Elgeyo, Njemps, Ndorobo, Giriama, Digo, Segeju, Boni, Bajun, Pokomo, Konongo, Boran, Sakuye, Gabbra, Pare, Adjuran, Gurreh, Rahanwein, Gosha, Suba, Juria, Swahili; beside the Somalis and Sudanese, some of whom live in a settlement known as Kibera, near Nairobi, which was made available to them in recognition of their services in the First World War.

Where do the people composing these tribes mainly live? The urban areas have attracted people from their traditional areas. Mombasa and Nairobi, in particular, have plural tribal, as well as racial communities. Nairobi's permanent African population is mainly Kikuyu, Wakamba and Luo.

People and their Religions

It would be too confusing to attempt a detailed description of the entire tribal areas, which are not, in any case, very clearly delineated in some parts. It is possible, however, to indicate broadly where the principal tribes, or tribal groupings, are located. Some of the smaller tribes inhabit the coastal regions, and inter-marriage is found with families of Arab descent. The Giriama, Ndorobo and Swahili are examples of these coastal tribes. To their north, and stretching away across the North-Eastern Province, where it borders Somalia, Ethiopia and then the Sudan, a considerable number of Somalis and Sudanese are to be found living in scattered pockets, the chief centre being Isiolo. They taper off eventually into the interior tribes of the Lake Rudolf–Sudan–Uganda frontier areas, which include the Rendille, Samburu, Gabbra and Turkana.

South of Mombasa, and running west along the border of Kenya with mainland Tanzania, the Masai country forms a wide arc, partly in one country, partly in the other. The claim used to be sometimes made that Nairobi itself lies in what used to be Masailand, but nowadays the Masai, still engaged in their traditional cattle rearing, skirt the capital, their area of occupation extending along the fringes of the Rift Valley to Kenya's Western Province.

Primarily, the West is the home of a group of tribes known as the Kalenjin, among them the Kisii, Kipsigis, Tugen, Nandi and Elgeyo. These people are mainly centred on land around Kericho and Sotik, and out towards Eldoret, merging into the Luo districts of Nyanza and the shores of Lake Victoria. The lake port of Kisumu is the main commercial hub for Luo agriculture. The Elgeyo, however, are separated from the other Kalenjin tribes, in that they live across Luoland, near Kitale and Mt. Elgon. The Abaluhya, who are sometimes associated with the Kalenjin grouping, form a tribal unit of their own, but one that is split by the arbitrary Kenya–Uganda frontier, so that, like the Masai, they are divided between two countries.

This leaves only one further main group, the Kikuyu and their "cousins". Though the Kikuyu (President Kenyatta's people) are predominant among Africans in Nairobi, their densely populated and intensively cultivated lands of the Central Province reach in a wide horse-shoe from Kiambu, on the city's outskirts, all the way through to Fort Hall, Karatina and Nyeri, stretching over the Aberdares, to Nakuru and Naivasha, and so back to Nairobi at Dagoretti Corner.

Close to Nyeri are the two areas of Embu and Meru which, as their names imply, are inhabited by the two tribes, Embu and Meru, who are closely related to the Kikuyu. At the other side of Kikuyuland, south-east of Nairobi, live another branch of the Kikuyu ethnic family, the Wakamba, whose principal population centres are Machakos and Kitui.

Many nationalities are numbered among the Europeans, but they are mainly British (a goodly number of Scots and Irish besides the English); Dutch either direct from Holland or through Afrikaaner descent having migrated from the Union of South Africa (the great majority departed soon after independence); Danes and Italians. Nairobi is a very cosmopolitan city for, in addition to the permanent residents who have settled from overseas, including a large Jewish community, there are trade or consular representatives from most countries of the world.

There has been no intermarriage of a really significant order, so there is no "coloured" problem, such as intervenes in South Africa. Mixed marriages there are, but they are the exception, though increasing as more Africans and Asians go to Europe and America for their education.

The Asian group falls into the main religious divisions of Muslim, Sikh, Hindu and Buddhist. Hindu subdivisions are the priest and upper class of Brahmins, the warrior Kshattriya, merchant Vaishya and the remainder mostly Shudra. Muslims are divided principally into the Sunni and the Shia, the latter being those Ismailis who owe allegiance to the Aga Khan, while the Bohra are confined mainly to the Mombasa area. The Ahmadiyya missionary movement, with the other Muslim branches, are all of the Islamic faith, which has also claimed many thousands of African converts.

As I have mentioned, Arabs are most numerous on the Coast, though some are found living inland. They, too, are Islamic. Goans, a most hard-working and thoroughly respectable people, whose discipline has held juvenile delinquency in check, are of mixed Portuguese and Indian descent from Goa which used to be a Portuguese enclave in India, and are almost all devout Roman Catholics.

With such a galaxy of races and religions living cheek by jowl, places of worship range from Sikh and Hindu temples and Islamic mosques to cathedrals and churches of the Roman Catholic, Church of England and Nonconformist creeds. Cathedrals of both the Roman and Anglican Churches are to be found in Nairobi, where a new Roman Catholic cathedral of the Holy Family has been built adjacent to the original church of the same name.

In Nairobi, too, the Anglican Cathedral of the Highlands, built in traditional English style of stone hewn in Kenya, contrasts in architectural style with the near-by St. Andrew's, the Scottish Kirk that is walled with plate glass. In final contrast, just across the way stands the (former) Dutch Reform Church, one of the earliest Christian churches in the country, originally Scots, but taken over and restored by South Africans of Dutch Reform persuasion. This tiny place retains its corrugated iron roof, as do so many of the older buildings in the country, and is now the Lutheran church.

Up-country townships all have their own places of worship, according to the presence of individual Church representatives. Missions have percolated to remote areas and there you will find congregations of different Christian Churches frequently sharing the same chapels for their worship. Among the Nonconformist Churches with missions in Kenya there is a quite bewildering array of denominations—Church of Scotland, Presbyterian, Congregational, Baptist, Methodist, Pentecostal Mission, Seventh Day Adventists, Friends, Christian Scientists, the ubiquitous Salvation Army and others.

African Christians attend these churches, both as ordained priests and ministers and worshipping in the congregations. African clergy serve side by side with Europeans as Bishops and in other appointments, both the Anglican and Roman Churches having Archbishoprics. Sad to relate, there is also much splintering among African Christians, some having formed breakaway groups of their own.

After independence—indeed, the process was under way in the years before—many nations extended helping hands to Kenya, classed in the politico-economic jargon as "an under-developed, emergent country" among many such countries in Africa and Asia. They offered bursaries for Kenya students in their colleges and universities; provided aid in loans or gifts of money to help development and educational projects; and they sent their technical experts by the hundred. The range of experts and the diversity of their advice have sometimes aroused amused, if caustic, comment.

Roars of wry mirth were provoked at a conference of the Kenya National Farmers Union when one lady farmer from Koru said Kenya suffered from "expertitis". Since *uhuru*, as she related in some dudgeon, very many experts had visited the country, to stay only a short time and leave without achieving what they set out to do. This is too severe and general a judgement, of course, but she sardonically recalled:

"On one occasion, I was advised by a German to plant sugar-cane in the furrows. A Dutchman told me to plant the cane on the ridges. An American told me to plant it on a Louisiana bed and an Australian advised me to stick the cane downwards. I managed to get all of them together and we nearly had a third world war."

Elspeth Huxley, who writes so perceptively about the country where she was born and which she loves so well, once explained the system crisply, saying the basic qualification for such appointments was that candidates should never have been to Kenya before, or preferably never have set foot in Africa.

This is all rather apocryphal, but illustrates the touch of ironic humour we have in Kenya, where you will find every African loves to laugh, at you, himself or anybody else. As I was writing this passage, I was telephoned by an American author who had earlier written asking for a little advice on a project. He and his family were on a journey to various points round the world to discover what he aptly termed "Proof Positive".

"Not so long ago," he recounted, "it occurred to me that, with so many negative opinions being expressed all round us about the current state of world affairs, the spread of violence, racial hatreds, collapse of moral values, revolt of youth and so on, it might be a good idea to write a simple, honest-to-goodness book about some of the positive things happening in the world." In effect, had Kenya any to show?

I scarcely knew how to answer; not for lack of the organisations he would wish to see but because there are so many. The American and British Governments, I told him, have volunteer people at work in many spheres. There are the Cross-Roaders and the Peace Corps. The British have their Volunteer Service. People in these organisations are employed as teachers, doctors, nurses, field officers in agriculture and other activities, besides missionary work. The Swedish Government made a big grant for the erection and maintenance of the Science Teachers' Training College, a splendiferous affair at Dagoretti, near Nairobi. One might wonder how a small country like Kenya is going to keep the college filled with students.

The Danes have converted Bogani, the home of the late Baroness Karen von Blixen, in the rural suburb of Karen, named in her memory, into a domestic science college. There are relief organisations at work such as Oxfam, Save the Children Fund, Freedom from Hunger, the Flying Doctor Service; schools for training the deaf, dumb, blind and physically handicapped; Dr. Barnardo's Homes for children, of which, in Kenya, Mr. Njonjo is the President; the Edelvale Homes to care for wayward girls; and among places to look after the elderly and destitute the Amani-Cheshire Home, with which Group-Captain Cheshire, the British V.C. Dambuster pilot, is associated. All these, and many more, are contributing outside aid to the spirit of *harambee* abroad in the country, while people in the remotest parts, many eking out a subsistence living themselves, join in self-help schemes to build dispensaries and *harambee* schools.

[With reference to the population figures given on pages 29–30, the preliminary results of the 1969 census surprisingly give the total as 10,890,000 which indicates that Kenya's population has doubled in the last twenty-one years, though some account must be taken of the numbers omitted for various reasons in previous counts. The growth rate has risen from 3 to 3·3 per cent, giving some cause for alarm since such an increase offsets benefits from the economic growth rate, set at 6·7 per cent for the first half of the 1970s.

While by far the greater proportion of the population lives in rural areas, the chief urban populations are: Nairobi 477,600; Mombasa 246,000; Nakuru 47,800; and Kisumu 30,700.]

CHAPTER IV

The Great Rift Valley

Right across the world, from Chile to Tokyo and back to Persia, 1960 was the year of geological violence. In East Africa, at least three earthquake tremors were recorded though, fortunately, the shocks were not severe.

Uganda had its worst for nine years: during the month of May at Masaka, 80 miles south-west of Kampala; another was felt at Tabora in June; and yet another in Nairobi during July. These shocks were associated in the public imagination, though probably without any reliable scientific evidence, with accounts of activity in the volcanic crater of Ol Doinyo Lengai, which rises 10,000 ft. over Lake Natron, near Tanzania's border with Kenya. Stories of Lengai's puffs of steam and bubbling mud pools fired the public fancy.

Dr. Leakey, who has undertaken much exploration in the area, intervened to soothe people's minds. He dismissed the reports of "renewed activity after six years' silence" by saying that, between its major eruptions, Lengai is perpetually stirring into the state described by those witnesses who approached the crater on foot, or took photographs from the air. "Time enough to get excited," he reproved, "when the next major eruption starts. Which might be next year or some years hence, for intervals between the eruptions are not regular, as far as we know."

Lengai erupted in 1922, again in 1925, in 1940–1 and in 1954. Taken together with the hot springs and other signs of suppressed volcanic activity, at Ol Olbutot and Longonot, Menengai and Mt. Buru, the Lengai eruptions and earth tremors in succeeding years suggest that The Great Rift Valley, while for the most part dormant, is by no means extinct as a volcanic area. The Great Rift Valley—shortened in Kenya conversation to The Rift—is the dominant geological feature of the country, indeed of the whole continent. With its chain of lakes and network of mountains, The Rift is yet another reason why Kenya can only be considered in its East African physical setting.

42

The Great Rift Valley

This colossal fault in the earth's surface, at which the imagination of mortal mind boggles, must be seen to be understood. It is as though some gigantic thermo-nuclear plough had dug an enormous furrow striking right across Africa from Nyasaland to the Red Sea. The subsidence, contraction or whatever is the correct technical description for such a geological phenomenon, must have convulsed half the world in some prehistoric age. The resulting valley, flanked by steep escarpment walls and mountain ranges, looks fit to let the sea in, right up to the doorsteps in Nairobi, striking into the heart of Africa from Egypt, the Sudan and Somalia. Indeed, The Rift must have been a gigantic inland sea once upon a time, from which the waters have receded, leaving a succession of lakes to this day.

The Rift crosses the country from south to north and can be most distinctly seen in bewildering views from the railway which follows its eastern escarpment for some time and then crosses to the west side, climbing the far escarpment and so on to Uganda; or from the main road joining Nairobi and Nakuru. The road from Nairobi climbs through fertile country farmed by Europeans and Kikuyu until it reaches a spot that is familiarly known as The Escarpment where, in a series of hairpin bends, it descends to the bottom of The Rift, into countryside that seems to be the very floor of the earth itself.

Pause before you start to drive down; stop in a layby at the left side of the road and look at the view (see plate p. 46). There is nothing like this anywhere else in the world. African men and women in colourful dresses will offer for sale their basket-work, their carvings representing heads and animals in polished wood. You stand on the edge of a steep cliff face and look across a wide and desolate valley to the mountains somnolent in the distance. Over all this scene of emptiness there is a brooding air of silence; emptiness and silence accentuated by a curl of smoke where a herdsman has lit his fire. For, among the stunted vegetation, there are grazing lands and the wide acres are divided into scattered farms.

The Escarpment, clothed in trees, drops from heights of 2,000 or 3,000 ft. and the valley, running straight ahead, varies from about 30 to 40 miles in width. Volcanic rocks lie strewn everywhere in the coarse grass that browns in the scorching sun.

The sky is rainbow lovely at sunrise and sunset. At high noon the sun blazes from a blue sea where stately galleons of cumulus cloud sail grandly behind their flying pinnaces. In the stillness of twilight, or when the storm clouds pile up in the louring sky, The Rift changes its moods. Now the whole shrouded valley is eerie, foreboding. You will shiver and drive on.

Along the floor of The Rift, on from the Escarpment near Mt. Margaret, there is an incongruous invasion of the prehistoric natural scene by the space-age engineers. Here, East African External Telecommunications Ltd. has sited a statellite earth station having a deadline of April 1970 to open up its services, sending messages across one-third of the earth's surface, via an Intelstat communications satellite to all intents and purposes stationary nearly 22,500 miles above the Indian Ocean. The station is linked to Extelcoms House, built at a cost of £525,000 and rising twelve storeys among the skyscrapers in Nairobi. This building houses both the headquarters of the company and the main relay station for telecommunications to and from the station out in The Rift.

The main road to Nakuru has a fine tarmac surface; it was built by Italian prisoner-of-war labour after the campaigns in Abyssinia and the Western Desert in the Second World War. On either side of the road, cattle graze on the ranches. Giraffe poke their long necks out of the thorn trees and munch the foliage on the topmost branches. The thorn trees look like umbrellas, some of them those strange Whispering Thorns which get their name because the breeze whistles through the holes in nut-like growths festooned in the branches. Sometimes the shy gazelle will skip across the open savannah; loitering zebra are conspicuous by their stripes which are quite the wrong camouflage for this kind of country. On rare occasions you might even see a lion lurking in a thicket at the roadside, but lion are unwelcome prowlers because of their raids on the cattle.

This stretch of country is not unlike the plains between the Coast and Nairobi, except that it has been tamed by scientific farming methods and irrigation schemes have taken water to concreted watering points, opening up acres all around for grazing on the paddock principle. Another difference is that, beyond Nairobi, and continuing north and north-west, through Naivasha, Gilgil, Nakuru and on to Mau Summit, Kericho and Sotik on the one hand and Eldoret and Kitale on the other branch, the scenery becomes mountainous as you climb ever higher.

As the farmlands drop behind, cultivation and grazing fade into the semi-arid bush and the desert of the Northern Frontier Province beyond Isiolo and Archer's Post. Access to this part of the country is permitted only at certain times of the year, for the roads are only tracks and in wet weather impassable. Finally, if you drive far enough or, better still, fly, you come to the land of the Turkana (plate, p. 95), the Rendille and the Gabbra, who tend their goats and stringy cattle from the *manyattas* (enclosures for huts and night-time protection of livestock) they build, which are surrounded by circles of prickly thorn branches. Lake Rudolf juts down from the junction of Kenya, Ethiopia and the Sudan, where the police fort and lookout stand near Namoroputh, a place with an airstrip but no houses!

From Mt. Kilimanjaro—Africa's highest mountain at 19,340 ft. —on the Tanzanian border, all the way to Uganda and the Mountains of the Moon (the Ruwenzoris), the country is strewn with volcanic ranges and lone conical peaks. In such a country, mountaineering is obviously popular and each Territory has its Mountaineering Club, Kenya's having its headquarters in Nairobi (P.O. Box 5741). Rock-climbing abounds for the specialist, but the novice must take extreme care on Mt. Kenya, for instance, where many climbs are not for the beginner. You say you are only a walker, but enjoy a good ramble? This is also the country for you, since most mountains are within walking capacity, including the top of Kilimanjaro and Kenya's snowline and glaciers (plate, p. 79). However, you need to be fairly fit and be sure you will have no difficulty with your breathing at such altitudes.

Kilimanjaro has twin peaks: Kibo at 19,340 ft and Mawenzi at 16,896 ft. Expeditions of quite ordinary folk frequently set out to climb the mountain, taking rest and a night's sleep at one or other of the huts situated at various levels. You do not have to be an expert climber to reach the topmost, Kibo Hut. Early in 1969, a party of blind mountaineers made this climb, principally to prove what the blind can do in their everyday lives.

A quaint little airport at Arusha, in Tanzania, lies under the enormous and snow-capped walls of Kilimanjaro which disappear into cloud. The runway is capable only of taking aircraft on the internal flights but a new one, to cost £3,000,000 sterling, is soon to be constructed near Moshi under an agreement signed between Italy and Tanzania. This will be big enough for airliners flying direct from Europe and America, for tourists who want to land "close in" for their visits to Kilimanjaro, the Serengeti Plains, Lake Manyara and the Ngorongoro Crater.

Like Kilimanjaro, Mt. Kenya is an extinct volcano, and chief among the abodes of God in Kikuyu folklore. The others were Donyo Sabuk, the Aberdares and the Ngong Hills, which are set around the boundaries of the Kikuyu country. Mt. Kenya's highest peaks are the twins Batian (17,058 ft.) and Nelion (17,022 ft.), which are hard rock cores exposed by the erosion of the volcanic crater. These two are the province of only the most expert climbers, but several subsidiary peaks, below them but above the snowline, may be climbed by people who have some experience and are reasonably hardy. Visitors usually go up to the snowline at 14,000 ft., where you can put a girdle round the mountain and its glaciers straddling the Equator, and see the most wonderful views, with the sun striking diamonds out of the frozen snow and all Africa at your feet.

Huts and camping sites there are, as on Kilimanjaro, and you would be best advised, coming new to the hazards, to join an organised mountain safari, equipped with mules and the necessary gear. Point Lenana, at 16,355 ft., is known as the tourist's peak, lying away up the scree and snowy slopes to be scrambled from the last rest hut. There are several points in Kenya where, when visibility is favourable, you can see both the giants, Kilimanjaro and Kenya faintly in the distance.

The nearest towns are Nanyuki and Nyeri, with fine views of the mountain from the hotel windows. The Outspan, at Nyeri, is a delightful retreat set in beautiful gardens, and is the hotel to which the famous Treetops is affiliated. This is a lookout post built in the trees, a comfortable hotel on its own account, where you can pass the night watching wild game coming out to drink in a scene bathed by artificial moonlight. The present Treetops is a new version of the old, which was destroyed during the Emergency. It was there Princess Elizabeth and her husband spent the night before her father died and, in the morning, she learnt she was Queen of England.

Kenya now has several of these hotel observation posts in the trees; another in Secret Valley is attached to the Sportsman's Arms at Nanyuki. I have already mentioned the fabulous Mount Kenya Safari Club, run by the American film star William Holden

Mail train ascending the Great Rift Valley, on its way to Nairobi and
Mombasa. Mt. Longonot in the background

Fort Jesus, Mombasa

and some associates, who love to "get away" to Kenya. In his time Lord Baden-Powell, the founder of Scouting, wanted to "get away", was attracted by the wondrous scenery and he spent the last years of his life at the Outspan. His grave at Nyeri draws pilgrimages of Boy Scouts from all over the world. Kilaguni is yet another, where you can sit on the verandah after dinner and watch the elephants and other wild game disporting themselves at the water-hole in a floodlit pageant in the surrounding darkness. Near by, at Mzima Springs, you can enter a submarine glass tank and watch the fish glide by, or have closer acquaintance with a crocodile.

Another extinct volcano, Mt. Elgon, lies away beyond Kitale on the borders of Kenya and Uganda, 14,140 ft. high and in densely wooded country where elephants are often seen. Incidentally, I never drive along the road that winds across the plateau between Nyeri and Thomson's Falls without getting some wry humour out of the notice-boards placed here and there at the wayside. Instead of "School", they read "Beware Elephants".

Mt. Elgon gives its name to one of the loveliest of woods in a country that boasts many fine specimens. It is the Elgon olive, whitish, with a deep grain and a faintly green sheen, not unlike English oak except for this peculiarity in hue and not quite so hard, but a beautiful wood for carving and household furniture. The nearest to the traditional English oak is, perhaps, the Meru oak which is really hard. Kenya's ubiquitous mvuli is used as an all-purpose wood and there are many others—but I digress. Mountains not trees. . . .

Come back, now, to central Kenya, to the Central Province itself, where the Aberdares rise as a watershed between the fertile, densely populated Kikuyu land between Nyeri, Karatina, Sagana and Fort Hall on the one side and the farming country between Nakuru, Gilgil and Navaisha on the other. No mountaineering skill is required for the Aberdares, since you drive across the back of the range which is an equatorial replica of the Berkshire downs. This is one of Kenya's loveliest areas, besides being very fertile. Once the land has been cleared of bamboo, I cannot think of any farming activity that may not be carried on. Rainfall is variable but, in the two seasons of the long and short rains, high ground like this will get 1,000–1,250 mm. (40 or 50 inches) and the climate is temperate, around 10–30°C (50–80°F). The nights have a cold snap in the air, so all the farmhouses pile up log fires.

The best-known farming areas of the Aberdares are the North and South Kinangop, where the first and main brunt of the transition in land ownership was felt. The former European mixed farms were brought out and divided for resettlement as smallholdings. In the centre of the range lies the dense forest on Kipipiri; at the northern end Ol Doinyo Lesatima stands sentry at 13,104 ft.

Coming round towards Nakuru, you will see Menengai which, if I am not mistaken, is one of the widest extinct craters in the world, covering 35 square miles. A rocky outcrop on one side at the top provides a perfect crow's nest observation post. The sides drop sheer, 1,000 ft. in places and the view is unobstructed to the north as far as you can see through your binoculars; to your left, miles away across The Rift; and round behind you, back across the farms of Subukia.

There are many more interesting mountains and peaks, such as Longonot, whose "old crater" covers 24 square miles and can be climbed relatively easily from a track leading off the main Rift Valley road. There are the Taita Hills, Mau Escarpment, Ol Doinyo Orok and Ol Doinyo Sabuk, while the four conical points of the Ngong Hills rise on the blue-green horizon of Nairobi, looking out beyond the Game Park. Masai legend had it that a god scooped up the ground along the brow of the hills, leaving hollows between the protruding points where his giant fingers passed.

Reverting, for a moment, to the Aberdares, I must not forget to say that here is the fisherman's delight in a country which has deep-sea fishing off the Coast for marlin, sailfish and other big 'uns, and sport in the rivers and trout streams. Tucked away in the Aberdares you will come across glades where tiny streams tinkle along between the trees as in an English dell. I shall never forget the first time I visited the North Kinangop, early in the Emergency when this was reckoned to be a dangerous area. Mr. Humphrey Slade had a farm there with the cosiest farmstead, where fuchsias grow round the door. In the late afternoon, we wandered down to the stream and there took the trout for our supper, at least he did, for I am no angler. It was so very peaceful.

You will have gathered the Aberdare range is fairly wet and riven by many streams. It is there that the Nairobi City Council

48

has dammed an artificial lake, Sasumua, which is also an angler's dream, but is really intended to supply Nairobi with water! And supply the city it does, through pipelines, with pure and very soft drinking water from the tap. Only a mile or so back along the track from Sasumua you used to be able to find an oasis of an inn called The Brown Trout, where again there is fishing at the bottom of the garden, literally at the bottom, because the lawns and flower gardens suddenly end in a bank dropping down into the gorge where a stream gurgles on its way. Unhappily, The Brown Trout was closed as an inn some time ago.

Finally, about these enthralling Aberdares, the range is now crossed by a motor road from Naivasha to Nyeri, which was opened by the Queen Mother. The road is a legacy from the days of the forest fighting, one of the few benefits, when a track was bull-dozed through the bamboo to supply troops engaged in operations. The forest was so dense and the countryside so remote that nobody had apparently ever been there before. This is a delightful drive nowadays, with landscape views of unexpected beauty and much wild game. Believe it or not, the new road led to the discovery of a magnificent waterfall. Now the traveller can rest near by and find lodge accommodation.

Kenya has a series of lakes, big and little, and at least fourteen waterfalls on its rivers. In the west, in Nyanza, the country is lapped by the waters of Lake Victoria, an inland sea covering 24,300 square miles, complete with a steamer service, ports and a thriving fishing industry. I have already mentioned Lake Rudolf, 154 miles long and 20 wide, which slices down from the triangle where Ethiopia, the Sudan and Kenya meet at Namoroputh; a mysterious lake, its origins still not fully explained but it has a fishery and a pleasant club for bathing and fishing away from the madding crowds.

In this remote corner there is a hill station called Lokitaung, surrounded by desert and at the end of a long gorge, the route Sir Richard Turnbull strode all the way from Namoroputh, down along the shores of the lake and then striking up into the hills in a famous walking contest. He was then an administrative officer and later became Chief Secretary (a kind of Prime Minister in the colonial Government and head of the Civil Service). Later still, he became Governor of (then) Tanganyika, which he took into independence and was appointed Governor-General until the country became a republic. And still later, he was Governor of Aden, with its internal troubles and fighting across the border with the Yemen, before Aden, in turn, gained independence.

I do not want to bore you by cataloguing all the rivers, lakes and falls, so I will mention only a few of the more interesting facts about some you can most easily reach. Down in The Rift you drive past three lakes in a row—Naivasha, Elmenteita and Nakuru. All are renowned for their bird life, especially the two last-named where the flamingos live and, taking off in banks of pink glory, hold you spellbound. This is a scene that has been filmed in colour to be repeated in cinemas where, perhaps, the people have seen only the homely sparrow or starling of the dark, industrial districts. Part of the circumference of Lake Nakuru has been declared a bird sanctuary and was so commissioned—if he will forgive the word—by Peter Scott. However, Nakuru can be temperamental and is a seasonal lake in that its area varies with the rainfall and, at times when the waters have receded and the banks dried, the wind can whip up clouds of soda dust. Fortunnately, this does not happen very frequently and the town of Nakuru itself, Kenya's agricultural capital, is attracting tourists in ever-increasing numbers.

These lakes also harbour odd characters like the hippos who were paddling in the papyrus growing thickly round a tiny island in Lake Naivasha one early morning when I had a place, duck-shooting, remarkably near their home. The garden of my host's farm ran out on to the shores of the lake. He explained that it was frequently visited by hippo who would gouge up rows of potatoes by using their snouts as harrows. Wherefore, he erected an electric fence. The wary hippos discovered that, by pushing the wooden stakes down, they could get across without a shock!

Amboseli, the game reserve in the south-west, has a very erratic lake which varies in size from almost nothing to forty or more square miles. And at Magadi there is a lake that is in parts solid enough not only to walk on, but to hold trucks. Magadi lies to the south of Nairobi and can be reached by car along a rough track which skirts the National Park, traverses the Ngong Hills and crosses the plain close to the prehistoric Olorgesailie. There you will find a self-contained township, complete with airstrip, hospital, shops, schools, where soda is mined from the lake first discovered and developed by the Germans before the First World

War. Some of the original heavy Krupps machinery is still in use.

Though Kenya has a dozen or more rivers, only two are navigable for any distance: the Tana for 200 miles by launch and the Athi (having by then become the Galana) by canoe. The Tana is the principal river, 440 miles long, rising in the Aberdares and flowing in a wide curving arc northwards over the waterfalls at Seven Forks, towards Garissa and then, turning away from Somalia, heading due south for the Indian Ocean at Kipini below Lamu Island. The Athi River rises in the Ngongs and begins by flowing north to take in the waters of Ol Doinyo Sabuk before changing its mind and, turning south, heading across the bushland, to become the Sabaki and then Galana, before emptying just above Malindi. This flat coastal area was submerged by deep floods, when 16 ins. of rain fell in one continuous downpour at the end of September 1961 and the two rivers burst their banks, submerging the neighbouring African villages.

The great drought lasting two years had ended when violent rainstorms lashed the country until nearly Christmas, causing serious floods, damaging roads and railways, destroying bridges, smashing down crops, and causing loss of life and havoc without recorded parallel. Famine and flood relief funds were opened, while the Royal Air Force, British naval and military forces went to the help of the Administration in reserve operations. Periods of drought and floods have alternated over the years since then, but nothing of the disastrous magnitude then experienced.

Some of the waterfalls are in faraway places which are difficult to reach, but others are just as easy to find. Nothing in Kenya can compare, of course, with Murchison or Victoria Falls, but cascading water is always inspiring to watch. The highest are the Seven Forks (440 ft.), away to the east of the Nairobi–Nyeri road where it passes Fort Hall. This is the area where a gigantic hydro-electric scheme is taking shape, the first phase having been completed and come into action to supplement electricity supplies from Owen Falls in Uganda. Along the same road, but nearer to Nairobi, are the Chania Falls, where the River Thika falls 80 ft.—at Thika.

Of all the waterfalls, my favourite is at Thomson's Falls, a township beyond the Aberdares, between Nanyuki and Nakuru. How the place got its name is easy enough; but how did the falls get theirs? Visiting Barry's Hotel, I saw a newspaper cutting framed in the entrance hall, giving some account of the exploits of that extraordinary young man Joseph Thomson. The falls are right alongside the hotel, nearly 100 ft. deep in a narrow gorge. The waters of the Ewaso Narok pour down the rock face, 200,000 gallons every minute. It can be very cold there at night because of the altitude and, lying in bed with a snug fire burning in the hearth, you can hear the boom of the rushing waters.

Joseph Thomson, the first white man to set eyes on the falls, was one of the great explorers of Africa. At the age of twenty, he was appointed to accompany a Royal Geographical Society expedition to the interior of Africa, led by Keith Johnston in 1878. Johnston died soon after setting out, so the youthful Thomson took charge. He covered the country between Lake Nyasa and Lake Tanganyika, discovered Lake Rukwa, and was back in London with his story of incredible adventure at the age of twenty-two.

Two years later, the Society asked him to go out again and he was off with alacrity, this time to the Masai country, with the idea of prospecting a caravan route through what was dangerous terrain peopled by hostile tribesmen. He set off in March 1883 from a place near Mombasa, visited Kilimanjaro and reached Naivasha, in The Rift Valley, by September, having by then covered at least 500 miles on foot.

On went Thomson to explore the plateau around Laikipia and Lake Baringo and he was the first white man to reach the eastern slopes of Mt. Elgon, marching successfully to Lake Victoria before the end of the year.

CHAPTER V

The Country's Economy

As Kenya is part of East Africa, the country's economy cannot be effectively disentangled from the remainder of the Common Market. For many years the three countries enjoyed various common services—Railways and Harbours, Posts and Telecommunications, East African Airways, Customs and Excise, currency and the diversity of research organisations are examples—and suffered no trade barriers. Their partnership was formalised in the Kampala Agreement signed by Presidents Kenyatta, Nyerere and Obote which brought the East African Community into being as from December 1, 1967.

This was the outcome of recommendations made by the Philip Commission, which had been set up to examine means for continuing and strengthening the common services, fostering trade between the partner States. Within a short time, neighbouring countries, notably Ethiopia, Somalia, Zambia among them, were applying to join. The Authority, as it is called, at the apex of the administration of the East African Community, is composed of the three Presidents, whose ultimate policy control widens out through Ministerial Committees on which the member States are equally represented. The permanent administrative machinery is directed by the Secretary-General. On the political and economic sides, the East African Legislative Assembly is a Parliament whose Members are drawn from the three countries, meeting regularly to debate their annual Budget for the Community, the balance sheets for the component Corporations administering the common services and other topics deemed appropriate.

As with other parliaments, the East African Legislative Assembly has its Ministers who report on their portfolios and are available for questioning during the proceedings. The Ministers are appointed from the three States but do not carry forward their individual national interests, having to deal with the broader outlook, so they are designated East African Minister for this or that.

One of the most, if not the most controversial provisions of the treaty lay in the inclusion of what is known as the Transfer Tax. In simple terms, the tax is meant to protect an embryo or struggling industry in one country against extreme competition from one well established in another, devolving from the fundamental principle of endeavouring to secure balanced development throughout the Community. The Transfer Tax had been accepted as the best, perhaps the only feasible, way of saving the trading partnership essential if a reasonable market is to be offered in order to attract investment and the expansion of industrial undertakings. Nobody knew quite how the tax would operate, for I believe this was a kind of economist's scheme which had never been worked out in practice in any other country. Consequently, there were many disquieting rumours and fears that the tax would set up trade barriers instead of freeing inter-statal trade from restrictions. As Kenya had become the most advanced of the three States in commerce, most international countries having their East African headquarters in Nairobi or Mombasa, clearly Kenya stood to lose most if the Transfer Tax worked harshly.

Moreover, the concentration of the former East African Common Services Organisation, which had superseded the colonial East African High Commission, in offices in and around Nairobi had given the impression that the whole set-up was fabricated for Kenya's advantage. Though this was far from true, the natural sentiments of national interest caused jealousies and suspicions of "what's going on up there in Nairobi". Under the Kampala Agreement, the headquarters fanned out, decentralising the postal authorities to Kampala, splitting the Railways from Harbours, with the head office of the former remaining in Nairobi and the latter moving to Dar es Salaam and so forth. The moves were not carried out without bitter opposition from many members of the staff who complained about being uprooted and understandably demanded accommodation.

The Community is centred at Arusha, which has become a sort of inter-territorial enclave and, although situated just across the Kenya border in Tanzania, is regarded not so much as Tanzanian as the East African capital. A vast building programme for offices and housing is being pushed through and the projected international airport has already been mentioned.

With statistics for only the first year of the Community's life available, it is difficult to assess the effects of the Transfer Tax and the complicated system of trading licences which has been introduced in each country. However, the East African Minister for Common Market and Economic Affairs, Dr. Ivan Majugo, had this to say to a meeting of the Legislative Assembly in Dar es Salaam:

"Goods subject to Transfer Tax have increased during 1968. Members will agree that the Transfer Tax has not killed trade within the Common Market as some prophets of doom forecast last year."

None the less, the full effects, and the changed pattern of trade and development between the three countries remain to be seen; for a full and reliable appreciation cannot be obtained until the Community and the Common Market have been operating for some, maybe ten, years. As a corollary, the three partner States set about affiliation to the European Economic Community on Associated Status, securing agreement after protracted negotiations in Brussels. Thus they accomplished something they had been unable, indeed, unwilling to do (because of its political connotations and suspicions) during the pre-independence era under British rule.

During the first year of the Community's existence, East Africa's external trade amounted to approximately £446,000,000, an increase of 6·8 per cent on the previous year, according to a report tabled in Kenya's National Assembly. For the first time, Zanzibar's contribution had been included in the figures; without it, the increase would have been 5·1 per cent.

Kenya's net imports stood at £115,000,000, Uganda's at £44,000,000 and Tanzania's £76,000,000. Nine or ten years ago, Kenya's imports totalled £90,000,000; but only a proportion of the total of these imports is destined to remain in Kenya, since the port of Mombasa serves as an inlet for goods consigned to Uganda and, to a decreasing extent as its own ports develop, for Tanzania.

This re-exporting accounts to a substantial extent for the colossal trade deficit Kenya appears to enjoy year after year; "enjoy" because such an adverse balance between the value of exports and imports implies machinery, plant and raw materials entering, with capital being invested in, a developing country.

Compared with the earlier figure of imports worth

£115,000,000, in the same year Kenya's exports were valued at £58,000,000, to which must be added the "invisible" items, mainly earnings from tourism. Kenya's exports showed a rise of about 8 per cent; at £65,000,000 Uganda's rose by 1·3 per cent; and at £79,000,000 Tanzania's rose by 2·1 per cent. Both Uganda and Tanzania, it will be observed, had favourable balances of trade. Re-exports that year declined in Kenya and Uganda, but increased by 24·3 per cent in Tanzania.

The report showed interesting trends—and all these figures are quoted to illustrate patterns since the actual totals will inevitably change year by year—in the trade conducted in local products and manufactured wares. Tanzania's exports to Kenya and Uganda rose by 12·6 per cent; Uganda's to the other two dropped by 15·2 per cent; Kenya's to Uganda fell by 10·3 per cent but rose by 14·8 per cent to Tanzania. Of the overall volume totalling £446,000,000, Kenya's share came first at £178,000,000, Tanzania's next at £158,000,000 and Uganda's third at £110,000,000.

When the three countries went into independence, they shared a common currency through the East African Currency Board, which had functioned for many years and had fairly recently moved its head office from London to Nairobi. Though it was thought the Currency Board would become the nucleus of an East African Central Bank, this was not to transpire; for Tanzania led the way, followed by Uganda and Kenya, in setting up separate Central (or State) Banks. From this it was an easy step, indeed inevitable, to create different currencies and monetary systems, an expensive exercise but dictated by the national fervour of the times and the varying policies. However, the three Central Banking systems work in close liaison and no overall policy decision is resolved unilaterally.

Thus it came about that, when Britain devalued the £ sterling, the East African countries remained aloof. By not devaluing alongside Britain, many millions were knocked off the value of the sterling assets they held, but they stood to gain 14 per cent plus on the costs of servicing and repaying loans and there was no change in parity with the dollar. The overall effects are still difficult to assess; some industries, especially tea and various agricultural lines, complain of heavy losses and increased competition; others say they are not affected and, generally, the Treasury and Central Bank in Kenya have continued to be optimistic. In terms of relative currency values, the effect of devaluation was to change the rates of exchange so that £1 British was worth approximately 17/- Kenyan; the other way round, 20/- Kenyan equalled slightly over 23/- British.

Currency Exchange Control regulations had been in force for some time prior to devaluation, necessitated by the flight of capital immediately before and after independence, when some business people were in a state of uncertainty. The situation was aggravated in Kenya, particularly, by the departure of Asian non-citizens, while it is obvious that one of the countries cannot have different regulations which would open up an escape route for money illicitly moved from a neighbouring country.

Permits are issued for remitting money for savings and payment of insurance premiums, school bills and other expenses; limits are put on overseas holiday allowances (at present £200 per person per two years) and the amount a returning non-citizen may take out on finally leaving Kenya (at present £2,500 followed by £1,000 a year of the capital for five years, then the remainder, together with annual drawing of pensions and dividends). It should be remarked that, although Britain applies restrictions to overseas holiday allowances, Kenya is within the sterling area and visitors therefore escape the ban.

Like the other States in East Africa, Kenya's money is based on the shilling, a "silver" coin. There are 100 cents to the shilling, issued in ten- or five-cent "copper" coins. "Silver" coins are issued for 25 and 50 cents, 1/- and 2/-; notes in denominations of 5/-, 10/-, 20/-, 50/- and 100/-. Officially, bills are calculated in shillings, but as the gross totals often run into unmanageable millions, it is customary in everyday usage to knock some of the noughts off by converting to pounds, 20/- equalling £1.

To the extent of money, at any rate, Kenya was already on the metric system when the Government decided to "go metric" fully. Weights and measures began to be changed over to grammes, kilos and so on, metres and kilometres in 1969, with an accompanying publicity programme. But the problems are so widespread, percolating to the very ends of this scattered country and affecting millions of illiterate or semi-literate people, that the "Imperial" system is running parallel with the metric and will do so for a considerable period in some respects. With miles still observed as road distances, and speedometers in car dashboards still marked in miles, how can K.P.H. take the place of M.P.H., with appropriate signs, as the speed limit? The change-over which has begun with the weights and measures in the shops will eventually overtake every activity and the country will become fully metric early in the 1970s. Meanwhile, not all the conversions have been made and people are inclined to think in the old terms, even if they can readily work out the sum and think "dual". That is why measurements are sometimes given in this book in miles or feet and sometimes in the metric method—including the very complicated conversion from Fahrenheit to Centigrade which has been already introduced by the Meteorological Department.

Raw materials must be imported for the steel rolling mills, a £750,000 plant due to be in production at Miritini, Mombasa, in 1970, which will put the country into the steel export business, as well as satisfying domestic needs. The plant's annual capacity is put at 36,000 tons of rolled steel bars and wire rods, some 16,000 tons a year more than Kenya requires, so the surplus is intended for export to neighbouring countries. Unlike Tanzania, Kenya has no diamonds and, at any rate as far as current discoveries go, is poorly off in mineral wealth.

Explorations are constantly being made for oil, mainly in the desert areas of the North-Eastern Province and off shore down the coast from Mombasa, but so far without any real success, though drilling has located the presence of some oil in these regions, encouraging the search to continue. The refinery built by Shell–B.P. at Mombasa draws its crude supplies from the Persian Gulf. Agriculture chiefly, and tourism to an ever-developing extent, are Kenya's economic mainstays.

East Africa in general, and Kenya in particular, is becoming a tourists' Mecca, because of the unrivalled combination of sunshine, scenery and wildlife within comparatively easy distance. Sometimes, this area is regarded with a little apprehension because of the political uncertainties and upheavals in other parts of Africa, which are reflected on other—and innocent—countries and the reputation derived from over-dramatised and sensational reports often appearing in the overseas press.

Once during a broadcast to New York, I remember being asked by the commentator about the dangers, or otherwise, of becoming involved in trouble. "Every country and city in the world has its crime," I replied. "Tourists will see little or nothing of Kenya's political problems and you should certainly not worry about getting mixed up in any Wild West shooting stuff." Immediately after the Zanzibar revolution a chain reaction set in of army mutinies but Kenya's was localised to one unit at Lanet and was of only passing consequence.

Sometimes the country gets a bad name unintentionally, and even by mistake. I recall, also, meeting a visitor who was most annoyed, and very frightened, having been surrounded, as he graphically said, by a menacing crowd of Africans while driving with his family along a road in the remote Abaluhya country. He complained that they stopped his car, they were armed with bows and arrows, wearing their "war paint" and accompanied by a band of tom-toms.

This story was given wide play in the British newspapers; but I do not recall any British newspaper publishing the explanation. It came from Mr. Musa Amalemba, himself a Baluhya, at that time a Minister in the Government and now holding a senior post with East African Airways. It seemed the visitor had met a procession on its way to a funeral ceremony and the "warlike and menacing appearance" was nothing more dangerous than some understandable irritation at the disturbance of their serious rites. Another occasion when troubles were given "big play" in the overseas press and on the radio and television was when a series of disorderly scenes followed Tom Mboya's murder, the people being incensed with grief and anger.

Within the foreseeable future travel will become the world's biggest industry and it seems that unquestionably tourism will be East Africa's biggest industry, far outstripping the others. In this sense, the tourist industry must not be considered solely from the point of view of the pleasure given to visitors, important though this is, or the money they spend, but also as to the contribution the revenue so earned can make to raising the general standards of living, providing more schools and hospitals, developing the roads and other communications. In short, strengthening the general economy, which is too reliant on agriculture and, accordingly, vulnerable to the vagaries of "pricey" chance that beset primary producing countries.

Even before *uhuru*, a remarkable forecast was made by Mr. John Keen, whose people, the Masai, had taken over the control of the

Amboseli game reserve, a Number One tourist attraction. Mr. Keen was speaking in the Legislative Council as Member for Kajiado soon after he had visited Cairo.

"Egypt is making £24,000,000 a year from tourism," said Mr. Keen, "and there is nothing to see there but the pyramids and a few dead kings lying around." He firmly believed Kenya should aim at boosting the tourist trade to £50,000,000 a year, which is flying high but—nothing venture . . .

How far has Kenya progressed along the road he signposted? Inside ten years, the tourist expansion was stupendous, with all this entails in the hotel business, game lodges, travel agencies, transport, photography and the making and sale of wood carvings, drums, shields and other souvenirs in "cottage industries". On the eve of the Jumbo-jet age, which will further increase the tourist traffic, it was computed that 257,690 visitors came to Kenya in a year, including the immensely popular "package tours" from Switzerland and West Germany and those beginning from England. Tourist revenue was then put at £16,400,000 for the year by the energetic and capable Minister for Tourism and Wildlife, Mr. S. O. Ayodo, who contributes a section to this book on his special subject. For the first time, tourism overtook coffee to become the country's leading "export", earning 18 per cent of all the income in foreign exchange.

Almost all the domestic exports listed in the trade statistics bear witness to the superabundance of agriculture in the national economy. Previously, the major portion of the national wealth was earned by the European farming areas, but African production has swung in to take its place, as thousands of African families have become farmers as a result of the agrarian revolution. Moreover, African farming methods have become more modernised and their productivity given a tremendous impetus by the application of the Swynnerton Plan.

This was a far-sighted, imaginative and most expert scheme for the development and modernisation of African farming, drawn up by Mr. R. J. Swynnerton, then Director, later the Permanent Secretary of the Ministry for Agriculture, and put into operation during the darkest years of the Emergency, costing many millions of pounds and the expenditure of enormous scientific know-how. Not the least problem for all farmers is the deficiency in sulphur properties which must be made good in the soil.

Perennial difficulties beset Kenya farmers, as they do in every country: difficulties of the prices obtained, measured against production, as well as natural hazards. Mr. Bruce McKenzie has talked often and straight to the Food and Agriculture Organisation about the necessity to stabilise world prices in order to give the primary producing countries a reasonable return which will facilitate the purchase of up-to-date machinery which the less-developed countries require so that they can develop. All this is a vicious circle, with low prices for agricultural produce and products constantly chasing but lagging behind the rising costs of manufactured goods from the sophisticated and industrialised countries. "Aid through trade" is the surest creed, and overseas trade for Kenya lies chiefly in agricultural lines whose values on the competitive world markets are constantly in jeopardy.

Then our farmers experience the natural hazards, another vicious circle of droughts and floods. Prolonged drought also results in a plague of army worm, a form of striped caterpillar which will cover a field and strip it bare of vegetation before moving on; much as the locusts would if swarms were not kept at bay by the incessant vigilance and spraying in their breeding grounds as far away as Ethiopia by field workers of the Desert Locust Survey.

Almost anything, it is claimed, will grow in Kenya. This is more or less true, given the right fertilisers and water, though the height has to be taken into account, and the temperature. For instance, a night's frost will curl up the leaves of coffee. It is said this happened on Baroness von Blixen's estate in the 1920s at Karen and there have been much later sorry experiences at Limuru, though this is an area turning over to tea. Lack of daily water—and here the rain which comes almost without fail every day is a great advantage in the Kericho district—will similarly ruin the tea bushes.

The country's principal agricultural activities are in ranching, dairying, pigs and sheep; coffee, tea, pyrethrum, maize, wheat and barley, sugar, sisal (though diminishing), pineapples, cashew and other nuts and market gardening. There is an ever expanding demand for Kenya's strawberries, avocado pears, beans and other vegetables, carnations, roses and exotic flowers including orchids, in the European capitals, being exploited especially in the European "off seasons" by air freight services reaching these markets within 12 hours.

You will note the reference to the diminishing demand for sisal. This has been caused by the flop in world prices, which hit Tanzania very heavily, due in turn to the synthetics. Here is a grave threat to natural produce which will have to be taken into serious planning account, as Mr. McKenzie never tires of warning. After all, it comes to something when you can get a synthetic lunch all the way from the cocktails, through the meat and on to the sweet, which he and Mr. Gichuru sampled in New York.

Maize being the staple foodstuff, strategic supplies have to be maintained in stores scattered throughout the country. A statutory authority has been set up to control the industry—the Maize and Produce Board—and regulate strategic stocks against exports (which are invariably chancy and generally at non-remunerative prices subsidised by cess). Prices to the farmers, and consequently to the consumers, are fixed by the Government through the Board. The Government also influences the general farming pattern by fixing prices for other principal lines, together with a variable guaranteed mean return per acre for wheat, over-produced recently against demand, so the acreages under wheat are being whittled down.

All in all, the gross farm revenue from marketed production, which stood at £60,378,000 in 1964, had risen to £70,634,000 by 1968, the last year for which complete statistics are currently available.

Organised agriculture began with the arrival of the very first settlers and, as everybody knows, where two or three farmers are gathered together, there you will find a show. The (then) Royal Agricultural Society of Kenya (which obtained its "Royal" in 1929 after a visit of the then Prince of Wales) celebrated its Diamond Jubilee in 1961 with a Royal Show at Mitchell Park, Nairobi, worthy in its setting and the quality of the exhibits of a Royal Show in England though not, of course, nearly as big. A few months before, the Jubilee of the Nakuru Show—which was first held in 1911—attracted many thousands of people to the permanent showground on the outskirts of the Agricultural Capital of Kenya. After independence, the word "Royal" was dropped from the title of the society and the show, which became the Nairobi Show, held at Jamhuri Park, that name also having been changed. The society spread its activities to organise district

Old Harbour, Mombasa

Sardine fishing, Old Port of Mombasa

shows, in all eleven in different places, albeit at considerable financial strain which ultimately curtailed this sphere of activity.

What one might describe as "mechanised farming" vastly increased the production of settled areas, where capital was invested far beyond the means of African smallholders in early times. Nevertheless, Africans have made great progress, by their own efforts and under the encouragement of the Swynnerton Plan. Difficulties have been encountered by the Government's Agricultural Officers, for the African farmer, like many another, is conservative at heart. Opposition was at first shown to immunisation of stock against diseases, but has been almost entirely worn down. Measures to prevent soil erosion have not always been eagerly accepted, but the bench terracing seen alongside the road to Nyeri, and similar improvements on Banana Hill, are typical of the advances made as the African farmer becomes more enlightened in scientific measures to aid intensive farming, and can acquire more capital. Banana Hill is something of a showplace, quite near to Nairobi and about half-way to the country club on the heights of Limuru. There you will see a bizarre contrast between ancient and modern: women file along the side of the road bowed down under the burdens of wood or water, which their menfolk are seldom seen to shoulder.

Flying low over the Central Province, you see a panorama of progress in the densely farmed countryside. Fields are laid out for pyrethrum, coffee, pineapples and other crops; roads run along the tops of the parallel ridges and tracks branch off into the valleys between.

Much of the produce grown by African smallholders finds its way to the markets in the towns and villages and is of good quality; produce including almost all the vegetables known in America or Britain and some more besides. The old dependence on subsistence farming, when peasants eked out a meagre existence on their strips of land, is disappearing in the face of economic necessity. The transformation has been helped by—indeed it would have been impossible to achieve without—land consolidation. This process started during the Emergency when scattered families living in their *bomas* were moved into villages in the areas of the Central and Rift Valley Provinces. They had never been accustomed to living together at such close quarters; the social problems were not easy for the Administration and voluntary organisations to master. The original purpose of collecting the people into villages was security: their own protection and closer supervision. Soon, the villages took on a different complexion as the people began to enjoy some of the benefits of modern ways of life, such as piped water, electricity, clinics and schools handy to their homes.

Meanwhile, the process of land consolidation had been causing a social and agrarian transformation in the Central and Rift Valley Provinces and among the Luo of Nyanza. By immemorial custom, a man's land was divided between his heirs after his death. The permutations and combinations of this custom often resulted in one man living with three or four wives in a *boma* and owning strips of land in a dozen or more different places, minute strips as often as not, separated by several miles so that the journey alone made cultivation difficult. Full economic use of the land was out of the question in these conditions. By a system of exchange and adjustment, these fragmented holdings were consolidated into an area of land which was both manageable and economic. Surveys were undertaken, title deeds prepared and the hope is that, with the adoption of the system of primogeniture, farms will be preserved as fully productive units down the years. It must not be imagined that this era of change passed without trouble and the legacy of trouble.

The enclosures way back in English history brought their political and economic consequences; so did land consolidation in Kenya. First, the lands of those people, chiefly Kikuyu, who were convicted as Mau Mau fighters or sympathisers under the colonial régime, were confiscated. When those who were sent to prison or otherwise detained were released to their home districts, naturally enough they demanded the return of their lands. The independent African Government was faced with heavy, and tricky, responsibilities, but through the exercise of wisdom and patient skill managed to resettle almost all those who were dispossessed and what could have welled into a dangerous crisis of discontent was overcome.

Second, consolidation meant fewer landowners. Though they then began to employ African labour of their own, many people were forced off the land and driven to seek urban employment. A similar change-over in Britain was facilitated by the industrial revolution which, in the midst of its evils, did provide alternative work in the factories. Kenya has needed, but lacked, the corresponding upsurge in its urban and industrial development to provide the cushion against change. However, land consolidation is one colonial measure adopted and furthered by the independent African Government, if only for the value of land titles and deeds for security against loans essential for development purposes.

Leaving aside the political consequences of the agrarian revolution, what has happened to affect the nature of agricultural production itself? "The cry for cash crops to strengthen the financial viability of agriculture in the African areas had become dominant and produced a deeper interest in the science of better farming than was thought possible ten years ago," Mr. Swynnerton reported. This point is illustrated by the increase of acreages under coffee and tea, started much later in African areas. Because of the capital involved, the processing and need to organise marketing, much of this activity, including sisal and pyrethrum, is carried on through co-operative undertakings.

Pyrethrum, a plant with tiny white daisies turning the fields into snowdrifts, has given the farmers, and especially African smallholders, a financial boost. Sales of pyrethrum extract and flowers had risen in value from under £1,000,000 early in the decade to nearly £2,630,000 by 1968. All this is owed to exploitation of the discovery during the Second World War of the chemical properties of pyrethrum as a base for insecticides but, if the industry is to be maintained at such a high level, the pyrethrin content will have to be improved above the average of 1·34 per cent being obtained in 1967–8. Headquarters of the Pyrethrum Board and Marketing Board are situated in Nakuru, the centre of this industry.

Pyrethrum is so relatively easy to grow, and commands such a quick and sometimes profitable return, that the expansion has been extremely rapid; so rapid and widespread that there is an ever-present danger of over-production. African smallholders do not take easily to the economic reasons for quotas, but pyrethrum production had to be rationalised and quotas proved an effective means.

The dangers of over-production are not confined to pyrethrum, as is seen so often in the story of Kenya's agriculture and with stock, where a man's wealth is calculated by the number of cattle he owns, irrespective of whether the animals are thin and scraggy.

Where stock are paid over as the bride price for a wife, the owners are additionally disinclined to cull their herds. Unless they will take such measures to keep the herds down to the grazing capacity of the land, huge tracts are in danger of being converted into dust-bowls. It must be remembered that, in some parts of the country, the land will at best support only one head on four or five, even ten acres.

Culling is necessary, also, to conserve wildlife, despite the objections continually made by those protectors of game who hate to see any animal slaughtered.

Some comparative figures, as listed in the *Economic Survey* for 1969, and referring to 1968 production, will serve as a guide to Kenya's agricultural and allied industries. After tourism, coffee exports earned £12,808,000, a decrease of £2,867,600 from the previous year. The coffee crop, which suffered in quality and quantity because of the ravages of Coffee Berry Disease (C.B.D.) fell by 17·5 per cent. Looking ahead, the forecast is a recovery to the extent of 25 per cent and the outlook is improved as a result of the success achieved against C.B.D. by spraying with newly developed chemicals, and a recovery in prices, though they remain below the 1964–6 levels.

In a world groaning under the surplus of Brazilian and other coffees, Kenya has no great cause to worry over competition, because the supreme quality of its Arabica coffee meets steady demand, especially in West Germany, even at high prices; in contrast with the lower prices and uncertain demands for the hard coffees, such as Robusta produced in Uganda. Nevertheless, there is a perpetual struggle to maintain reasonable quotas under the International Coffee Agreement, with efforts to find booster non-quota markets. Sometimes, production has to be pegged, or cut back by uprooting the bushes. However, the toll of C.B.D. wreaks the same reducing effects in bad seasons.

Tea production, especially from new smallholding areas, has shown a spectacular increase of more than 30 per cent over the last year or two. Despite the financial returns suffering from devaluation, tea exports earned an additional £2,645,000 in 1968 and, standing at £10,041,000 rank second in agriculture. This rapid expansion is based on African planting of carefully reared seedlings under the supervision of the Ministry of Agriculture and with help from the research and other services given by the established tea industry. The international groups have redoubled their activities as they have met difficulties elsewhere in the world, notably in Ceylon.

Kenya's tea-growing country centres mainly, but by no means exclusively, on Kericho, a delightful town in the Western Province, where the lines of closely planted bushes shine a vivid green in the sun. The high-altitude climate is near perfect, for rain falls regularly almost every afternoon. The Tea Hotel, as its name suggests, was originally built for the convenience of staff and visitors to the tea industry, but is now open to other guests who find the place delightfully restful. The world's increasing tea supplies are creating a situation in which yet another artificial curtailing is threatened under the international fixing of quotas.

The bumper maize harvest in 1968 added a welcome £4,774,000 in foreign exchange, though not without drawback, since the prices obtained overseas were lower than those paid out to the producers, necessitating another subsidy. Over-production of maize (£5,361,000) and wheat (£6,779,000) continue to be serious, more so for wheat than maize, which provides the staple foodstuff called *posho*, a form of yellow flour. In the immediate years ahead, many farmers will have to move out of wheat, turning perhaps to maize or livestock as alternatives.

There has been a steep decline in the production and earning capacity of sisal. In 1964, sisal output was valued at £6,691,000, but in five years declined to £2,193,000. Sisal is the product of a plant having stiff green fronds (the process of extraction is called decortication) and is the raw material for rope and matting being woven in ever more attractive forms, with artistically coloured designs. What with hybrids yielding treble the output per plant, and world trends towards synthetics causing falling prices for the natural fibre, the acreage planted with sisal will undoubtedly continue to shrink.

There is a considerable trade in wattle bark extract and wattle bark (£702,000) from the tree of this name which bursts into a mass of tiny yellow flowers resembling mimosa, to which some people are allergic on account of the pollen giving them hay fever. The product is used in the manufacture of leather.

In a country such as Kenya, with its ranches, dairies and wildlife, one would expect to find these sources making a direct contribution to the national income, and one would be justified.

The total value of cattle and calves for slaughter, sheep, goats and lambs, pigs, poultry and eggs topped £13,155,000, with dairy products at £6,360,000; wool was worth £550,000 and hides, skins and undressed furs £653,000 in the year under review. Leopard skins are popular with the ladies, and fetch fantastic prices in the fashionable salons, but killing leopard is highly unpopular in Kenya lest the species should die out.

All the meat is exported by the Kenya Meat Commission, a quasi-Government organisation functioning at Athi River on behalf of the producers. The counterpart for dairy farmers is the Kenya Co-operative Creameries. These and several other parastatal trading organisations existed before independence. Since then, a notable feature of the country's economy has been the development in co-operatives and State trading corporations.

There is even one for the wine trade, besides transport and the giant National Trading Corporation which covers a wide range of imported commodities.

To conclude this review of agriculture's massive contribution to the general economy, sugar-cane has climbed the list to reach a value of £2,185,000, coconuts and by-products (grown only on the Coast) fetched nearly £500,000 and the range of fruits £810,000.

Cotton, which is in its infancy compared with Uganda and Tanzania, is making headway and the 1968 crop was worth £700,000. Scanning the cash crops which have expanded, cashew nuts return more than £325,000 for growers, also at the Coast. The nuts are exported mainly to India for processing, but plans are on hand for processing to a far greater extent in Kenya. Cashew nuts are also exported to the U.S.A. in bulk, to be sold in small packets. An interesting departure is being made in the East and Central Provinces, where a great number of trees bearing Macadamia nuts have been planted. At present, world production is low and prices consequently high. Though no significant output has been produced so far, Kenya hopes to become a leading supplier of Macadamia nuts as the plantings mature.

Manufacturing experienced its fastest rate of growth in 1968 for several years. Most of the increase in output was directed towards internal consumption, but the *Economic Survey* records that exports also moved ahead, notably to Tanzania after the abolition of quantitative restrictions under the East African Treaty.

The Country's Economy

On the other hand, in some industrial groups, particularly textiles, stocks accumulated to a high level. The Quantity Index of Manufacturing Production in 1968 showed an overall increase of 7·2 per cent; the groups contributing the greatest weights were food, transport, beverages and tobacco, followed by paper and printing, chemicals, non-metallic minerals and metal products.

Sales of timber and other forest products (e.g. charcoal) have fallen away, but an active policy of afforestation has greatly increased the acreages planted with indigenous softwoods and hardwoods, cypress and pines.

The only sizeable chemical or mineral output is in soda ash from Magadi, gold, Kaolin, carbon dioxide, Diatomite, limestone, salt and copper from the Macalder mine in Nyanza. The soda production was valued at £1,225,000 but copper declined steeply from £655,000 to £14,600 in the course of five years.

Between the two world wars, rumours about gold strikes ran through the country, echoing overseas, leading to the formation of exploitation companies. Nowadays, gold (its output more than doubled in the same five years when copper declined and now worth nearly £450,000) is to be found in the vicinity of the Macalder mine and in the Kakamega area, where once there was a regular "gold rush". Prospectors carry on hopefully, some of them picturesque characters, looking for diamonds and rubies as well as gold. Nowadays they are armed with Geiger counters and they fly around in aircraft, as well as trekking on safari, searching for uranium or other radio-active deposits. The discovery of radio-active minerals in Mrima Hill, down on the Coast towards the Tanzanian border, created a stir some years ago, but the difficulties of working relatively low concentrations have prevented any major development.

Electric power is supplied through a conjunction of the grid from Owen Falls in Uganda and the Seven Forks generating station on the Tana River. President Kenyatta officially "switched on" the Kindaruma Dam power-house after the first phase of this immense project was completed. Additions estimated to cost many millions of pounds are being planned to take shape in the early 1970s by the Tana River Development Co. Ltd. In addition, there is renewed interest in exploration to harness geothermal steam deposits in the Lake Hannington area to generate electricity. Completion of the transmission line linking Mombasa to the main Kenya grid at Nairobi, together with additional Coast electricity capacity, is scheduled for 1970–1 at a cost exceeding £8,350,000.

The chairman of East African Power and Lighting Co. Ltd., Mr. Vincent Maddison, recalls that geothermal steam exploration was undertaken without success in the Lake Naivasha area in the 1950s; new techniques since available appear to justify further search around Lake Hannington. At any rate, international aid is being sought to carry out the survey.

Lacking an industrial prime mover, secondary and light industries are attracting development money and enterprise. Huge amounts are being invested in building super-hotels up to international standards. A new Hilton and the Inter-Continental (associated with T.W.A. and Pan-Am respectively) tower into the sky, the former literally with its rotunda, as the latest additions in the centre of Nairobi, supplementing the original New Stanley and Norfolk, with the Ambassadeur and Pan-Afric also opened in recent years. Old hotels have been refurbished and extended and new ones built at the Coast: Lawfords is an example of the former, the Dolphin of the latter. There is no doubt that "selling services" is becoming one of the country's main occupations which will grow steadily as tourism develops.

Talking about secondary industries, I must not fail to mention the Kamba carvings, which are not only made for sale to visitors but have acquired such fame that great quantities are now exported for sale at souvenir shops in many parts of the world. These carvings are not exclusively the work of the Wakamba, for the Kikuyu and other people are also adept at wood sculpture, fashioning beautiful figures of wild animals, lithe in their lines and curves, and warriors' heads, often adorning wooden salad spoons and so on.

Where do Kenya's exports go and whence come the imports? Trade with the sterling area continues to expand. Over the past five years, there has been an increase of £5,000,000 in exports to sterling countries, raising the yearly total to £24,529,000 of which Britain took the lion's share at £15,879,000. Exports to the U.S.A. were worth £4,202,000; Canada £1,311,000; West Germany £5,861,000; the Netherlands £2,882,000; Italy £1,293,000 and the same for France; the Soviet Union and Eastern Europe £1,374,000; non-sterling African countries £4,989,000; and, in the Far East, Japan took £1,697,000 worth, with China trailing behind at £437,000.

Imports from sterling area countries stood at £46,050,000 Britain accounting for £36,110,000. Going down the list once again: Imports from the U.S.A. were worth £7,922,000; Canada £773,000; West Germany £9,112,000; Italy £4,841,000; France £4,103,000; the Netherlands £3,440,000; Soviet Union and Eastern Europe £2,555,000; and, in the Far East, Japan sent £7,969 worth of goods and China £1,592,000. Imports from Iran totalled £8,944,000, accounted for mainly by oil.

In every town, and in many tiny settlements, banking and insurance facilities are provided by international companies, with Kenya entering the financial field through its own insurance corporation and building society. These incursions are signs of the particular attention being paid to investment from internal resources rather than seeking finance from outside. The State's Provident Fund and private funds of a similar nature represent savings which accumulate into considerable sums available for investment, while Currency Exchange Control had the effect of keeping much more money inside the country.

The late Minister for Economic Planning and Development, Mr. Mboya, had been explicit in his warnings that developing countries must move away from their dependence on the financial fluctuations of the big Powers, such as Britain and the U.S.A., having watched with some alarm—fortunately not borne out in the event—the successive monetary crises in Europe. Few of the major trading nations are following expansionary politics, Mr. Mboya pointed out, stressing "the serious consequences of such stop–go movements for development efforts in countries such as Kenya". Consequently, "we must adopt a growth strategy to reduce the impact of these movements on developing nations".

Only a month before he died he was able to report, triumphantly, that the target of an average rate of growth, set at 6·3 per cent in the Development Plan for 1964–70, had been achieved despite all the external vagaries of world trade and the internal uncertainties of weather, harvests and the changes caused by the introduction of the entry permit system to control employment in certain categories and the operation of the Trade Licensing Act.

During that first planning period, the estimated investment of £92,000,000 was exceeded by something over £8,000,000. The successor five-year plan for 1970–4 sets its sights even higher, providing for a steady growth in development expenditure. Actual expenditure for the first of these years, as provided in the Budget for 1969–70, is likely to be around £26,000,000, which is in excess of any previous year.

How does the development money go? The biggest item is nearly £8,000,000 for roads, agricultural projects take £3,800,000; new housing £2,300,000; about £2,100,000 is being spent on land settlement, but substantially for farm development instead of land transfers, marking a sharp change from previous years when the transition in land ownership was taking place; £2,000,000 for health services includes £950,000 to convert the Kenyatta National Hospital in Nairobi into a teaching hospital; education takes £1,900,000 for development, on top of the recurrent costs; and rather more than £1,000,000 has been allocated for commerce and industry, to include loans for new African traders.

How is this money raised? Loans and grants from overseas total about £14,000,000, to which the World Bank is expected to contribute nearly £5,000,000. Then come loans from the U.K., principally for purposes associated with the land, West Germany for roads, agriculture and irrigation, and from the Scandinavan countries. Significantly, because of the insistence on more and more self-reliance instead of overseas borrowings, it is expected to raise slightly more than half of the total expenditure from internal sources.

When, as Minister for Finance, Mr. James Gichuru, was answering a parliamentary question put by a K.P.U. Member (Mr. Okelo-Odongo) he stressed that Kenya's policy is to borrow less and less from foreign countries and eventually rely on its own resources. The questioner wanted the Government to stop borrowing from Britain and switch to the Soviet Union and China—"in view of the fact that Kenya's debt to Britain was staggering and almost equal to Kenya's national budget and in view of the fact that the country would come to a standstill if Britain demanded immediate payment of all money due in the event of a quarrel between the two on such matters as Rhodesia".

A demand for immediate payment seems out of the question, but how much does Kenya owe to countries overseas? Mr. Gichuru said £42,704,800 to Britain; £3,280,300 to the U.S.A.; £3,679,000 to West Germany; and £162,900 to the Soviet

Union. Kenya, he insisted, had sufficient resources to back its economy and is quite solvent.

His Budget for 1969–70 provided for recurrent expenditure amounting to £67,000,000 besides the money required for development purposes. This figure ran £5,620,000 higher than in the previous year. About one-fifth of the total spending goes on the combined costs of the armed forces, police and the judiciary, standing at more than £12,000,000 and the highest in any field of activity since security, internal and external, is the foundation of the country's stability, hence its progress.

Education took the greatest single allocation, at £9,552,000, which was ahead of agriculture, grossing £8,202,000, but the latter attracted the biggest of the appropriations-in-aid leaving only £3,650,000 to be met from the Budget yield. The Ministry of Local Government accounted for the next highest, at £5,536,600.

Fiscal policy in many respects is co-ordinated between the three countries in the East African Common Market, but recent years have brought some divergencies. Most imported commodities are subject to *ad valorem* duties. Motor-cars, especially the bigger models, attract heavy duty but petrol, at around 5/- a gallon, is cheaper than in most countries. Direct taxation—personal income and company taxes—though still below British rates, is considered by some critics to be on the high side for a country anxious to attract development investment. A Graduated Personal Tax applies to everybody, rising from a few shillings a month for the lowest paid workers to £20 plus a year at the top scales. Taxpayers also pay a Hospital Tax to provide for State relief towards the cost of hospitalisation and contribute to the State Provident Fund as compulsory saving. Monthly deductions are made by employers under the Pay-As-You-Earn system to meet Income Tax demands. The standard rate is at present 2/50 cents in the £. Surtax, mounting as the level of income rises, is payable on taxable salaries above £1,000 a year, and collected in two half-yearly instalments.

Industrial relations are well and widely organised, with a strong trade union movement and employers' organisation. Mr. Mboya began his public career as a trade union organiser and rose to become Secretary-General of the Kenya Federation of Labour, alongside being a vibrant nationalist campaigning for independence. He relinquished the union post after he was appointed a Minister and, presently, it passed to Mr. C. K. Lubembe, who was to become a figure of some controversy in political and union affairs.

The Federation at one period splintered, when a group of unions formed themselves into a rival Congress. Ultimately, they were fused into a monolithic body under the title of the Central Organisation of Trade Unions. Mr. Lubembe remained as Secretary-General for some time, until the 1969 elections resulted in his defeat and Mr. Dennis Akumu replaced him. A very able trade union administrator, Mr. Akumu is also a knowledgeable economist, well qualified to lead the workers' movement.

The employers are organised under the Federation of Kenya Employers. Sir Colin Campbell, a man of fair views and forthright expression, has held the office of President with distinction for a number of years and it will be sad to see him return to his native Scotland, as he must in the early seventies on account of private business commitments—he is engaged in the tea world.

Conciliation machinery is maintained by the Government, working through the officers of the Ministry of Labour for, as in most countries, disputes will occur from time to time. If no settlement can be reached at that level, final recourse lies to the Industrial Court, where Mr. Saeed Cockar, a barrister who has shown a notable flair for enlightened industrial relations, sits as President. I first met Mr. Cockar when he was Kenya's star tennis player!

CHAPTER VI

How the People Live

When they hear Kenya mentioned, many people think at once of "The Happy Valley Crowd" and they are thinking back. This was the name given to a happy-go-lucky set among some of the older generation, who gave rise to the question: "Are you married or do you live in Kenya?"

There certainly were some high-jinks in the roaring twenties and thirties, which was nothing unusual in many another country in the years between the wars; but the real backbone of Kenya, the people who made the country, were never as feckless and amoral as some novelists make out. It is true a few people lived in Happy Valley and behaved as its name implies, so its murky reputation continues in the imagination of many.

Nowadays, the people of this polyglot country have their lives to lead and they behave with as much propriety, and no more, as the people of any society in the world. Mini-skirts are worn by many young women and girls in the towns, African and European, though the Asians mostly remain faithful to their traditional dress, and the young African male outlook is critical about taking on "Western culture" in this fashion. The antics of the permissive age have not, anyway as yet, turned this cosmopolitan place crazy.

Some years ago, and this was before *uhuru*, a London liberal Sunday newspaper published an *exposé* of the lavish living of "the settlers", saying all the luxurious cars that went swishing past were driven by Europeans. Today, that reporter re-visiting Kenya would get an eye-opener. With the advent of Africanisation, the face of society, as of the economic scene, has radically changed, and for the better. African men and women hold posts throughout the fabric of national life. Many are well-paid administrators and business people; it is perhaps true to say that top salaries are often fixed too high for people working in their home country because of the inflated rates paid to attract expatriates, past and present, which are the legacy and comparison.

75

No longer do barriers rigidly confine the families of different races to specified areas, although aggregations do remain, as we shall see, for Africans and Asians have percolated the formerly exclusive European districts such as Muthaiga, which is Nairobi's fashionable suburb and a magnet for the seniors among the Diplomatic Corps. Many of the cars that swish by are driven by Africans with happy faces; and good luck to them in their climb from the under-privileged class. What this country is engaged in is a war against poverty, ignorance and disease. Though it is being fought the socialist way, this does not mean everybody must be reduced to a common low denominator, with all the enjoyment screwed out of their lives. Anyway, it would be impossible to lead a drab existence in this sunshine.

Not long before his death, Mr. Mboya had something telling to say on this subject of the so-called African *élite*, holding that African socialism implies levelling upwards, not downwards; the poor should be made richer, not the rich reduced to poverty. Interviewed by the *Sunday Nation*, he said:

"You can't really think you are going to try to create a colourless society in this country, or any other country in the world. It has been tried before, in Russia, and it was decided that nobody should earn more than 300 roubles, regardless of his job, his station in life and so on. This is the kind of attitude or approach which is really negative, because it can lead people to assuming things that are not going to happen."

To drive a Mercedes-Benz is something of a status symbol in Kenya, as owning a Rolls-Royce or Bentley, Pontiac or Cadillac in other countries. What had Mr. Mboya to say about this? the questioner pursued.

"The mere fact that a Cabinet Minister drives in a Mercedes car does not mean he is removed from his people or from identifying with the *wananchi*," Mr. Mboya replied. "I drive in a Mercedes because it is the most convenient means of transport that I think is suitable."

Under the traditional clan system, the more well-to-do Africans are honour bound to help their less fortunate relations; wherefore, one frequently finds a high income reduced in real terms to the individual because the money is shared round to help support several other families.

"What is not recognised by some of our critics," said Mr. Mboya in the same interview, "is that the new African *élite*, so-called, is not really the kind of person they think he is. When I look at the senior civil servants among our people, the host of family relations who feed on them and hang on them, is nothing compared with what a European District Commissioner used to have to contend with.

"An African Permanent Secretary is looking after such a large family unit—this extended family problem—that it is virtually dragging him to the ground. The higher you go, and the more salary you earn, the greater responsibility you undertake."

A Permanent Secretary is paid approximately £3,000 a year, with certain fringe benefits such as housing and a car loan. When considering the progress being made toward a Utopian State based on the equalities of socialism, Mr. Mboya was right in saying:

"It is naïve to think that, with the kind of colonial institutions we inherited at the time of independence, we could have moved to the final goal in five, six, ten or even twenty years."

Tom Mboya met his death in the prime of life, aged 38, having already attained world stature as a politician and orator. The manner of his assassination was at once a wanton display of pointless killing and an illustration of the informal behaviour in everyday life to which the Ministers and other public dignitaries were accustomed. He left his office at lunchtime one Saturday in July 1969—having returned only the previous day from a conference in Addis Ababa—and drove himself, unescorted, to a chemist's shop in the city centre, as he had often done.

Having parked his car at the kerbside, he went into the shop to buy several articles of toiletry. It was after normal shop hours, so the doors were closed behind him. When he emerged, accompanied by the chemist's wife, a gunman shot him twice in the chest, point-blank, and he was instantly killed. The gunman melted away in the ensuing confusion, possibly down one of the alleyways from the main street, Government Road.

His death shocked the nation. Kenya has had a robust existence, but the political underworld had not been so vicious as to pose any real threat to life, even in a period when many African countries went up in flames of *coups* or internecine strife, when assassinations in established countries, the U.S.A. for example, had become only too appallingly common. Sadly, the Kennedy brothers were Tom Mboya's friends, as was Dr. Martin Luther King.

One previous murder was ascribed to political motives, when Pio da Gama Pinto was shot in the driveway of his house. He veered towards the extreme left in his views and the companions he kept. During the Emergency he had been held in detention; but at the time of his murder he was an M.P.

After a week of lamentation, and a state funeral at the Holy Family Cathedral in Nairobi, for Tom Mboya was a Roman Catholic, his body was taken in solemn procession to Kisumu, thence to Homa Bay to lie in state once more, before the final journey by ferry to Rusinga Island, on Lake Victoria. To increase her woe, his wife, Pamela, was injured in a car crash in the mist at the foot of the escarpment, as were others in the funeral party.

The burial in Rusinga Island returned the body of an outstanding son of Africa to the land of his forefathers. Tom was born there of humble origins, had no advantages of education beyond local schooling and, later, a period at Ruskin (where he came into the orbit of Dame Margery Perham) but rose to international renown on sheer personality and brilliance as an organiser. One day, he might have become Secretary-General of the United Nations. He will be revered as the angry young man of African nationalism who outwitted successive British Colonial Ministers and Governors; a formidable figure in debate; not always easy to work with in the Government; but the ideal public man to journalists (he never complained about being misreported); and one whose surface appearance of arrogance was caused by his innate shyness, as he would confess to close friends.

The motive for his assassination, which deeply angered the Luo people and provoked a wave of demonstrations, anger welling through their anguish, was officially ascribed to "political execution", by the Vice-President, Mr. Moi. Subsequently Nahasha Isaac Njenga Njoroge was tried and convicted on a charge of murder. He was previously little known but had been a Kanu supporter and an acquaintance of Tom's in Nairobi's politics.

Expatriates, contrary to popular report in their countries of origin, have not funked a hard life at home to be lay-abouts in the sun, with servants at their beck and call. Almost all Europeans work extremely hard alongside their African colleagues and the

Giant groundsel on Mt. Kenya

The "Curling Pond" below Lewis Glacier, Mt. Kenya

Asian dedication to work is a by-word. They do not observe a five-day week; not infrequently many put in six or seven.

If you were to ask a real Kenyan, and not "a bird of passage", why he or she stays on despite frustration and difficulty in some respects, as against the Welfare State in Britain and the "mod. cons." of the sophisticated countries, you would get a blank stare of surprise and—

"But this is my home, I love the country." Which is so. As a matter of psychological fact, it is impossible to be depressed in the early morning sunshine; so whatever happened yesterday, at any rate we start the new day well. What with the sunshine pouring into the study, and the pair of ostriches who used to come up the paddock to gaze across the fence, inquiring how I am getting on and ruffling their war feathers when I answered "not making much progress today", you will understand this is an unusual kind of country and we live, perhaps, a little strangely compared with standards in the Old Country.

Opinion about whether we live better or worse than we would in England (or anywhere else in Europe or America) depends upon the individual. Let me whisper my own: "We live well according to our station and we love it all—all the criticisms and crises, the conferences and the constitutional changes". For Kenya is a disputatious country, always has been and will be for evermore; everybody loves arguing and especially the African, more particularly if the subject is a political *shauri*.

As to myself, I live out at Karen in a house best described as an English farmstead, its stone walls white-washed, woodwork picked out in blue and a resplendent roof with red-brown tiles shimmering in the sunshine. But in the evening it is cold enough for the cosiness of a log fire burning in the hearth. In the paddock, we have carved out a patch of kitchen garden, where lettuce, radishes, beans, spinach, celery and mealies all grow profusely, for we are lucky in having a bore-hole and almost anything will grow in Kenya, given water. Moreover, this is red soil, where Karen von Blixen had her coffee estate in the years between the two wars, as she describes in her classic, *Out of Africa*, but where the bushes eventually withered away.

Her manager lived at this end of the estate and, as I write, I look out to his house, wooden walls and a corrugated iron roof painted a dull red, just across the lawn and over the hedge topped with a shower of "Golden Rain". For this plot has been subdivided: the occupier of the manager's house lives on one half and we have the other.

Karen Blixen had lines of trees planted as wind-breaks to protect the coffee. Although Karen is a "forest area" and trees are susceptible to a grey, scaly growth, many still stand as stately reminders of her day and times. Among them are the Mugumo, or wild fig trees. We have one whose branches spread out across the border of flowers around a sweeping lawn at the back of the house—well, really it is the front, facing to the Ngong Hills, but that is just another of the roundabout ways things often are in Kenya. The lane leads up through the white gates to the back door and there is no way to get in by the front except to step out on to the verandah from inside the house, turn round on the lawn and come back.

Do you believe in foretelling the future? The Mugumo tree, which is legendary in the Kikuyu traditions, has a relevance for *uhuru* in the story mentioned by President Kenyatta in his book, *Facing Mount Kenya*. The plate opposite, p. 31 shows the withered trunk of the Mugumo at Thika, surrounded by a cement wall built by the Administration to keep the tree upright when it began to droop and shrivel during the Emergency. A Kikuyu *mzee* and "seer" at the turn of the century, Mugo Kibiru, who had predicted the arrival of white people and the building of the railway, which he described as "an iron snake with many legs like the centipede" had prophesied that when the tree withered "the imperialists will leave the Kikuyu country and the land will be returned to us". Another Mugumo has been planted, this one in the centre of "Uhuru Field", on the spot where Kenya's independence was received by Mr. Kenyatta's hands.

Among the other trees in our garden we have citrus, heavy at the moment with golden oranges and lemons, grapefruit, tangerines (or *nartches*) though, admittedly, the fruit is all rather too tart for eating and would best be made into marmalade. Except for the lemons, which are wanted for Martinis. You do not cut a slice of the peel and drop it into the gin mix. What you do is squeeze the oil through a lighted match, and a display of sparks leaves a pungent lemon aroma in your glass, which is what you want.

We have mangoes, peaches, an inhibited apple tree and a clump of avocados, all bearing pears heavily. The seed for one, which has the purple, not the customary green pear, came from Miami and the tree was in fruit inside eighteen months instead of the usual seven years. And we are just putting in bananas, sinking the roots into a deep pit filled with compost, which is recommended as the professional method.

Our gardens do matter, as you can tell from Mr. Sharpe's loving chapter later on in this book, and no wonder considering that anything will grow and everybody has "green fingers", provided, as I said before, there is irrigation and the soil is right, for instance red soil for coffee, black cotton soil for roses. The lawns and variegated flower beds of State House, in Nairobi, set the standard. The big difference between houses in Kenya and in Britain or America is that we have space. There are no terraced rows of houses, or even very many semi-detached as yet, though suburbia has its housing estates, newly developed for the new African artisan and clerical workers; with here and there a survivor from the old days, flaunting a defiant tin roof among the concrete.

Flats are coming into vogue, as land becomes more expensive. Plots fetch up to £2,000 or more an acre in some parts of Nairobi, which is getting very built-up, for all that occasionally a lioness will amble out of the Game Park to have a look round. Housing is expensive, but, compared with prices in England, no higher and offering better value for money. Rents are universally high, from 40/- or 50/- a month for a one-roomed billet to the £200 a month for the "diplomatic" or "executive" type of detached residence.

Some of the farm-houses are on the grand scale with an odd admixture of Cape Dutch to English traditional style, and they all have lovely gardens. Sir Michael Blundell, who was twice Minister for Agriculture, is a farmer at heart and a great gardener. His farm-house at Bahati was built on a shelf cut from the hillside and surrounded with lawns and landscaped gardens containing at least a thousand different specimens from many parts of the world. Sir Michael knows all of them, and very often the Latin names as well.

Some houses have their own guest houses (or rondavels) detached in the garden. These do very well for young couples and new arrivals, though it is not difficult to find accommodation in the suburban hotels around Nairobi. People who live in England, with all its shortage of domestic help, are invariably astonished by, and no little envious of, the servants employed in most European and many Asian and African homes. They must not think this is entirely without problems of its own as a mixed blessing. Houses, therefore, have what used to be known as "boys' quarters" in their gardens, but are now called "servants' quarters", since the word "boy" (cf. the French *garçon*) has fallen into disrepute because of its inflection of disrespect, though this is the last feeling most householders have towards their domestic employees.

Maybe families employed many African retainers in years gone by; the very rich can still afford (on their firms) to keep a retinue these days; but the average houshold makes do with one or two servants.

Whereas it used to be quite common in the urban areas, if not "the thing to do", for wives to work in offices, shops, hospitals and schools, this is becoming outmoded, mainly because young African men and women are coming out of the schools and colleges to fill such jobs. Those expatriate womenfolk who carry on working do so on permits of up to two years. They will be phased out of clerical and shop work and, ultimately, will be recruited only for special duties, for example, as nursing sisters and in other expert fields.

A queer aspect of the traditional African outlook which lingers on finds nothing amiss about their menfolk being employed to do housework and cooking in other houses, yet most of them would never lend a hand for such chores in their own homes. African women are gradually being employed in professional and secretarial posts, as *ayahs* to look after children, as domestic servants and more often to work in the garden; but it has always seemed a weakness to me that African women are not much more emancipated and doing these household jobs, from which they would learn so much of value to them in their own homes.

Asians employ Africans in their homes as well as in their businesses. Some Asian homes are unusually large establishments and then, when you go inside, you discover the secret: by tradition, married children frequently stay on with their parents, so that presently several families are sharing the accommodation under one roof. We have many Asian friends, some who regard England as their home, but alas, they have not really provided a bridge between black and white. Generally speaking, more affinity exists between European and African than between Asian and African people.

Africans live in a variety of ways. Some tend their goats and their cattle in faraway semi-desert places. They wear few clothes and go barefooted, carrying their spears or bows and arrows. The Masai among them are notable for their aquiline features and the custom of anointing their heads with an ochre-coloured clay, mixed with fat. The homes of the nomadic and pastoral people are sometimes *manyattas* constructed from the branches of thorn trees, sometimes mud and wattle huts built in circular form on a framework of bamboo struts. Houses of similar design, though walled with aluminium sheets, have been erected on housing estates as Government or railway quarters.

Workers on the railway or in the public service, and in the employment of the bigger firms, enjoy better living quarters than their kinsfolk, generally in housing estates. In the towns—and this is certainly true of Nairobi, Nakuru and Kisumu—there are usually whole areas, or locations, taken up by African dwellings which vary tremendously, from well-laid-out estates resembling municipal housing in Britain, to slums and shanty towns. Seldom is there a European living in these conditions, but thousands of Asians share the squalor in overcrowded, insanitary areas, of which Eastleigh in Nairobi has appalling examples.

Africans join Europeans in the congregations of the Christian churches. Many thousands have been converted to the Muslim faith and can be seen at their devotions in the mosques, with their domes and minarets reflecting the sunshine.

"The sunshine"—it is the most well-worn phrase of all to describe Kenya, but the weather is not by any means all sunshine. What is Kenya's weather like? The answer, for Nairobi and the highlands, is that it is the best anywhere in the world; but the country's variable conditions are too complicated to describe in detail. What is more, the climate has been out of joint these last few years. As there is, strictly speaking, no summer or winter, the seasons are counted from the short and the long rains. The short rains should last six weeks, according to the oldest inhabitant, but never seem to start when they should, in mid-October, or end as they should, in November–December.

The long rains are due to start in mid-April or so and last

four months, until the end of June or beginning of July. In between, ideally there are grass rains for a fortnight in February, but they seldom seem to keep the date. The country hots up into a breathless suspense in March, a nervous waiting for the rains which caused March to be known as "suicide month". After the long rains are over, the temperature drops and even mid-morning can be chilly, with the nights really cold. All I have said about the weather must be taken with reservation, for what climate you will experience depends on where you are, from the humid Coast regions where the temperature is generally well above 30 degrees C. (85–100 degrees F.) to the cool Highlands, where it may range between 10 and 30 degrees C. (50–85 degrees F.).

Rainfall varies considerably and there are parched areas where the Government has initiated major irrigation schemes, such as those known as Mwea, the Tana River, Perkerra, the Kano Plains (Ahero) and Yala Swamp in order to bring them under cultivation, with rice fields and cotton. By contrast, vast areas are sometimes seriously flooded. One scheme has been propounded, which seems more fanciful than practical—but who knows in these days of snaking pipe-lines?—to tap the waters of Lake Victoria and irrigate the Athi Plains. Facetiously, one of the protagonists of this scheme was asked at a public function during a period of heavy flooding:

"The point is—can such a pipe-line be made to work backwards and empty the floods into the lake?"

If any rainfall figures can be said to be average, here are some (as a basis for consideration!): In the Northern desert areas, under 500 mm. (under 20 ins.); along the Coast, in Nyanza and some Rift and Central areas, 1,000 to 2,000 mm. (40 to 80 ins.); elsewhere, 500 to 1,000 mm. (20 to 40 ins.). There is perpetual dispute over exactly when the long rains should start. To quote that astute observer, Karen Blixen once again, she maintained "before the end of April".

Let me now refer to the Meteorological Department which reported that rainfall in April 1969 was the lowest for any April since 1945 and that 19 out of 52 selected stations this was the driest April on record. The department's Director for Kenya, Mr. J. K. Muriithi, had this to say about the changeable weather in recent years:

"Normally, the rains start in mid-March and last until early June. This year they started fairly heavily at the end of February and continued into early March. Since then, we have had long dry spells."

These alternated with rain-storms during the next two months. Nevertheless, the rains cannot be said to have done their best, as in 1968, though they did not entirely fail.

"Studies of the variations of rainfall show periods of deficits alternating with excess in a more or less cyclic rhythm," Mr. Muriithi explained. "Droughts have occurred at an average of one in five years during the last two decades. Years in the middle and at the end of the decades have been particularly vulnerable."

Scientific explanations of the anomalies have not been found; but the reality is that rainfall was previously well below expectations in 1945–6, 1949–50, 1955, 1960–1 and 1965.

Because the Equator crosses Kenya, the sun's rays are almost vertical at midday. Residents of long standing are rather careless about exposing themselves to the sun; sometimes, as a result, they get burnt through the joint effects of the sun and the wind, especially in the high-lying open countryside. Visitors should beware and have sunburn lotion handy; also, as a protection from the glare, dark-tinted spectacles are advised. Both, incidentally, can be bought or renewed at the chemists' shops found all over the country and in their dozens, it would seem, in Nairobi.

Strangely enough, few men or women wear hats in the towns and the topee is such a rarity as to be an oddity. Out of doors on the farms, people wear what they find comfortable, bush jackets and slacks more often than not, and there they do wear hats, the slouch trilby, the wide-trimmed sombrero, or the jungle-green type of forage cap bequeathed from the war. Straw hats, scarves wound round the hair gipsy fashion, do for everyday wear among farming wives and daughters. Office and shop workers of both sexes wear very much the same clothes as in Europe or the U.S.A., but of light material and the men seldom wear waistcoats by day. They do, however, wear collars and ties, generally shirts with collars attached and now drip-dry for ease of laundering, occasionally the more conventional "business shirt" with separate collar. People have long since dispensed with the necessity to dress for dinner just to keep up a semblance of civilisation in "darkest Africa". True, they wear dinner jackets on formal occasions, and are expected to sport ties in the smart hotels and clubs in the evening, but, in general, there is an informality about clothes which breaks out into whatever you think most comfortable during week-ends and holidays.

For advice about what women should wear in smartest Africa I turned to Michaela Denis, who lives with her husband Armand at Langata, between Karen and Nairobi, and who, over the years, has constantly gone off with him on safari to make the entrancing television films so popular in Britain and America. This is what Michaela said (with special application to visitors):

"One of the most important aspects in a woman's life is to wear the right clothes for every occasion. The right clothes are usually the most comfortable and the most practical, and are not so eccentric that they scream 'foreigner' or 'tourist'.

"In planning your safari wardrobe, the most important items will be one or two washable, drip-dry type of cardigans. There are so many warm synthetics which I find just as warm as wool and I would bring at least two of these from Britain or America. You need at least three pairs of khaki slacks and shirts. I usually get a small man's size, which fits me. You can have the waist altered or any minor alteration of that sort, and still have the superb cut which you find in men's garments. If you have your shirts made for you, I advise khaki or olive green colour—when you are photographing you want to be as inconspicuous as possible.

"I always carry a large leather handbag with a shoulder strap: nothing is more irritating than not to know exactly where your handbag is. You can wear it as a sort of knapsack. You will find that, having been in slacks for some weeks, you long to put on a dress, and the occasion may demand it if you are being entertained or you suddenly arrive in a small town on your journeys. I do not buy this kind of dress abroad: there are dress shops in Nairobi specialising in drip-dry dresses, so chic and elegant that nobody would know how practical and hardy they are. These are the ideal dresses which can be spick and span and elegant wherever you go.

"I buy my shoes in Kenya, too. I wear a man-type shoe for safari and always carry a pair of Japanese sandals in rubber to wear during bath-time. It is unwise to run around camp with bare feet, even in your own tent. I never wear a hat, but that is purely a matter of choice for the visitor. You do not wear a sun helmet: you are likely to find that you are the recipient of several amused stares if you do. If I have to wear a head covering, I wear a scarf either Babutchka or turban fashion.

"Don't forget to take moisturisers, cleansing creams and astringents. These can all be bought in Nairobi. You will be astonished when you see our city: there is hardly anything you cannot buy here, so don't load yourself up with a lot of things you will find in every shop when you get here. They are more expensive than in England, but don't forget that you will probably be coming by air, with baggage charges and perhaps Customs duty to pay, which will cancel that out."

Passing from clothes to food, I do not suppose there is any kind of food in all the world you cannot ask for and get in Kenya; though there is no "local pub" at the corner of the street and most entertaining of a convivial nature is done at home, in the hotels, clubs and night clubs. There are at least a couple of fish-and-chip shops in Nairobi. Chinese dinners may be ordered precisely as the Chinese prepare their food, running to twenty or more dishes, interspersed with two sessions of hot face towels and tiny porcelain tot after tot of warm *saki*, a kind of Chinese sherry, though not quite. With so many Indians living in the country, curries are really curries and not powder boiled up in water, as you find almost everywhere in Britain. It is one of the wonders of life to order a full curry dinner for six to be prepared at an Indian restaurant and, half an hour before your guests arrive, turn up with your car and an assortment of saucepans to collect all the courses, ready to serve at home. Kenya cheeses of high quality are made in a wide range from Blue to Cheddar.

Some of the politicians, more patriotic than gastronomic, have been demanding the introduction of traditional African dishes in the hotel menus. While certain people—around Lake Victoria and on the Coast—are fish-eaters, others go for meat. Each abhors the other's fish or meat diet, but a national publicity campaign is being conducted to persuade people to "eat more fish", "drink more—milk, coffee or tea". The staple diet of the Kenya African is *posho* which, as I previously mentioned, is a form of yellowish flour ground from maize corn (corn on the cob). Add to this fruit and meat and the fare is simple but not highly nutritious. As they have turned over to a more balanced diet, foodstuffs higher in protein value, they have become better trenchermen and, in physique, look all the better for their new eating habits. This is especially true of the womenfolk, who have stronger limbs, rounder figures, and carry themselves with a natural swinging ease.

The staple diet of the Britisher is (would you believe it?) beef steak for dinner, bacon and eggs for breakfast. With toast. At times, the steak can equal the best English or Scotch, pork is almost always of a high quality; but the best of all Kenya meat is assuredly Highland lamb, which melts in your mouth as though it had come from a Welsh mountain and not around Molo, though Molo is about nine times higher than most sheep-rearing parts of Wales.

With food goes good drink, as the Food and Wine Society will aver, and the whole gamut of beer, wines and spirits is available in Kenya. Beer is bottled, never draught. A hint on wine: red travels best in the heat and Chianti can stand the rigours of safari road shaking so is the most suitable choice for a picnic. Very few houses have cellars, hence keeping wine is a problem. Please, never keep your wine in the refrigerator or the sideboard. The best place is on the stone floor of a store where people are not constantly going in and out, for then the temperature will vary least of all, and it is variation in the heat of the room that affects wine worst of all.

The products of most vine-growing countries are on sale with the exception of South Africa and Portugal, since Kenya has cut trading and diplomatic relations with those two for political reasons. Consequently, there is no Portuguese port, but you can get the Australian type, among a wide range of Australian wines.

Associations catering for group interests flourish as they do in England. In some ways, the East Africa Women's League is a counterpart of the Women's Institute but then, also, of the Towns-women's Guild, since it covers the entire country, embracing rural and urban activities, with cultural and social work, including a club for teenagers. Its counterpart among African women is the Maendeleo Movement. The Housewives is an organisation active on the shopping front, vigilant about prices and getting value for money.

Apart from the sporting fraternities, there is a wide array of clubs and associations of the professional, learned, Services and "Old Boy" varieties. The main towns have their branches of the National Chamber of Commerce, along with Rotary Clubs,

Lions' Clubs and Round Tables. Accountants, architects, doctors, engineers, lawyers and so on through the professions, all have their appropriate associations and there is a common meeting ground for the erudite in the Nairobi Scientific and Philosophical Society.

Asians and Europeans add their own "tribal touches", besides the heavy round of "National Day" parties given by the diplomatic missions. So you will find the Caledonian, the Welsh and Irish Societies, the Royal Society of St. George, the Anzacs, with the Sikh Union, Goan Institute, and many activities grouped under the wing of the Aga Khan foundations.

Among the last named, the outstanding is unquestionably the Aga Khan Platinum Jubilee hospital, started by the late Aga Khan and opened by his grandson, who succeeded to the leadership of the Ismaili community on his grandfather's death. The hospital lies near the Aga Khan Club at Parklands, on the outskirts of Nairobi, and is a fine addition to the group of hospitals in the city.

Kenya is, in general, a healthy country except for endemic diseases among the indigenous peoples which the Government's medical services, through clinics and dispensaries, maternity and child welfare, are endeavouring to stem. If you are unfortunate enough to fall ill, you have highly qualified private practitioners at your call in the urban areas, but difficulties of time and distance have to be encountered in the distant parts.

Except for the Aga Khan and a few smaller hospitals or nursing homes, the main hospitals are centred "up the hill" just outside the city along the Ngong Road. King George VI has been renamed the Kenyatta Hospital and is being expanded into a teaching hospital. On an adjoining site, the Forces Memorial Hospital is being built on public subscription handsomely started off by the Munitalp Foundation. This hospital will cater for all serving members of the Security Forces.

Again part of the "hospital complex", is the Infectious Diseases Hospital where much successful treatment has been given to patients suffering from poliomyelitis and research carried out.

Determined immunisation campaigns have greatly reduced the incidence of polio, as of tuberculosis, but the doctors still have to cope with various tropical diseases and the surgeons with the heavy toll of accidents to which the roads are regrettably prone.

To complete the "complex", the Nairobi Hospital, composed from the former Princess Elizabeth and European Hospitals is a general hospital with an impressive reputation for treatment, medical and surgical, with X-ray and other facilities required for modern techniques. A long-felt want has recently been filled with the provision of a centre for the treatment of cancer.

Malaria is no longer a potent danger, so effective have the anti-malarial control measures proved. It is not even necessary to sleep under nets in the higher altitudes, though some people continue to do so. At the Coast you should use nets and, as this is one of the few areas where mosquitos are active and can be dangerous, anti-malarial tablets are recommended—you will find any one of several reputable brands completely effective if taken regularly according to the prescription.

International regulations require all travellers to have immunisation against yellow fever and smallpox and it is advisable to add poliomyelitis if you have not already taken the anti-polio course. T.A.B. (anti-typhoid) is an optional which newcomers often take, but residents seem fairly indifferent to this, and seldom bother to get the injection, unless they have to travel overseas, particularly to the Far Eastern countries.

CHAPTER VII

Athletics and Sport

The third of the Three K's stands for Kipchoge Keino, symbolic of all he and his team mates have done for Kenya in the international sports' world.

Kip Keino is a policeman who has been promoted, "in the field" of sport as it were, to the rank of Chief Inspector. Naftali Temu is a soldier (see Plate, p. 126). Most of the top athletes come from one or other of the branches of the Security Forces. Their truly fantastic doings at the Olympic Games in Mexico City late in 1968 had their origins in the previous Games at Melbourne in 1956, and in Rome and Tokyo, when Kenya made modest beginnings. They have continued along the trail blazed by fine runners like Nyandika, Arere Anentia and Seraphino Antao, who competed but never won Olympic medals.

In the 1964 Games at Tokyo, the first medal won for Kenya was a bronze by Wilson Kiprugut (another soldier) in the 880 yards. Something startling happened in the succeeding years. Training at home, experience in events abroad, reached their climax when Kenya's competitors in the Games at Mexico City won three gold, four silver and two bronze medals, doing better in the athletics events than any other country but the Soviet Union, and coming fourteenth in the overall table. This was the year of the bitter "altitude controversy", when the sea-level athletes—or more correctly some sports writers on their behalf—complained about the "unfair" advantages of those runners who, like Kenya's, live at 5,000–7,000 ft. with their lungs adjusted accordingly giving them better staying powers in high-altitude Mexico.

Tequila is a traditional and fierce drink in Mexico. So, to the Sports Editor of the *East African Standard*, John Downes, who went with the team, all these arguments about "athletic whitemail" and "blackmail" seemed like sour grapes in the tequila. One cannot do better than quote his final cable, summing up the extraordinary feats of the Kenyans. Before doing so, however, it must be said that the international stars of sea-level countries have been remarkably reluctant to come to Kenya and "have another go", presumably because they do not want to see their reputations run into the ground at 5,000 ft. This is the summing-up John Downes cabled from Mexico City:

"The Nineteenth Olympiad has been described as Kenya's because of the great performances of the athletes who have completely shattered the British National Union of Track Statisticians who predicted some of the slowest times in the history of the Games would be recorded because of the altitude. Although some runners had to receive oxygen after events, nobody was admitted to hospital, but 43 world and 118 Olympic records have been broken . . .

"Naftali Temu was the first to bring glory to Kenya. He won the first gold medal of the Olympics in the 10,000 metres, which he ran in 29 mins. 27·4 secs. Temu astounded everybody as he sprinted to the tape on the last lap, completely pulverising the opposition, including Australia's record-holder, Ron Clarke.

"Then it was Amos Biwott's turn in the 3,000 metres steeplechase. His runaway victory came in 8 mins. 51 secs. Benjamin Kogo, considered to be Kenya's top steeplechaser, took the silver in 8 mins. 51·6 secs.

"At a Press conference after the race, Biwott was asked why he always cleared the water jump and did not splash through it, and he replied: 'Why get your feet wet when you don't have to?' . . ."

This answer was typical of the unaffected and direct approach of the Kenyans to the task in hand, or rather, on foot. Another illustration—Kip Keino was travelling in a bus to the stadium to compete in the 1,500 metres, but they were crawling along in a traffic jam so he got off the bus and jogged along on foot so as not to be late!

Downes went on: "Keino, the world 3,000 metres champion, was not to be outdone and in the 1,500 metres beat the Olympic record in 3 mins. 34·9 secs. Earlier in the Games he failed in the 10,000 metres but had taken second place in the 5,000 metres in 14 mins. 7 secs. After the 1,500 metres, newspaper headlines said: 'Keino the Lion of Kenya' . . ." (No wonder, seeing that Kip Keino was not in the best of health, having developed an internal ailment which required treatment.)

"Temu took the bronze in the 5,000 metres", Downes recorded. "One of the most popular of the athletes competing in the Games was the 800 metres runner, Wilson Kiprugut, who always received a special round of applause whenever he competed. He won Kenya's third silver with a time of 1 min. 44·5 secs. breaking the old Games record. Kiprugut ran a great race, but just could not beat Australia's R. Doubell, who clocked a new world time.

"Kenya's fourth silver medal was won by the 4 × 400 metres relay team with a time of 2 mins. 59·6 secs. . . . Philip Waruinge completed the medal collection for Kenya when he won the bronze in the featherweight boxing tournament. . . . Later he was acclaimed the best boxer in the tournament by the International A.B.A."

So there is the record and you may well wonder what it is the Kenya athletes have that others lack? Endurance, certainly, and a simple dedication. Also, they are used from childhood to walking long distances, from home to school or to the nearest village, and running when the rain begins to pour! With their fame as the spur, the National Council of Sport is planning to erect a National Sports Stadium, or Sportsdrome, with a natural amphitheatre banking the Nairobi Dam out on the Langata Road opposite "Uhuru Field". There, in the years to come, Kenya hopes to entertain the All-Africa Games, the Commonwealth Games, and who knows? even the Olympiad.

Many promising youngsters are coming along, one of them Robert Ouko, an up-and-coming schoolboy who, at a Mombasa meeting, forced Kiprugut into second place in the 800 metres event, which he won in 1 min. 55·3 secs. Moses Nyagoti, a medical student, is another—he beat the Olympic sprinter, J. Sang, in the 100 metres at the same meeting.

You may wonder whether there are any women athletes and the answer is "yes"—Tecla Chemabwai, voted one of the finest 400 metres and quarter-milers, Lydia Stevens the sprinter and Elizabeth Cheshire in the 800 metres, all Olympic class.

Athletics and football claim the keenest following among Africans. Asians are best at hockey (the Olympic team has always acquitted itself well), cricket and tennis. Europeans, at any rate those of British stock, go in for all the sports, from horse to car racing, polo to golf, tennis to hunting, fishing and, of course, football and cricket.

Mainly, however, football—the soccer variety—is an African

game, since the closure of Caledonians and other clubs. The leading soccer clubs are Gor Mahia, drawing chiefly on Nairobi and Kisumu Luo players; the Kisumu Hot-Stars, who are again Luo; Nakuru All-Stars; Abaluhya, a Nairobi team which is probably the best turned out for Kenya in a major African competition reaching the semi-final of the Africa Club Cup in 1968; Ramogi F.C., a Luo team at the Coast; and two other Coast clubs, Feisal and Liverpool. The standard of soccer is such that a representative Kenya team gave West Bromwich Albion a close game when Albion, as F.A. Cup holders, were on tour.

Visiting teams of national standing often tour the country; from India, Pakistan and England to play cricket, including the Cavaliers and Worcestershire when County champions; from England to play rugger (and enjoy the social life of the tour as is their wont!). Perhaps the strongest link is in rugger. From 1929 onwards some excellent touring sides have played games in Nairobi and elsewhere in East Africa: teams like Combined Universities, French Parachute Regiment, Springboks, Barbarians and British Lions, Wales, Paris University, Harlequins, Richmond and Blackheath, Middlesex County and the north-country Anti-Assassins. The Tuskers—named inevitably after a popular brew of beer—are a representative Kenya side which has toured the Copperbelt in Zambia and the U.K.

One of the extraordinary features of Rugby Football is that, despite so many European families having left, the clubs continue season after season, their ranks strengthened by young men posted from the U.K. (and latterly the U.S.A.) on business contracts or as teachers. Latterly, too, the game is getting a grip on the schools and armed forces, so that many more African players are becoming available. Already, there are several good players, fleet of foot, in the Harlequins club which, as at Twickenham so in Nairobi, is located at the R.F.U. headquarters—along the Ngong Road from Nairobi towards Dagoretti Corner. Impala, great rivals, play on the sports ground cheek by jowl, where, incidentally, the sight of rugger, tennis and even cricket being played simultaneously is not uncommon. Across the city, Nondescripts have their headquarters at the Parklands Sports Club. Some twenty miles away, the township of Thika has a handy team; so has Nakuru and the area round Mt. Kenya; while a Coast club is centred on Mombasa.

Cricket is played on grounds near and far—the Sikh Union,

Traditional dancers from Embu

Traditional Turkana

S.V.I.G. and Nairobi Club in Nairobi in particular. The Commercial Cricket League brings together teams from companies for week-end matches. Kongonis represent Kenya in the annual tour of England. Some of these players, and very many of the Asian exponents, would be well worth their places in English county sides—and have so played.

In a country enjoying so much sunshine and warmth, it goes without saying that swimming, as an outdoor sport and pastime, is second nature for young and old. So, too, is tennis where, again, Kenya's top players are able to give visiting stars a good game.

To understand golf in this country, it is necessary to go back to "once upon a time", I am told by Michael Roe, one of my newspaper colleagues who is no mean exponent himself. As I know next to nothing about this cult followed with such consuming dedication, allow him to tell you the story:

"Long, long ago", he begins, "two officers serving in what was then the King's African Rifles formed the Northern Lake Rudolf Golf Club. It had only two holes and, as the first stretched for 27 inhospitable miles from the Ethiopian border, not surprisingly it was never played. The 'short second' was a mere eight miles. In one memorable match, a lieutenant in the K.A.R. beat a superior officer over this hole by 3,923 shots to 3,950".

This may be an apocryphal story, though it has been recorded with apparent sincerity by that doyen of golf writers, Henry Longhurst. Certainly the type of golf played in those far-off days when pioneers carved courses out of the bush, has no relation to the game today. The Nairobi district now has several courses which would be the envy of many clubs overseas.

"Those early pioneers who started converting Nairobi from a swamp into a city, around the turn of the century, brought their *fimbo* (clubs) with them and soon designed a course," Michael Roe continues. "The Royal Nairobi Golf Club, as it is known now, is still going strong, having celebrated its diamond jubilee in 1966. This is one of the 'big three' in Nairobi—the others are Muthaiga and the Karen Country Club, where the first Kenya Open was held in 1967, with the encouragement and participation of one of the world's leading golfers, Peter Thomson. The championship was carefully timed to fit in between the end of the Far East circuit and the opening of the British tournament season and proved a great sucess, Guy Wolstenholme winning the title.

"The Open was held there again in 1969 and it is illustrative of our game that three of the leading players, Maurice Bembridge (the winner for the second consecutive year), Bernard Gallacher and Brian Barnes, all won major competitions in Britain during the ensuing weeks."

Karen Country Club's course is situated on part of Karen von Blixen's old estate. Nestling under the Ngongs, the course benefits from heavy dews which keep the fairways pleasantly lush most of the year. Its setting, dappled with flowering trees, may be one reason for its choice as the location for one of the films in the *Wonderful World of Golf* series. The three players flown out for the "shooting" were the then reigning British Open champion, Roberto de Vicenzo, Tony Jacklin and the American Bert Yancy. "Roberto" shrugged off his years and the par 73 of the course, striking his finest form and going round in a record 67.

Membership of the many clubs is still predominantly European, though African and Asian participation is growing rapidly. Many Africans show great talent for the game. Their "shining year" came in 1968 when Burhan Marjan became Kenya's Amateur Champion. Marjan, affectionately if incongruously known to fellow golfers as "Blondie", is the Peter Pan of Kenya's golf. When he won the title he was 53, yet was hitting the ball probably further than anybody else in the field.

Some idea of the standard of the leading golfers, and the growing rôle of African players, can be gauged from the entry in that championship. The handicap limit was seven and in a field of 69 players, 16 were African.

Wildlife does not pose such a problem nowadays on the courses as once it did; but only a few years ago the Karen club committee had to summon the Game Department to trap an inquisitive lion which was constituting an unusual hazard on the fairways. A few days ago, I hear, a Royal Nairobi golfer used a sand wedge to deal with a spitting cobra which came sizzling out of the undergrowth.

Up-country, there are many attractive and sometimes highly challenging courses. That at Molo, some 130 miles from Nairobi, has the highest tee in the Commonwealth, at over 9,000 ft. The Kisumu course has to be altered from time to time on account of the fluctuations in the level of Lake Victoria, and the committee has passed special rules to counter the intrusions of hippos.

Until quite recently, golfers at Nanyuki could play one hole in the Northern Hemisphere and the next in the Southern. Unfortunately, this club has been closed because so many people have left the district. "There are plans", my informant states triumphantly, "for package tourists to combine golf and wildlife safari holidays."

With the intense interest sparked by the East African Safari, no wonder motor rallying and racing attract so many enthusiasts. Kenya's roads offer ideal contrasts for rally competitions, varying from the corrugations and twisting hairpin bends of the rural areas to the long, flat stretches of tarmac on the main arteries radiating from Nairobi to Mombasa, Nyeri, Nakuru and Eldoret. Race-tracks for the thrill of speed events have been built just outside Nairobi, alongside the airport road, and at Nakuru.

Principal interest centres in the Safari, which began as the Coronation Safari, an event to mark the coronation of Queen Elizabeth II in 1953, and was sponsored by the *East African Standard*, together with what is now the Automobile Association of East Africa. Incidentally, the A.A. of E.A., formed by the late Mr. L. D. Galton-Fenzi, celebrated its fiftieth birthday in 1969, membership having grown from 35 at the outset to nearly 14,000. Mr. Eric Cecil, who finished first overall in the 1956 Safari, has been connected with its organisation right from the beginning, functioning in recent years as Chairman of the Committee.

The Safari, which attracts world-wide television and press attention, is recognised as a qualifying event for the international championship, on account of the nightmare conditions severely testing the drivers (men and women) and their machines. The first year's maxim has continued to hold good—"It is a greater honour to finish the Safari than to win many another international event."

Indeed, most cars in the field usually fall by the wayside and it is not uncommon for only seven or nine to finish out of 100 or more starters; the largest number ever to finish was 78. The Safari is run over the Easter holiday period, starting out on the Thursday evening and finishing on Monday morning, with various halts and a half-way rest. Because of the time of year, nobody can forecast the kind of weather; some events have been shrouded in dust, others bogged down in the mud left by heavy rainstorms. For 17 years in succession, Nairobi was the start and finishing point. This led to some inter-territorial rivalry. Why should not the Safari live up to its name and become truly East African in its

97

start-point? enthusiasts (and Governments) began to ask in Tanzania and Uganda.

When, in 1969, the committee refused to move down to Dar es Salaam for the start–finish, the Tanzanian authorities boycotted the event, prohibiting Tanzanian drivers from competing and banning the use of its roads. Consequently, the Safari was re-routed into two huge elliptical sectors, 3,200 miles in all, covering Kenya and reaching up to the Mountains of the Moon (the Ruwenzoris) in Uganda. One outcome of the controversy is that Kampala has been nominated to take Nairobi's place as the start–finishing point for 1970. Up to the present, overseas competitors have still to win the event against the skill, daring and especially the experience of East Africans who are used to the changing conditions of heat and cold, sunshine and blinding rainstorms at night, sea level and 9,000 ft.; mud, dust, tarmac and murram. The plate opposite p. 127 is an unusual picture of one competitor passing a village, caught in the slanting rays of the sunset.

Asian enthusiasts, who take a lively interest in all motoring events, are successful in many of the rallies. In 1965, Joginder Singh won the Safari overall, partnered by Jaswant Singh; and three years later, the redoubtable Joginder was placed second, this time with Bhardwal Bhardwaj as co-driver. African motorists are developing the rallying technique, entering the Safari and other competitions. The Safari, of course, has been a "winner" from the outset with African spectators. Many thousands congregate at vantage-points along the route and collect in dense throngs, bubbling with excitement and good humour, to cheer their favourites down the starting ramp and home across the finishing point. The Kenya Rally Drivers' Club, to which most of the African competitors belong, is fostering their interest and improving support for the entries. Mr. Peter Shiyukah, a senior civil servant who is himself a Safari entrant, was responsible for the drive which went into forming the club, of which Mr. Charles Njonjo, a keen motoring fan, is President.

Motors—and horses. All over the country you will find "the horsey people" who go in for racing under Jockey Club rules, and gymkhana, show-jumping and riding across the wide ranges of their farms or for personal pleasure in town and country. The racecourse adjoining Jamhuri Park, lying between Dagoretti Corner and Karen, is as delightful and jovial a spot as you could wish to find, small by American or European standards, but intimate and in even more pleasant surroundings than Cheltenham's. Every holiday, and frequently at week-ends, meetings are held there which draw thousands of racegoers. The horses are entered from stables near by and distant, such as Lord Delamere's at Soysambu, near Nakuru, trained locally and ridden by lady and gentleman riders or professional jockeys from Britain, reinforced as the years have passed by some very able Africans. Replicas of the English classics—the Derby, St. Leger, Cambridgeshire and so on—are the highlights of the calendar. On course betting is allowed but the betting-shops in towns have been closed to stop widespread gambling, though the Charity Sweepstakes continue.

A sight I think I shall never forget because of its idyllic beauty, and as an example of the diversity of sport in Kenya, occurred one week-end while visiting my good friend, John Hillard, retired to Dorset now, after spending 44 years in Africa and we miss him sadly. He served in the Sudan (one of the Rugger Blues in that Service!) and in Kenya was a businessman who held many public offices, including Chairman of the Police Service Commission and Chairman of the Governors of Limuru Girls' School, established by the Anglican Church. John took us to the Limuru Country club to watch the cricket (he is also an Incognito) and there we saw a gymkhana going on at the same time. The game (on a grass wicket) stopped for the players to watch the horses racing round the boundary (see plate, page 111).

Almost all the agricultural shows boast their show-jumping sections, which have become outstanding at Nakuru and Nairobi. These events are organised by the Show Jumping Association of Kenya, where a former R.H.A. Master Gunner, Mr. "Pip" Piper, is the leading light. Separate show-jumping events are arranged by the Horse Society and the Pony Clubs. The Molo and other Hunts were disbanded after so many farming folk left, but the Limuru is still with us, meeting in the rural adjuncts to Nairobi.

The other day, a piscatorial friend was mentioning (offhandedly) how he had taken a 4 lb. 6 oz. trout up at Ngobit. This was his personal second best, as he had once before taken one of 5 lb. 8 oz. from a stream in the Aberdares. You keep a poker face when such stories are told, carelessly adding something to the effect that "well, you know, trout of ten and even twelve pounds are not uncommon".

In fact, some big trout have been caught, particularly in the Sasamua Dam (from the Aberdares watershed) and there have been reports of fish weighing about 10 lb. I hesitate to suggest what the expert anglers of the Fly-Fishers' Club will say about this in their camps at—no, I will not give away their secret and expose the location of their heavenly retreat to the inquisitive, even if anybody had sufficient curiosity to endure driving over many miles of rutted tracks from the nearest main road.

The average weight nowadays has dwindled to around 1 lb. 8 oz., mainly because of the depredations of poachers. Most of the rivers in the higher areas carry rainbow or brown trout. The best stretches which are more easily accessible are at Embu, on the Sagana River and the Naro Moru. I should tell you (using Izaak Walton's parlance) that originally the streams had no indigenous trout, but were stocked by enthusiasts who imported supplies by air from hatcheries in Britain and suffered extraordinary hardships to liberate them at chosen spots in the head-waters.

Most of the lakes contain black bass and tilapia. The Kenya record, a large-mouthed bass weighing 9 lb. 8 oz., was caught in Lake Naivasha. This lake, midway between Nairobi and Nakuru and "on the tarmac" all the way except for a short turn-off, abounds in tilapia, but sport fishermen usually hope a bass takes the lure. Lake Rudolf is famous for Nile perch, the biggest caught on rod and line weighed about 160 lb., but the best area for Nile perch is the Nile at Chebe, where fish up to 200 lb. have been boated. Lake Rudolf also has tiger fish.

Sea fishing cannot be bettered anywhere in the world than at the Coast, where there are many varieties of game fish. The most popular among sport fishermen (for there is a thriving fisheries' industry there and at one or two of the lakes) are marlin, sailfish, kingfish, felusi (these are also known as dolphin but should not be confused with the porpoise), karambesi, barracuda and tunny. Some people go for shark, but most fishermen prefer not to have one take the bait since they are so strong and do not generally put up a spectacular fight, like the marlin and sailfish.

For the record: As far as I can verify the facts, the largest fish caught in Kenya waters was a Mako shark weighing 638 lb.; the biggest marlin a 510-lb. Black Marlin; and the heaviest sailfish accepted for record purposes was one weighing 145 lb. Countless "Africa records" have been caught there. Malindi is most famous for sailfish, as many as 1,400 having been landed in a season. Shimoni is your place for the big marlin and Mako sharks. Mombasa and Kilifi in general are very productive areas. It was off Mombasa that a world record cobia (Black Runner) was landed, weighing 110 lb., but it could not be accepted internationally because the rod used was not of the standard length.

Nobody knows more about the Coast, its history and oddities than Edward Rodwell, who has been mentioned before, a writer who is an authority as much on Coast lore as on fishing and boating. He lives in one of the most lovely settings on Mtwapa Creek, 10 miles up the North Coast from Mombasa. His wife, Olivia, runs a 15-acre farm, breeding grade goats from pedigree Swiss Toggenberg billies. Let him tell you something of life in this world apart. While we talked, four dogs sprawled around the verandah, geese cackled as they grabbed at the early grass on his lawn which leads down to the orangery and a trim grass tennis court. Creekwards, the water flowed on the ebb. Two woolly-necked storks pecked in the shallows and a skein of whimbrel flighted low upstream. "Roddy" put his drink down on a whale's vertebra weighing 30 lb.—one placed by each chair as a drinks' stool—and this is what he said:

"When I first came to the Coast—it was in 1933—the only boats available were those belonging to the Customs, two rowing boats and one motor launch. Youngsters used the rowing boats for racing, until the Rowing Club imported some fours from Salters of Oxford. Sometimes, we managed to borrow the motor launch for deep-sea fishing, using handlines and sisal string lures. Some of our catches were almost beyond count, for apart from the African fishermen, no others were aboard, but as there were no fridges in those days the fish had to be eaten at once or given away."

—And was this the beginning of angling at the Coast?

"Heavens, no," he replied. "The first record was made some 1,500 years B.C. and if you don't believe it you can see the evidence in the murals in the Temple of Deir-el-Bahri near Thebes, on the Nile. They depict the fleet of Queen Hatschepsut moored on the shores of the Land of Punt—you pronounce that *pwane*—and while the sailors were loading orange trees, ivory and what-all—

else the official artist of the fleet was drawing a signature of the fish they caught when off-duty. These included sailfish, or marlin, ray, parrot and so on. Give and take a few years, piscators have been at it on this coastline for the past three-and-a-half thousand years."

—How things have changed.

"Not as much as you think," he cracked back. "Oddly enough, the art of fishing has hardly changed a scrap. We still use rods, hooks, live bait or lures. We still fry, boil or roast the catch. This record"—he held out a copy of the Egyptian mural—"proves the seaboard here probably has one of the oldest sporting connections in the world's history."

—Then perhaps gear and boats had improved during the centuries under mention? As he chatted on, I could see his own boat, Judy II, lying at her moorings in the creek, a 13-ft. Fisherman, an all-purpose craft used for racing, fishing, water-skiing and goggling. Sometimes, but not often, for just messing about in and taking a skim ride north or south of Mtwapa.

"Only during the past hundred years or so have better boats been introduced," Roddy was saying, "and it is only during the past twenty-five that fishing tackle has changed from the traditional blood-soaked thick cotton line, held in the hand and trolled over the stern of a rowing or a sailing boat. My first fish by this method was a forty-five pound Karambezi, a deep-bellied fellow who went straight to the bottom while the line dug to the bone of my hand. In a way, it was fun, but painful fun. Ten minutes after boating this Karambezi, a twenty-five pound kingfish drew the line through the same gash in my hand."

—How do you carry on nowadays?

"Oh well, we now use the most beautiful of rods, reels and artificial fibre line. Lures have changed, too, and our boats are vastly different from the slow old shadeless craft. They are slick and comfortable cabin launches having a burst of speed that takes us out to the fishing grounds in a matter of minutes rather than hours. I should say we have reached a point of no-break-through in deep-water fishing, except possibly with electronic gear and the use of this will take much of the fun and excitement away from the piscator."

—What advice would you give the visitor?

"The point about now is that you don't have to beg a Customs boat any longer, or buy a couple of hanks of line boiled in blood", he ruminated. "From north to south, at Lamu, Malindi, Watumu, Kilifi, Mtwapa, Mombasa, Tiwi and Shimoni, you can hire the whole lot—boat, gear and fishermen. For a few pounds, anybody, just anybody, experienced or novice can enjoy a day's big-game, fishing. The odd thing about all this is that many of the record-breakers have been caught by anglers who have never handled a big rod before in their lives."

Politely, he inferred that perhaps I might loaf off and find something else to do because—"now I must get Judy ready for tomorrow's race". Next day, I was not surprised to hear he had won. I did not see him again that time because, on the third day, he flew off to Switzerland, or somewhere, for a directors' meeting. You will hear more from him later, but I ought to say here that, past sixty, he weighs 200 lb. but his size is deceptive. He is a power-boat driver and Commodore of the local club. For a scribbler, he has diverse interests—on the board of several companies, Chairman of the Kikambala Association, Vice-Chairman of the Coast Tourist Association, a Fellow of the Royal Geographical Society, contributor to the *Encyclopaedia Britannica* and mixed up in public relations as a consultant.

Every sport is organised under its own association, e.g. the Football Association, Rugby Football Union and the Three A's of the Amateur Athletics Association, and all fall under the ultimate control of the National Sports Council. Mr. Isaac Lugonzo, a Kenya international footballer in his day, is chairman of this Council, which works under the aegis of the Ministry of Co-operatives and Social Services. Inevitably, therefore, a measure of politics is introduced into sport, in the sense of the deep-seated repugnance to apartheid and colonialism, seen in the refusal to allow Kenya's athletes to take part in meetings where South African, Rhodesian or Portuguese representatives are competing, and the ban against teams or individuals from these countries competing at meetings in Kenya. Apartheid in sport is anathema, causing Kenya to oppose vehemently South African membership of the Olympic movement.

Aside from the National Council of Sport, the Commonwealth and Olympic Games Association exists to popularise and arrange for such international participation as its name implies. Mr. M. Mbathi has succeeded Mr. Reggie Alexander as its chairman but Mr. Alexander remained a member of the International Olympic Council, since this was a personal appointment. Kenya owes its Olympic beginnings to his ambitions for the country where he was born, his zeal in travelling the world to make the necessary contacts and his persistence in raising funds by public subscription to meet the expenses up to the year of the Games in Mexico.

CHAPTER VIII

Town and Culture

As the Egyptian piscatorial murals show, the Kenya coast was known in the otherwise forgotten history of 3,500 years ago. Because of its accessibility to the Arab dhows and other sea-going craft, the coastal region was the first settled area of Kenya and Mombasa—which was known in the first century A.D.—had grown into a metropolis of some importance under Arab influence by the Gedi era in the twelfth and thirteenth centuries. When the British began to arrive at the turn of the nineteenth and beginning of the twentieth centuries, it was only fitting that Mombasa should be the seat of Government. Anyway, there was no other town in the length and breadth of the whole country.

Mombasa, or rather the town of Mombasa as it is known today, lies on an island in a bay of safe anchorage, linked with the mainland by ferry and causeway and it is the main port and railway terminal. Its docks and naval installations, developing industrial area (including Changamwe where the oil refinery is sited) and the shipping offices in the shopping centre, all add their quotas to the bustling air of activity, despite any lassitude that may be induced by the hot and humid sunshine. Here is a town reflecting, in character and in architecture, the mixed cultures that have come together, Arab, Asian, African and European.

Mombasa's continued existence as a thriving Indian Ocean port is crucial to Kenya's economic health. Southbound shipping via the Suez Canal stopped abruptly with the Middle East war in 1967; but the passenger and freight services from India, to and from the off-shore islands and coastwise have been supplemented by ships routed from Europe round the Cape and northwards, calling at the various ports including Dar es Salaam and sometimes Tanga before arriving at the port of Kilindini, which has thirteen busy deep-water berths and two more projected.

By one of those quirks of fate, Mombasa was dethroned from the seat of Government because of the railway having its origins there. As the railroad penetrated the interior, Mombasa lost its administrative significance, so that in 1907 the Administration moved to Nairobi. This duality accounted for the two sets of State (formerly Government) Houses, Roman Catholic and Anglican cathedrals, one in Nairobi, the other in Mombasa; not, as might be supposed, a convenience for moving from Nairobi to the Coast, as there was seasonal movement to hill stations in India.

The railway and its parallel road pass through many wayside stations and tiny townships on the route to Nairobi. At Voi the branch line and road swerve away left-handed to round the Taita Hills and cross the Tanzania boundary for Moshi and Mt. Kilimanjaro. Beyond Voi the train chugs steadily onwards to Machakos, the scene of the missionary Stuart Watt's early experiments with orchards and farming, which is nowadays a busy administrative centre and market town on the stock route to Athi River, where the Kenya Meat Commission has its installations.

Nairobi lies about 20 miles beyond Athi River and now both railway and road skirt the National Park, presently passing by the airport at Embakasi. In 70 years, Nairobi grew from a malarious stretch of swamp—remembered in the name of one of the streets, Swamp Road—to a city with more than 450,000 inhabitants, and one of the most cosmopolitan in the world. Many other streets have connections by name with antecedents and with pioneers: Delamere Avenue which runs at right-angles out of Government Road was renamed Kenyatta Avenue after independence, Sgt. Ellis Avenue, Sclaters's Road, Eliot St., and many others. One, which is called Grogan Road, is not the most fitting of tributes to the late Col. Ewart Grogan, a Churchill contemporary, who walked from the Cape to Cairo and settled in Kenya to become a prosperous landowning farmer and one of the most controversial political personalities. He died in his eighties, in South Africa, very soon after his illustrious contemporary.

Most street names were retained after independence, but a number took new ones, including Haile Selassie Avenue, honouring the Emperor of Ethiopia, Uhuru Highway instead of Princess Elizabeth Way—a beautiful dual carriageway flanked by two parks at the entrance to the city centre and lined by flowering shrubs and trees which are a joy to behold—Koinange Wabera and Muindi Mbingu Streets. Another, Dedan Kimathi Street, commemorates the leader of the forest fighters who fought the

British during the Emergency, holding at bay the troops and "pseudo-gangs" set to catch him for several years until he was finally captured in operations under the leadership of his arch-foe, the Police Superintendent Ian Henderson. Dedan Kimathi was tried and later executed, so that his memory is revered as a popular hero of the liberation movement.

Modern Nairobi is a remarkable jumble of architectural styles, from its ramshackle shops in River Road to the imposing shops and multi-storeyed buildings of Harambee Avenue and City Square and the Arabian Nights fantasy of Parliament Buildings which, with its attendant Secretariat, Treasury and other departmental buildings, is so very far removed from the tin-roofed headquarters of the original colonial Administration.

After the initial development had spread westwards from the railway, in contradistinction to most other cities recent development has turned back eastwards towards the railway station. Vast office blocks and stores built in reinforced concrete and plate-glass tower over the remains of the original town. Here and there you will find a diminutive stone building, perhaps retaining its "tin roof", incongruously sandwiched between skyscrapers. As physical signs of differing cultures and religions, the Khoja Mosque of Government Road, and the Jamia Mosque adjoining the McMillan Library are within walking distance of the Cathedral of the Highlands (otherwise All Saints), the Anglican cathedral in traditional English style adapted to Kenya and built of indigenous stone, and the plate-glass façade of St. Andrews, the Scots kirk.

Nairobi, which could have been a town planner's dream had there been sufficient money and civic support for the early planners, has got itself into a landlocked traffic jam; for one reason because there are so few entrances and exits and, for another, because the cars *per capita* must be among the highest of any city in the world.

Besides being the seat of government, Nairobi is the commercial capital and, although people of the other countries are somewhat envious of its rôle, Nairobi has been for many years the commercial capital of East Africa. Yet it is a city that has not outgrown a parochial character in many respects; its people can think big but are still limited to the horizons of suburbia. The suburbs themselves range from sedate residential areas like Muthaiga and Karen to the squalor of Mathari Valley and

Eastleigh, while there are many pressing requirements for the rehousing of overcrowded Africans and Asians. Nevertheless, the African housing estates, of which Ofafa is typical together with the "higher income" estates, and the Asian area of Nairobi South, also of Parklands and High Ridge, will compare with the best in Africa. The shops, banks, the insurance offices, oil company blocks, garages and car dealers, antique salerooms, stock exchange, tea and coffee auctions, all add up to a city so modern that it has not had time to mellow but is not brash, either, a "city in the sun" which has become a conference centre of some renown in this age of conferences and seminars.

In the system of local government, Nairobi is administered under the policy-making control of its City Council. The first African to become Mayor was Mr. Charles Rubia who held the post for some years before returning to private life with his many business interests and political affairs in the Nairobi branch of Kanu. He was followed by Mr. Isaac Lugonzo, the sporting personality *cum* E.A.P. and L. General Manager. The first Kenya-born Mayor was Mr. Reggie Alexander.

The remaining towns are best taken in order along two routes running north-west and north from Nairobi. The first sends rail and road links on to Naivasha and Gilgil, both small farming townships of one main street and a cluster of shops, and then continuing through the Rift Valley to Nakuru, lying 100 miles away. Nakuru, with its agglomeration of races and occupations, being the agricultural capital is the centre of the farming area of the Highlands. The Kenya Farmers' Association has its headquarters there and the showrooms and repair shops of the car and agricultural machinery firms stretch along the main road out of the town, up the long climb to Njoro, Molo and Mau Summit, Londiani, Lumbwa, Kericho, Sotik and Kisumu on one side; and, on the other, Eldama Ravine, just across the Equator, the difficult and, in wet weather, slippery defile of Timboroa, to Eldoret and Kitale.

Kericho I have previously mentioned as the heart of the tea country, where the bushes glow greener than laurel polished in the rain. Kisumu, the Lake Victoria port, was at one time in danger of becoming a Kenya counterpart of Tobacco Road, but its fortunes have revived under the applied faith of its people and the progress of African farming (Luo and Kipsigis) in its hinterland. Its municipal buildings are cool and stately, for Kisumu has also attained the status of a borough, leading the way in civic Africanisation by electing the first African Deputy Mayor, Mr. Mathew Ondiek, and later the only woman Mayor, Mrs. Grace Onyango. In the 1969 parliamentary elections she again made history by becoming the country's first elected woman M.P. During 1969 Nairobi followed Kisumu's lead by electing a daughter of the President, Miss Margaret Kenyatta, as Deputy Mayor. Though it has been a criticism that women have been excluded from active roles in African politics, clearly they are now making a breakthrough.

Along the main road from Nakuru, or cross-country from Kericho via Kapsabet or Kakamega, lies Eldoret, the centre of what was an Afrikaans farming district settled by families who trekked from the Union, and called The Plateau. Efforts are being made to transform Eldoret into another Cheltenham with its schools in a healthy climate about 200 miles from Nairobi and within reasonable motoring distance of Uganda. Also, you could one day hear more of Eldoret in the space travel age. An imaginative Town Clerk once wrote to the U.S. State Department canvassing the town's advantages as a convenient site for a space station in the days of inter-planetary travel. This, he suggested, might well be the starting-point for journeys to the Moon, having the initial advantage of being 6,863 ft. on the way already!

The main road through Eldoret soon branches, murram and difficult to negotiate in places, straight on to the Uganda border and Tororo, and right-handed to Soy, where there is a restful and secluded country club open to visitors, and so on to Kitale, a pleasant little town with well-stocked shops and a theatre club. Some distance beyond Kitale lies Kapenguria, scene of the Kenyatta trial. Now, the country is getting distant, the vegetation sparse "at the end of the line", though there is another road that strikes away to Endebess, curling round Mt. Elgon, with some of the most glorious scenery in the whole country.

Taking the second main route, north from Nairobi, you come to Kiambu, the brewery township of Ruiru and industrial Thika, where there are also the sisal research station and the bag and cordage factory. Fort Hall lies beyond, well into Kikuyuland, one of the earliest settlements and nowadays a bustling market centre for African farmers. The main road runs, tarmac all the way, through Sagana, where the Royal Lodge stands, the country's wedding present to Princess Elizabeth and her husband, before she became Queen Elizabeth II.

Karatina is the next township, again almost all African and a trading post, with administrative offices. Beyond Karatina and the terraced Shambas of cultivation lies Nyeri, the Provincial centre of administration, and now you can see the snowcap of Mt. Kenya hanging in the heavens.

The road continues much nearer to the mountain, through Nanyuki and on to Isiolo, Archer's Post and Marsabit, though this remoter part is passable only at certain times of the year in the dry weather. Between Nyeri and Nanyuki a turn-off to the west skirts the northern tip of the Aberdare mountain range, a road that looks as though it is metalled but is constructed out of stones pounded solid in the murram by the passing traffic. This is one of the few lateral roads in Kenya, leading on past the three N's—Naro Moru, Ngobit and Ndaragwa—to Thomson's Falls, with its booming waterfall in the garden of Barry's Hotel, and the railhead surrounded by a neatly-laid-out shopping centre for all the world like the shops in one of England's new towns. Beyond Thomson's Falls, the road continues through farming country cleared from the bamboo forests, past Bahati and Subukia to Nakuru.

All the larger towns, and even some of the isolated places, have their cinemas, while the amateur drama flourishes in excellent "Little Theatres" such as you will still find at Kitale and used to exist in Molo until the farming families who provided the producers, players, stage mangers, scene shifters and finally the audiences, began to feel the strain of working all day and then motoring 20 or 30 miles to rehearsals. Nevertheless, the amateur drama movement carries on, based in the larger centres of Mombasa, Nairobi and Nakuru, and reaches its annual climax in the National Drama Festival when, as with its counterpart in song and dance, companies from all three races take part in a week of competitive performances at the National Theatre in Nairobi.

There are both the National Theatre as a physical building in the Cultural Centre, an area including the university complex, and the National Theatre Movement which its Director, Mr. Seth Adagala, is striving to spread throughout the country, generating enthusiasm among African players and aspirant playwrights.

Elgeyo warriors (traditional)

A cricket match pauses at Limuru with a race at the gymkhana meeting on the same ground

Indian dancing is a particularly expressive art form. The African is a born mimic, more inclined to comic than tragic, and much latent talent awaits proper encouragement, under experienced guidance, to throw up more and more artistes in the Danny Kaye strain like Kipanga, who can spread rippling good humour into any crowd within a few moments, and Mzee Pembe, the uproariously funny television star with his diminutive "son" of the dead-pan face, Juma. The National Theatre was built with the aid of a grant of £50,000 from Colonial Development and Welfare funds, via the British Council representative, in the early 1950s but, as a condition of the endowment, bears the financial burden of helping to support the Cultural Centre, of which it forms part.

Accommodation is provided at the Cultural Centre for rehearsal rooms and training in ballet, music and drama, mostly on an amateur footing, though Kenya has an astonishing number of musicians and stage folk of first-class professional accomplishment. The Donovan Maule Players, in their superb club theatre close to Parliament Buildings, consist of a repertory company drawn from London and the English provinces, supported by others recruited locally. Their consistently high standard does credit to "Mollie and Don" (Maule) who began their venture in a tiny theatre over a shop at the bottom end of Government Road, developing it into one of the leading theatres in the whole of Africa.

For all that Kenya is young, the country has a quite extraordinary flair for artists with the paint brush, who range from the academic realists and the portrait painters to the moderns and abstract, whatever these terms really mean. The Nairobi School has an established reputation for vigour, which is understandable if you only think of the striking colours, the scenery, the skyscapes, the sun, shadows and the people. When he worked as an art master at one of the schools, McLellan-Sim became a prolific landscape artist whose works are known far outside Kenya. Other painters include Bruno di Sopra, Joyce Butter, Robin Anderson, Bona Rabagalino, John Seldon (whose young son will probably have a brilliant future) and many more who must not feel slighted for lack of inclusion in only a fractional list. Mrs. Joy Adamson, whose books about Elsa the lioness and her cubs have made her a household name throughout the Western world where wild life is loved, has another claim to fame: she has painted some 350 African tribal heads, a fantastic performance for any artist, much more for one who has so many other preoccupations away in the bush.

The wildlife paintings by David Shepherd have an international reputation, since he is one of the foremost artists in this form. Much of his work has been done in Kenya, though the country cannot claim him as one of its own "products".

African art is burgeoning with the encouragement of the Paa-ya-Paa Gallery in Nairobi, its name allegorical as a literal translation would be "The Rising (or Leaping) Antelope". Eli Kyeyene is developing a style of his own in the use of bold colours. Another painter and sculptor, Elimo Njau, opened the Kibo Gallery on the slopes of Mt. Kilimanjaro as an exhibition hut for his own works.

Originally, the radio service was run privately by Cable and Wireless Ltd. from studios in Sclater's Road, Nairobi, developed in colonial times and with expert advice from the B.B.C., into the independent Kenya Broadcasting Corporation. Very soon its scope was widened with the opening of a television service, sound and television studios being located in a self-contained unit in the Cultural Centre, with transmitters on the heights near Nairobi.

The next stage in the development of the radio services lay in the Government "take-over", with the payment of compensation to the shareholders in the television venture, and transition into the Voice of Kenya, known as V.o.K. for short. V.o.K. is on the air from early morning to close on midnight, with the customary array of programmes including the news bulletins, broadcast in Swahili (National Service) and English (General Service), flanked by a variety of vernacular broadcasts. Its television counterpart puts out "live" programmes of important outside events—such as the Jamhuri Day parade and outstanding sporting occasions—but is composed mainly of American and British feature films, documentaries from different countries, discussion panels and news bulletins compiled in its own newsroom.

For many years, the *East African Standard* enjoyed a near monopoly in the English-language daily newspaper field. Like the Government, the newspaper had its origins in Mombasa, where it was started in 1902 by an early Asian immigrant, Jeevanjee (his name is commemorated in the Jeevanjee Gardens, Nairobi), and soon afterwards acquired by the Anderson family (who also ranch at Mt. Margaret in the Rift Valley). In those days it was the *African Standard*, taking in the *East* when it followed the Government to Nairobi in 1913, and since it has incorporated *The Leader*.

The *African Standard* became the *Mombasa Times*, reflecting the particular personality of the people of the coastal area, until economics enforced its closure a few years ago. News carried by wireless beam from several international agencies is received at the *Standard*'s Nairobi office via the official Kenya Government News Agency, which also transmits news gathered in the provinces, supplementing the newspaper's own reporting resources. East African news is exchanged over separate teleprinter circuits between the Nairobi office and the associated dailies, the *Standard Tanzania* (and *Sunday News*) at Dar es Salaam, and the *Uganda Argus* in Kampala.

A Swahili weekly, *Baraza* (literal meaning—a gathering to hear announcements) is published by the *Standard*'s parent firm in Nairobi, besides other periodicals. Modesty will not preclude me from claiming the *East African Standard* to be one of the leading and most influential newspapers in the continent.

For many years, the *Kenya Weekly News* (or "*Green 'un*" as it was affectionately called) was published at Nakuru under the erudite editorship of the late Mr. Mervyn Hill, having been founded by the Couldrey family. When the *Kenya Weekly News* fell upon lean times, having to contend with trading difficulties caused by the departure of so many European farmers, it was reprieved for a time by Consolidated Holdings Ltd., which owns the *East African Standard* and was transferred to Nairobi, under the editorship of Mr. Jack Ensoll, who had succeeded Mervyn Hill, to be produced by Printpak, a company in the C.H. group. Late in 1969, however, the *K.W.N.* alas, had to close and was incorporated in the news magazine, *The Reporter*. Mr. Claud Anderson, a son of the original Anderson in the *Standard*'s beginnings, has recently retired from the chairmanship (succeeded by Mr. Harold Travis) but remained on the C.H. board of directors. His wife, Mrs. Jean Anderson, has long given her service to charity and welfare work and is a past President of the East African Women's League. Mr. Jack Couldrey, son of the

K.W.N. founder, Commander Couldrey, is a lawyer practising in Nairobi and we see a good deal of him and his wife—who is a devoted audio-therapist working among the handicapped African children—for they, too, live in Karen.

East Africa's "cheerful weekly", the *Sunday Post*, was founded in Nairobi by the late Mr. Jack Rathbone, who had soldiered in (then) Tanganyika and Kenya during the First World War and afterwards settled in Nanyuki, where he tried his hand at a number of jobs—as he often humorously recounted—before starting his newspaper in Nairobi. In recent years, another week-end paper has appeared, the *Sunday Nation*, forming part of The Nation Series, established by Mr. Michael Curtis, a former editor of the *News Chronicle*. With financial backing from the Aga Khan and, later, an additional association with the Thompson group, he began to produce lively papers of a tabloid format. Alongside the English-language *Daily Nation*, this organisation also publishes the daily *Taifa Leo* (Swahili for "people", or "nation") in Swahili for African readership. The last three *Daily Nation* editors have been African journalists, at present Mr. Boaz Amori.

There are, or were, several magazines, *The Reporter* (previously mentioned) run by Mr. Henry Reuter, *Africana* (a wildlife periodical), Government papers such as the illustrated monthly *Inside Kenya Today* a "glossy" in colour, the *Kenya Mirror* and a galaxy of others, in English and vernaculars, too numerous to mention. Unhappily, the end of 1969 saw the last number of *The Reporter*.

African writers are coming along at a great pace. James Ngugi is already widely known for his novels *Weep Not Child* and *A Grain of Wheat*. Grace Ogot wrote *Promised Land*, the story of development pioneers who migrated to Tanzania. She dedicated this book to her husband, the historian, Dr. Bethwell Ogot. In a varied career, she has worked as a nurse, in community development, public relations and script-writer and announcer for the B.B.C.

Mrs. Rebecca Njau has not produced a great output by volume but is one of the most distinguished African writers and she is said to have spent ten years over her novel on life in Kenya. Pamela Ogot, who was the first African teacher to join the staff of the Kenya High School for girls, writes most attractive children's stories. *Potent Ash* is a joint book of short stories produced by the very promising brothers, Leonard Kibera and Samuel Kahiga.

Just recently, a tearing controversy was started by Dr. Okot p'Bitek, who wrote to the newspapers complaining about the English folk-song, *Bobby Shaftoe*, being sung by a Kisumu choir during the Madaraka celebrations. Who is Bobby Shaftoe, anyway? he demanded—and what relevance has this song to Kenya in this day and age?

In one of the *Saturday Essays* written for the *East African Standard*, I tried to sketch the answer and teasingly referred to Okot p'Bitek's character, Lawino, the village girl deserted by her snob of an undergraduate boy-friend, Ocol, in his poem which is a classic of African literature. Who, then, was Lawino and what were her origins? one quizzed.

A few days later, a long-distance telephone call came in from Kisumu.

"Did you write that *Saturday Essay*?" Okot gleefully asked. "Well, what bride price do I get for marrying my Lawino to your Bobby Shaftoe?"

Some folk had become mighty angry over singing a silly English folk-song on a national day, showing how sensitive a subject culture can be; but here was the originator of it all showing the humour natural to African people. So I wrote another piece describing the wedding, with Robin Hood as best man, an African choir singing traditional Luyia wedding songs and the Owl and the Pussy-cat dancing under the moonlight. He replied in a similar vein, setting the scene, and composing a lyric.

An Austrian musicologist, Mr. Gerhard Kubik, who made a study of traditional music in East and Central Africa, concluded it is quite wrong to describe African music as primitive.

"It is much more advanced and complicated than European music," he observed. "I think the music of that British pop group, the Beatles, is primitive by comparison."

African music certainly has a beat and a melody all of its own. Chuka drummers from the Meru district, the Wakamba traditional dancers, various Kikuyu and other groups all have distinctive styles. When it comes to individual composers, Daudi Kabaka's *Helule helule* was featured on the Hit Parade in Britain. Fadhili William, the guitarist who composed *Big City Blues* became top of the Hit Parade in Sweden with his *Malaika*. Two original Swahili songs by the Sing Out Africa group have been released for world-wide distribution. These are *Tujenge Pamoja* ("Let's build together") and *Tuishi Vema* ("Let's live straight"). As Harambee Africa, this group toured a number of countries making concert appearances. Almost certainly, you will have heard *Harambee, Harambee* and *Africa Nchi Yetu* ("Africa our land") being played and sung at one time or another.

Of all the national activities, it is justifiable to say education claims the deepest attention among the people. Is this not understandable, considering the craving for knowledge which was so long denied them, and the boundless possibilities opening up for those who are well-educated and trained for their careers? This yearning accounts for the Harambee schools opened by the score through self-help projects up and down the country to supplement the Government's efforts. It would be wearying to plough through all the statistics but, briefly to indicate the expansion, the number of primary schools has increased from 5,150 in 1964 to 6,135 in four years, while secondary schools have been sensationally increased in the same period from 244 to 617.

The enrolment of children in the primary schools, which stood at rather more than 1,000,000, increased to nearly 1,210,000; while secondary school pupils shot up from 36,000 to 102,633, illustrating the immense concentration on education at this level, and still there remained very many children leaving Standard VII in primary school who could not be found places in Form 1.

The tremendous growth in education is not without its consequential problems, since there has not been a commensurate expansion in the national economy, sufficient to find jobs for all the school-leavers. As the *Economic Survey* for 1969 put it: "Owing to the explosion in secondary education during the last few years, and the slow growth of employment opportunities, there are signs that the output of secondary schools is outstripping the expansion of jobs requiring a conventional secondary education. For this reason, greater emphasis is being given to scientific and technical subjects."

In order to improve the quality of education, the survey records, negotiations were opened with the International Development Association for a loan intended primarily to finance the provision of new workshops, laboratories and equipment in secondary schools and to develop secondary technical education.

Thus, there will be additional technical education and provision of special schools.

The Kenya Polytechnic has getting on for 2,000 students taking a wide variety of subjects and courses in technical and vocational training (including hotel management). The technical teacher-training course started at the Polytechnic in 1968 is being supplemented by training in the industrial arts at the Kenya Science Teachers College. These are only two of the many institutions—the Mombasa Technical Institute and the Kenyatta College are others—where emphasis is placed on the instruction of instructors, for the country remains woefully short of qualified teachers.

Kenya's own teaching resources are broadened by teachers recruited from overseas, mainly America and Britain, and they are filling a needy gap. However, with the best will in the world it cannot be said that drawing on other countries is the ideal method because of the environmental limitations. Teachers trained in the American or British or any other national tradition will work from their own backgrounds, alien to Kenya in so many fields of history and literature. This was the kind of psyche, if you like, which introduced Bobby Shaftoe with the silver buckles on his knee to the celebration of freedom from colonial rule.

Secondary and grammar schools exist in the main centres of population, from which pupils obtain entrance to higher institutions in East Africa and universities overseas. The outstanding Alliance High School has already been mentioned—the first two European boys, brothers, have just been admitted. Other establishments in this category include the Nairobi (formerly Prince of Wales) School, Lenana (formerly Duke of York), the Limuru Girls' School, Alliance Girls and Kenya High School, all well up to the standards of comparable pre-university levels in the U.S.A. and Britain.

Several schools are run independently to prepare for entrance to the English public schools, fulfilling a want especially among expatriate families spending a few years living and working on contract in Kenya, whose children will have to make their careers back home.

At the apex of the educational pyramid stands the Nairobi University College of today, soon to become Kenya's own University. The three branches—Makerere, Dar es Salaam and Nairobi—which formed the constituent colleges of the University of East Africa are blossoming into individual university status, in order to be able to match more closely the particular manpower requirements of each country and provide extended facilities for specialist study in their Faculties. In Nairobi, the close co-operation with the Schools of Medicine and Law will be continued under the new arrangement.

Alongside the conventional means of instruction in schools, the thirst for knowledge is being partially assuaged by libraries attached to places of learning or operated privately. Two public libraries attracting book-lovers are the McMillan in Nairobi and the Seif Bin Salim in Mombasa. The East African Literature Bureau carries on invaluable work in this respect, with religious and secular organisations taking a hand. The Literature Bureau, along with the East African Publishing House, encourages creative writing by publishing the works of new authors, while many of the leading American and British publishing houses are represented, for the sale of books and to discover new writers.

It is appropriate, here, to recall some of the discoveries made by Dr. L. S. B. Leakey and his wife and the general work of the Kenya National Museum, all having an illuminating bearing on the antiquities of the country and its place amongst the slowly emerging knowledge of prehistoric times. Parallel with finds at Olorgesailie, in the plains 42 miles from Nairobi in the direction of Magadi, Dr. Leakey discovered "Mr. Z" in 1959 at Olduvai Gorge in Tanzania. This was *Zinjanthropus boisei*, then thought to be the oldest tool-making man. Two years later, his team discovered remains of another branch of man's ancestors, *Homo habilis*, having a somewhat larger "brain box" and more "man-like" in appearance, who probably built in stone using tools 1,800,000 years ago.

In 1968, first on Rusinga Island in Lake Victoria, then at Fort Ternan, between Eldoret and Kisumu in Kenya, the remains of two *Hominidae* (not quite man) were unearthed. These were known as *Kenyapithecus Africanus* and *Kenyapithecus Wickeri*. In the age when this creature lived, Dr. Leakey said, man had not yet developed; but Kenya can claim that, 20,000,000 years ago, this area had the oldest representatives so far known of the family from which man eventually evolved. Dr. Leakey has become famous for his work, receiving international recognition.

Stone Age tools have been found in several localities. Dr.

Leakey's son, Mr. Richard Leakey, who is the administrative director of the National Museum, led the Kenya Group of the International Expedition to the Omo Valley region of south-west Ethiopia in late 1967. Remains of two skulls were found which were indubitably assigned to *homo sapiens*, showing the species to which modern man belongs was well established some 100,000 years ago, towards the end of the Middle Pleistocene period, in Ethiopia which would have had some relationship with the adjoining land mass, including Kenya.

Jumping, now, to contemporary times, I have spoken of the satellite telecommunications station near Kijabe. Kenya forms part of the network of telephone and telegraph, postal and radio services provided by the East African Posts and Telecommunications Administration. Telex links and radio-telephone services are available to overseas subscribers though, as to the latter, calls are best booked in advance, because the international channels are open for only specified periods every day.

The new arrival in Kenya is perplexed, perhaps a little dismayed, to discover there are no postmen to deliver letters through the letter-box after breakfast. Mail is sorted into Post Office boxes, rented privately or by firms, and must be collected by the renter. Which leads me to another peculiarity: though streets are named and houses, or some of them, have numbers, people rely on name-boards instead. The first time you visit, you will receive a description of how to get to the house in question, maybe with a sketchmap. One result of all this is the graveyard appearance at road junctions, where residents place their name-boards. And there is a mischievous story, perhaps apocryphal, about the old colonial days when it seemed every farmer, and most other folk, were at least Brigadiers or Colonels (which partly accounted for the country's individualistic character). Among the signs of rank at one turn-off, a resident who shall be nameless erected his: "Cpl. Blank".

CHAPTER IX

Security Forces

Security is the starting-point of progress. "The maintenance of law and order within the country is an essential function of the Government, in order to provide international security and stability which are necessary for the country's economic and social developments," the Vice-President, Mr. Daniel arap Moi once said. "Despite occasional upsurges of criminal activity, we are satisfied, by and large, that security has not only been maintained but improved and strengthened. It is only in the context of peace and harmony that the benefits of independence, particularly in the economic field, can be realised."

At independence, Kenya's armed forces consisted of no more than a small content of infantry battalions. It should be explained, perhaps, that the origins of the Kenya Rifles lie with the proud record of the former King's African Rifles. Six battalions of the K.A.R. existed up to Tanzania's independence at the end of 1961; three of them raised in Kenya, two in Tanzania and one in Uganda. Independent Kenya, then, began to construct its own armed forces on this nucleus of soldiers and its legacy of what was the smallest navy in the world, the Royal East African Navy, with a complement of 200 officers and ratings in three ships, which had been jointly maintained by the three Governments but disbanded soon after Tanzania attained independence.

"From small beginnings, we have expanded the army into a well-equipped force of all arms, with, in addition, an Air Force and a Navy," Dr. Njoroge Mungai explains. Dr. Mungai qualified overseas as a doctor of medicine and still carried on practising after returning to Kenya and entering politics. He became President Kenyatta's personal physician; but, as a member of the Government, he was allotted the Ministry of Defence, after a short while as Minister of Health and Housing.

Dr. Mungai also stresses the design of the armed forces primarily to provide protection for the country so that stability can be maintained for the Government's development planning to take effect. Secondly, he says, the forces have been formed in such a way that they themselves can play a big part in giving material assistance to civil development.

"To this end, priority has been given to the training of men in the technical skills which are equally necessary in both civil and military life," he explains further. "Such skills include those of mechanics, drivers, pilots, engineers of every description, radio and radar operators. Emphasis has been laid on instilling the arts of leadership and man management into the officers and senior N.C.O.s.

"The three Services have not been allowed to grow in isolation from one another. A unified Defence Headquarters has been established and, through this organisation, it has been possible to co-ordinate the progress of the Army, Air Force and Navy, and to rationalise such services as supply, medical, education, repair, documentation and records, pay, housing and other administration common to the three."

Defence Headquarters, under the Minister, retains control of all three Services, but their operational control and everyday running is vested in the three Commanders. President Kenyatta is Commander-in-Chief of the armed forces and, early in 1969, he promoted Brigadier J. M. L. Ndolo, who was Army Commander, to the rank of Major-General, appointing him as Chief of Defence Staff. There, he took over from Maj.-Gen. R. B. Penfold, the last in the line of British Generals serving in Kenya. There cannot be many soldiers who joined the ranks and climbed one by one to become Chief of Defence Staff, but that is exactly what Maj.-Gen. Ndolo has done. We often rib each other because it so happens he and I enlisted in the same year before the war and held equal seniority until he outstripped me by joining the "Generals' Union". Col. J. K. Mulinge, promoted Brigadier, succeeded him as Army Commander, with Col. P. Kakenyi as his Deputy. For the time being, on account of the technical duties involved, command of the Air Force and Navy is vested in seconded senior British officers.

The marked improvement in efficiency and the overall standards of training has been achieved despite "the minor war that was waged by the *shifta* in the North-Eastern Province and adjacent districts before the détente with Somalia", Dr. Mungai said. "Not only did the army, in co-operation with the air force and police, have to fight the *shifta*, but also escorted civilian convoys and provided protection for cattle round-ups and cattle drives to market areas.

"Army doctors attended civilians injured by land mines and aircraft of the Kenya Air Force transported sick and wounded civilians from remote villages to Nairobi and other hospitals.

"The Engineer Squadron, in particular, has been of great value to the development of the remote and previously more dangerous areas. Roads and airstrips have been built, water supplies developed, and this squadron, with its latest plant and machinery, is available to go anywhere at any time."

There are now an *élite* company of paratroops, armoured cars and Gunner units, besides the support troops and services, to back up the four first-line battalions of the Kenya Rifles. Their training is being assisted by a specialised team from the British Army. To see these troops on parade, with their band and drums, is a moving spectacle, for they love ceremonial, while their foot drill has the precision of the Guards. As Dr. Mungai went on:

"In lighter vein, our forces have actively participated in agricultural shows up and down the country, with the band and the colourful arena events proving immensely popular. And in the field of sport, despite its comparatively small size compared with the super Powers, the Kenya army holds more gold, silver and bronze medals won at the Mexico City Olympics than any other army. The names of Wilson Kiprugut, Ben Kogo, Naftali Temu and Philip Waruinge have resounded round the world.

"Unlike certain armies, our incomparable athletes are soldiers first and always, and not professional athletes or 'shamateurs' with soft jobs."

The Kenya Air Force was inaugurated by the President on June 1, 1964, and has come a long way since the earliest recruit pilots were helped into the cockpits of the fifteen-year-old Chipmunk training aircraft. As they qualified for their "wings", the young pilots transferred from Chipmunks to the Beaver operational squadron, which carried out sterling work in the operational areas during the *shifta* troubles.

By March 1967, some of them transferred to the Caribou squadron, where they started as co-pilots. Kenyan pilots are now serving as Caribou captains and, already, one has qualified as a flying instructor at the R.A.F. Central Flying School, where other K.A.F. pilots go for training as instructors. The K.A.F. has done a fine job in casualty evacuation, both of servicemen and civilians, from remote areas where the rugged Beavers, because of their short take-off and landing characteristics, enable them to use short (and rough!) strips.

The Kenya Navy, the youngest of the three Services, was inaugurated in December 1964, by President Kenyatta, when he accepted as a loan—later a gift—from Britain the seaward defence boat H.M.S. *Aberford*, later rechristened K.N.S. *Nyati*. The Navy settled into the old armament depot at Mtongwe and started recruiting and training its officers and ratings. In mid-1966, three new Vosper patrol craft, specially built to suit the Navy's requirements, arrived at Mombasa, having sailed out the long voyage from Britain, manned by joint K.N. and R.N. crews.

"With their arrival"—Dr. Mungai again—"we had a Kenya Navy in being, ready to patrol our shores, prevent smuggling or illegal immigration, protect our shipping and our fisheries and to show the Kenya flag in the Indian Ocean." All three are frequently practised in team working and combined operations.

As a mark of public appreciation of all the forces are doing to protect and develop the nation, it was resolved in June 1967 that there should be a separate hospital for members of the Security Forces, i.e. the Armed Forces and Police. The public appeal was handsomely started off by the Munitalp Foundation and subscriptions continued to roll in while the planning of this 150-bedded hospital continued and work started on the site.

As with the Kenya Rifles and the K.A.R., the Police Force succeeded the old colonial force. The great body of uniformed constables (generally called *askaris*, though incorrectly, since an *askari* is really a soldier) were then, and have remained, African. On rapid promotion, and as Asian and European officers thinned out, Africans entered the more senior gazetted ranks, only a handful of expatriate officers staying on. Mr. Bernard Hinga, a lifelong devotee to the policeman's lot, one might say "born to the job" as he rose swiftly on promotion, has remained the efficient Commissioner of Police since succeeding Sir Richard Catling not long after independence.

Police, Prisons and Probation Services, and the Immigration Department all fall under the Vice-President's Office and Ministry of Home Affairs which are linked in one ministerial portfolio. Reporting on their rôle, Mr. Moi said:

"The Police have played a most active part in bringing down the *shifta* war. However, its work continued in all those areas which were affected by the *shifta*, in order to ensure law and order is maintained and local citizens are able to live in peace and stability. This makes it possible for development projects to be carried out smoothly, while protecting the populace from the gangs of bandits and stock thieves who are likely to continue roaming these areas as an aftermath of the *shifta* activities, particularly in the Eastern and North-Eastern Provinces."

The Police have been very active, as Mr. Moi said, in combating crime in the big towns and have achieved excellent results in prevention and detection. Measures taken to stop payroll robberies have included more mounted patrols—Z cars and extremely smart police on horseback—and the highly trained and courageous dogs with their handlers. In the Dog Section, the famous Hugo has made well over 1,000 arrests, believed to be a world record.

One wing of the Police Force is known as the General Service Unit, a para-military force. The G.S.U. was expanded to reinforce the army in the anti-*shifta* operations. Since then, it has provided protection for the oil exploration teams working in the North-Eastern and Coast Provinces; also, for road construction parties building the Kenya–Ethiopian highway between Isiolo and Marsabit.

The Stock Theft unit is another police service, which, since its inception in 1965, has continued to operate with good results particularly in the Rift Valley Province, where the losses of grade cattle to rustlers have been minimised. Two mounted troops have been formed and proved the ideal mobile force to chase cattle thieves across the wide-ranging plains.

In any modern State, and especially over so wide an area as Kenya, radio communications are essential, within the country and to neighbouring Police headquarters. A comprehensive radio-telephone system has been developed enabling rapid and clear voice communications between the Nairobi headquarters control room and every Provincial H.Q., as well as almost all the divisional headquarters. The Police Air Wing has added to its fleet, flying aircraft varying from the DC-3 to a Cessna-185, enabling the Wing to undertake a wide variety of tasks, besides flying investigating officers, including casualty evacuation and rescue searches when civilians are involved.

Alongside the Police, the Prisons Service has continued, in Mr. Moi's words, "in a most exemplary manner". Unfortunately, as in most other countries, Kenya's prison population has increased during recent years, caused by a combination, perhaps, of more crime and more diligence in catching the culprits. The punitive aspect is not the chief aim—rehabilitation is the modern outlook. Prison industries have been extended and it is a lesson in positive work among criminals to visit the shop adjoining the head-quarters near Wilson Airport, or the permanent exhibition house kept at Jamhuri Park for inspection of handicrafts—and ordering —during the agricultural show. Increasing numbers of prisoners go back to normal life with trade-test certificates and are absorbed into industry and building as skilled hands. Prison farms cover more than 16,000 acres, so that nearly all the prisons are self-supporting in vegetables and some can supply maize out of their surplus to neighbouring institutions.

Corporal punishment has been made more severe as part of the deterrent campaign against crime with violence. The death penalty remains for capital crime and, recently, President Kenyatta warned of its extension in cases of armed robbery, in order to combat gangs. A heated controversy naturally started when the humanists opposed this departure, pointing to the abolition of capital punishment as a contemporary trend elsewhere in the world.

Justice is administered by a system modelled on the British pattern which was bequeathed to Kenya by the departing administrators, right through from the lowest courts to the High Court. Final right of appeal no longer lies to the Privy Council in London, but to the Court of Appeal for Eastern Africa covering the partner States. In his prosecution of the law, the Attorney-General is independent of the Government in his decisions, and so, of course, is the Judiciary. Mr. Njonjo, as Attorney-General, is an *ex officio* member of the Cabinet.

Though Judges of Asian and European stock still serve on the Bench, the long succession of British Chief Justices ended when the Hon. Kitili Mwendwa was appointed to that responsible office by the President. Mr. Mwendwa, a barrister who was called at Lincoln's Inn, after reading law and other subjects including economics, at London, Exeter and Oxford, had served in various administrative capacities, for example, Permanent Secretary to the Ministries of Social Services and Home Affairs, before becoming Solicitor-General during the years 1964-8. His elevation to the Bench, as Chief Justice, gave many people great joy, for he is a man of keen intellect and lively humour. I feel privileged to say he is one of my close friends.

Finally, with regard to the legal profession and the Judiciary, the School of Law, under Mr. Njonjo's encouragement, is turning out more and more African lawyers, who are practising as advocates in the courts and taking their places as magistrates alongside Asian and British colleagues.

[It should be noted that, in this chapter, Dr. Mungai was speaking as Minister for Defence. In the new Cabinet appointed for 1970 onwards, he took over Foreign Affairs and was succeeded by Mr. Gichuru, moved from Finance, to be followed there by Mr. Mwai Kibaki.]

Naftali Temu, Kenya's first Olympics Gold Medal winner, leading his compatriot Kipchoge Keino in the pre-Games race

The 17th East African Safari. A competitor's car drives along the escarpment road

CHAPTER X

Getting to Kenya: and Getting around when you Get There

Kenya, as we have seen, is less than twelve hours' flight from Britain by the jet-age clock, and the whole journey from New York can be completed in twenty-four. Since the flying-boat days soon after the Second World War, and even the two to three days' flying time, with two overnight stops, of the late fifties, Kenya's accessibility to the outside world has come a long, long way. By the same token, the radar flying and landing controls and all the safety devices of the modern airport at Embakasi are so very far advanced from the rudimentary devices at the old, original Wilson Flying Field.

Since Nairobi stands at a cross-roads of international flying routes, it enjoys the advantages of easy access, and egress: north to Paris, the continent of Europe and London; south to Blantyre, Lusaka or Johannesburg; east to Aden, Bombay, and Karachi; and west to the Congo, Ghana and Nigeria. It is possible to cross the Atlantic from New York to the West Coast by services flown under agreements with Pan-American and T.W.A. and on to Nairobi while another route from New York is via London, Rome or Paris. Day and night, all through the week, and every week of the year, aircraft arrive at or depart from Nairobi airport, on the international routes, besides the internal "round the houses" flights operated by the East African Airways Corporation.

British Overseas Airways Corporation, Central African Airways, British United Airways and other international airlines operate a pooling arrangement with East African Airways. Accordingly, frequent scheduled flights connect Nairobi with the major airports of Europe—in Britain, Scandinavia, Belgium, Germany, France, Switzerland, Italy and the Soviet Union. As the tourist industry has built up, airlines are flying "package tours" from Britain, Germany and Switzerland, at inclusive fares ranging from about £120 to £200 (sterling) depending on the duration of the visit and the type of hotel accommodation offered.

Air India fill in with E.A.A. to Aden and India; Air France take in Paris and fly on to Madagascar from Nairobi; Ethiopian Airlines and Air Congo operate flights to the West Coast and the Congo, respectively. All the major airlines flying scheduled services via Cairo, Athens, Rome and Paris permit passengers to break their journeys at these points in transit, if they wish, so that they may stay to see the sights, while there are connections from these airports to others, including Tel Aviv, Cyprus and Rhodes, all three from Athens.

Mombasa is a port of call on the main sea routes: before the canal was closed during the 1967 Middle East war, from London through the Mediterranean and Suez by Union Castle or one of several lines with cargo boats which also carry a limited number of passengers from European continental ports; from Trieste or Venice, after crossing Europe by train or car, in one of the Lloyd Triestino liners in which the Italian cooking is a great attraction. These voyages were re-routed round the Cape because of the Suez closure. Some travellers disembark at southern ports and, taking to the landlubber's car, motor north to Kenya. Ultimately, as sections of this highroad are improved, there will be a motorway connecting the Cape to Cairo, and this route is already interspersed with hotels at convenient daily intervals.

Despite the relatively long distances involved, travelling inside Kenya is remarkably simple and reasonably comfortable, at any rate comfortable by air and rail, if not always by road. When you get off the tarmac of the main roads, such as those leading north from Nairobi, southwards to Mombasa and north-west to Nakuru and beyond and to Nyeri, you find murram surfaces little better than cart tracks at some times of the year. The theory is that these roads are "graded" by strange mechanical monsters and all the holes and ridges ironed out in time for the surface to set hard in the sun after the rain; and so on before the next rainy season. Unhappily, one always seems to be driving at off-seasons and then the only course is to take your courage in the hands that also have to hold on for grim life to the steering wheel and career over the corrugated ridges, the bumps and the potholes at 30 to 40 m.p.h. In this manner, though it may seem crazy and car-breaking, you hope to achieve a form of sailing across the ridges instead of wallowing into every hole. You will find this method pays in the end, causing less damage to the suspension than more painstaking and slow progress!

As in Britain, you keep to the left in Kenya, hence most cars have right-hand drives. My advice is to treat as a somewhat sardonic joke the report that African drivers say: "The British made us drive on the left. After *uhuru* we drive as we please." Drivers of all races have been doing more or less that for years.

One of the fiercest arguments that raged for years was the Road *v*. Rail controversy, especially as it affected the road from Mombasa to Nairobi. Here is the country's main artery to the sea from its capital, yet for years the Mombasa road was allowed to keep its murram surface; at least, apart from each end, and the tarmac there crept slowly outwards. Finally, the road running parallel with the railway, joining the Coast to the capital, has been made up to a tarmac surface all the way, by direct labour supervised by the Ministry of Works and partly financed by a British loan. Now the petrol bowsers and heavy lorries bowl along and the surface suffers.

Many are the groups of people who have journeyed to and from Kenya as overlanders, making their way by truck, caravan, motor-cycle, scooter or even hitch-hiking. They ceased being news with the treks that took place from austerity-bound Britain in the years immediately after the Second World War. There is an amusing, typical and true story of a leathery news editor in Nairobi who was visited by two or three young hopeful under-graduates, making their way across Africa, looking for publicity and a little *pourboire* to help them along. With some acerbity, he snapped: "Not interested. Unless you crossed the Sahara on roller skates." And hopefully: "Did you, by any chance?"

However you travel, there is no need to clutter yourself up with motor spares, as some fearful visitors do, and three of everything at that. All the leading manufacturers of American, Australian, British, French, German, Norwegian, Swedish and Italian cars have their agents and their repair depots in the country and, for the most popular cars, it is easy to find a mechanic who can do a reasonable job at the service station in even the most remote township. Possibly it is a good idea to have a spare petrol pump fitted, and to carry an extra spare tyre but, again, these are readily obtainable almost anywhere.

If you are a tourist without a car, or just a business resident left stranded one morning, you summon a taxi. You will find them on ranks in Nairobi and the main towns; otherwise you telephone one of the taxi firms. Cars are also hired out by the day or week, with or without drivers, and some firms do conducted tours with all-in charges. All countries have their import and licensing peculiarities and Kenya is no exception. Anybody intending to enter Kenya with a car, therefore, should take advice from their local branch of a recognised international motoring association. For those leaving, entering or staying, the Automobile Association of East Africa offers a first-class service of advice, help with documentation and also operates a network of radio "first aid" for members who are in trouble. The address is P.O. Box 87, Nairobi.

Road and rail go, literally, side by side in many parts of Kenya. The railway, stretching all the way from the Coast to Uganda, has been mentioned many times in these pages, naturally enough since this is not only Kenya's backbone but its very origins and *raison d'être*. The original Uganda Railway was completed from Mombasa to Kisumu, a distance of 587 miles, on December 20, 1901. Sixty years to the day after the last rail was laid, a new station was opened at Kisumu, as the centre-piece of the Diamond Jubilee celebrations.

Some of the hazards which confronted the British engineers, working with labourers brought from India, have been described but there is one that may seem amusing in retrospect, but was intensely tragic at the time. It was commemorated once in a Railways' exhibit at the Nairobi Agricultural Show—a carriage with a life-size effigy of a lion peering through the window. Man-eating lions held up the construction of the line for some weeks at Tsavo. So many workers had been taken at night that all the others were so terrified they refused to work until the raiders had been shot. (See *Man-eaters of Tsavo*, by Col. Patterson.) The railways have become one of the East African common services under the full title of the East African Railways Corporation, operating nearly 3,500 miles of railroad throughout the three countries, together with several thousand miles of road, lake and river transport services.

Starting from sea level, at Mombasa, the Kenya–Uganda line rises to an altitude exceeding 9,000 ft. where it crosses the Equator, and eventually descends to 3,000 ft. at its terminus at

Kasese, near the Congo border, some 1,080 miles distant. Every evening a mail train leaves Nairobi for Mombasa, and vice versa, with passenger coaches having "sleepers" with a high degree of comfort, and restaurant coaches where dinner and breakfast are served *en route*. Overnight trains are also run between Nairobi and Kisumu. Both services may appear somewhat slow compared with the express schedules in Britain or America, each taking roughly 14 hours, but the difficult, climbing terrain must be taken into account. Ships' passengers who have a few days to wait in Mombasa can take a special return excursion at cheap rates, enabling them to visit the Game Park near Nairobi, see the Rift Valley, lunch at a hotel 8,000 ft. above sea level and so back to harbour in a day and two nights.

What other holiday tours can you make from the armchair comfort of a railway train? There are several to the principal wild game and scenic areas. Or you can combine the railway with steamship tours. The "Round Lake Victoria" trip, for instance, is a holiday that is quite distinctive. The five-day voyage on this inland sea, 250 miles long, 150 miles wide, is both a leisurely kind of steamboat procession from one picturesque little port to another and a concentrated study tour of the local peoples, their customs and surroundings, right in the very centre of Africa.

The Nile rises in Lake Victoria, so you can spend a holiday of some ten days navigating its upper reaches by launch, again part of the Railway undertaking. As you glide along, you will see elephant standing idly in the forests, or maybe charging through the trees; rhinos lurking in the undergrowth on the river banks and perhaps crocodiles thrashing the water. Also, you could take in a visit to the Murchison Falls in Uganda where the Nile rushes through a cleft in the rocks less than 20 ft. wide, dropping some 400 ft. in a series of cascades to the level of Lake Albert.

There are bus services inside all the towns and connecting most of them with long-distance services, but there is no suburban railway service. This accounts for the relatively low number of passengers carried compared with the mileage—the passengers number between 5,000,000 or 6,000,000 a year. For more than 20 years, the articulated type of Garrett locomotive was used extensively over the whole system, proving to be an ideal means of traction on what is, in reality, a mountain railway. In the early 1960s, new main-line diesel-electric locomotives came into service in increasing numbers. More and more, attention is being directed to the ambitious, and costly, plans for electrification.

If the railway came first, the airways came along with astonishing progress and particularly after East Africa's own public airline —E.A.A.—coupled "international" with flying. E.A.A., a Corporation launched in January 1946, has had an incredible career of swift expansion typifying the progress of the territories it serves. Revenue has risen from a minute £86,000 in that first year to around the £13,000,000 mark with—an unusual feature about State airline corporations—a respectable net operating profit. Over all the East African internal network there are 28 stations, while the E.A.A. insignia is seen on jet-liners flying the international routes serving 25 countries in three continents. At the present time, Super V.C.10 flights are advertised to Aden, Addis Ababa, Athens, Bangkok, Bombay, Cairo, Copenhagen, Dar es Salaam, Entebbe, Frankfurt, Hong Kong, Karachi, London, Lusaka, Mauritius, Paris and Rome, with New York upcoming soon.

The history of East African flying is interwoven with a human story of faith and individual enterprise, blossoming into a great commercial venture which is symbolic of Kenya's general development. It begins with the story of one woman, Mrs. Florrie Wilson, whose name has been attached to Nairobi's satellite airport now catering for light aircraft, including the Kenya Police Air Wing, charter services widely used for Governmental and business purposes, and club flying. Wilson Airways, which she founded as the first airline in East Africa, celebrated its 40th anniversary on July 29, 1969.

Her "happy little airline", as it was known, started out with one aircraft, a Moth christened "Knight of the Mist". When war started in 1939, the R.A.F. took over the entire fleet and flying crews. This is E.A.A.'s tribute, from the story of its own expansion: "Wilson Airways recorded an astonishing achievement in opening up vast territories of East Africa for air travel. Moreover, Mrs. Wilson and her happy little airline laid the foundations upon which the vast organisation that is known as East African Airways was built."

After the war, and as a result of the recommendations of a wartime committee set up by the Governors of the three countries, E.A.A. began operations with six de Havilland Rapides and 12 pilots flying 21 scheduled services a week. In those days there was an almost complete dearth of radio communications, while most airfields were little more than airstrips.

An official report records that in the early years: "It proved exceedingly difficult to recruit trained, or even partially trained, commercial staff. Thousands of pilots and engineers had been trained during the war but none, it seemed, to carry out the commercial side of civil aviation."

Nevertheless, in that first year close on 10,000 passengers were flown; by 1950 the total had risen to nearly 50,000; by 1960 to close on 150,000 and 344,000 in 1968. Within four or five years, the Corporation was set fair for steady expansion, retaining that "happy" spirit from Wilson Airways in the slogan "fly among friends". Progress continued, through ever-widening services and more advanced aircraft, Lodestars, Dakotas, Canadairs and Britannias to Comets and Super V.C.10's.

Meanwhile, E.A.A. had become the first airline in the world to carry a British monarch. On February 6, 1952, while Princess Elizabeth and the Duke of Edinburgh were in Kenya, breaking their journey to Ceylon, Australia and New Zealand, King George VI died. The new Queen of England at once decided to fly back to London. One of E.A.A.'s Dakotas, R.M.A. Sagana, flew to Nanyuki where they embarked at dusk, and took them to Entebbe to join an Argonaut for the flight back to England. Again, in 1954, an E.A.A. Dakota, specially refitted, flew the Queen and the Duke of Edinburgh when the main purpose of their visit was to open the giant hydro-electric generating station at Owen Falls.

A year later, E.A.A., in association with B.O.A.C., announced the intention of entering into the international sphere, a policy that met with some opposition from interests inside East Africa who believed more money and effort should go into the development of domestic services and township airfields.

After only a couple of years, all doubts about the justification for this change of policy were dispelled, since the revenue so earned helped to subsidise the internal services. Accordingly, the Corporation began pushing ahead with its long-distance flying, with additional Comets going into commission, Fokker Friendships replacing Dakotas and Canadairs in order to keep abreast of the developing techniques and requirements of economic and comfortable flying. Subsequently, the Comets were phased out of the scheduled international services and put to internal use.

Besides the scheduled international and internal services, E.A.A. offer special facilities for package tours from Europe, though "package tour" implying an organised party is really a misnomer since passengers receive individual attention. Regular cheap services flown from Nairobi to Malindi are especially attractive to week-end holidaymakers and to business visitors who want a short rest by the sea; and inclusive flying tours to see the wild game at Serengeti have proved immensely popular. Ships and aircraft are linked up in the Ship Side Safaris from Port Reitz airport. These flights enable passengers in transit to disembark, while their ships are tied up at Mombasa, and visit game areas and other interesting showplaces, returning in time to board before sailing time—however much they may want to stay behind.

As the Jumbo-jet era and space-age travel approach, E.A.A. looks to the future, intending to go in for new types of aircraft to succeed the Super V.C.10, while the Government has under consideration plans to extend the runway at Nairobi Airport and other extensions for the 1970s.

You will understand, from this account of facilities for travel, that there is no difficulty about getting around Kenya. Neither is there about finding accommodation to suit individual taste, though it is advisable to book in advance. Some folk prefer the simple life; others to make their safaris from "base" in one of the luxury hotels. All can be satisfied, in the tented camps and rustic game lodges in the National Parks and Reserves, or the hotels dotted around the country, especially in Nairobi and along the Coast.

The National Parks and Game Reserves are dealt with in detail by Mr. Olindo and Dr. Stewart in their contributions. Let it suffice, at this point, to say they receive getting on for 260,000 visitors a year. The most popular, because of its proximity to Nairobi and the astonishing range of wildlife to be seen so close to a metropolis, is the Nairobi National Park, which accounts for about half the total of visits; the others, in order of popularity by number of visits are Fort Jesus (Historic site), Tsavo National Park (West and East), Gedi (Historic Site), Lake Nakuru, Mountain and Meru National Parks.

Four new areas have but lately been gazetted—Mt. Elgon National Park and Shimba Hills National Reserve, with two Marine National Parks and their surrounding Marine National Reserves off the coast at Malindi. These marine areas cover 90 nautical square miles and may possibly be the first of their kind in the world.

CHAPTER XI

Snapshot Hunting Trophies

What impels people to travel? Many have to go abroad in the course of their business; many more are lured by the fascination of something new, something strange. Is it not true that people yearn more than they ever did to get away from the sameness, the drab routine of the workaday world of industry, the pressures and the monotony, the everlasting rush for trains and buses in order to save time to waste on saving time for something else? We, who live in the sunshine of Kenya, can so well understand people gasping to get away from the smog of the city, from the grime of industrial areas, from built-up streets and suburbia.

As Sir Julian Huxley so aptly remarked: "To see large animals going about their natural business in their own natural ways, safe and unafraid, is one of the most exciting and moving experiences in the world, comparable with the sight of a noble building or the sound of a great symphony." It is more than this, for it puts the noble building into the centre of a Constable landscape of illimitable horizons; here are the emotions of Landseer and Beethoven. All this is real and alive, with the wind blowing through the bush and the tang of the good brown earth.

If you live in Kenya, these sights and these emotions are always with you. If you are visiting, you must be selective for there is so much to see and to savour. Apart from the organised tours and safaris, holiday occupations are divided into three main classes:

The first is just messing about. Having chosen your headquarters, you can work out into the neighbouring countryside where there is always plenty to see, before moving on somewhere else. The second is the Coast, because where there is the sea, there will always be something to do, if it is only sitting on the beach looking idly at the surf.

Kenya's Coast has deservedly earned the reputation of being Africa's Riviera, for bathing, sailing, surfing, fishing or, if you want to laze in the sun, for sheer idle relaxation—only do take care about sunburn precautions and wear dark-tinted glasses. Its holiday period lasts all the year round except for a few weeks after Easter when most of the hotels close for rest and renovation while the weather is generally poor because of the seasonal rains.

When I asked Edward Rodwell what the Coast was like when he first arrived, he answered:

"By most standards primitive. European, Asian and Arab merchant princes lived fairly cloistered lives. The rest of us made our own fun. One track led to Nairobi and another to Malindi. There were elephant at Changamwe and along the Kilifi road. Herds of buffalo were found as near the island as Nyali. Lion prowled at Likoni.

"Arab and Indian dhows maintained a trade older than the Christian era and Mombasa was the entrepôt for everything from whisky to cotton-piece goods. Our money was East African, English, Maria Theresa dollars, Indian rupees—in fact, any recognisable currency offered was accepted.

"Most of the area where the town now lies was covered with coconut plantations and maize *shambas*. Water came from the wells. The railway terminus was where the post office now stands and all the main roads on the island were criss-crossed by railway lines.

"It was fun", he concluded, "but of course it had to change. Most of the romantics went after the war." Change the Coast has, into an enchanting mixture of ancient and modern. You can still find the coconuts, sometimes wild animals; the sea and the sands are eternal—but now there are splendid holiday hotels as well.

Finally, the third of Kenya's main attractions, and the best, is the wild game. Until they come to Kenya, many folk have never seen a wild animal outside a zoo, and they are the poorer for it. Kenya, indeed the whole of East Africa, has inherited an unsurpassed heritage of wildlife which is more than a pleasure for its peoples. Our wildlife is a sacred trust—and the Government is at great pains to preserve the trust.

The ex-Minister for Tourism and Wildlife, Mr. Ayodo, contributes an article to this book, dealing with game policy. All I would like to add here is a reference to Amboseli because it is renowned the world over as a tourist cynosure for wildlife and has been the scene of a remarkable experiment under African local control.

Amboseli was the responsibility of the Trustees of the (then)

Royal National Parks from 1948 until it was handed over to the control of the Masai, in whose traditional area it lies, in July 1961. Simultaneously, Ngong, West Chyulu and Mara National Reserves became Masai Game Reserves. The explanation for this integration of Masai interest in the preservation of wildlife and responsibility for the proper control of the area was given in a statement issued at the time by the Trustees, in which they said:

"It must be remembered that Amboseli is still, and has been for many years, a portion of the Masai Land Unit, and has never reached the status of a National Park. There is, therefore, no question of handing back the area itself to the Masai—it has always been theirs—since it is merely a change in the arrangements for the management of this wildlife sanctuary."

From Amboseli you can see Mt. Kilimanjaro in one of the grandest of all her perspectives. This double attraction was mentioned by the then Governor, Sir Patrick Renison, when he handed the care of the area over to the Kajiado African District Council at a ceremonial *baraza*.

"Amboseli's world renown is based on two main assets," he said, "its game and the splendour of this mountain, Kilimanjaro." He went on to warn against the evils of poaching by marauding gangs which has caused such widespread concern not only in Kenya but throughout the world where wildlife is valued. Game wardens, scouts, some of the Masai themselves and police supported by spotter aircraft, wage a ceaseless fight against the poachers, who snare or shoot animals with poisoned arrows, in order to get principally ivory and horn which can be disposed of to receivers at Mombasa and elsewhere.

Of all the game to be seen in Amboseli, the rhinos are, perhaps, the most interesting because of their tameness and willingness, even film-starrish anxiety, to pose for photographers.

"There is a danger," Sir Patrick continued on that day back in 1961, "that the rhinos may disappear. I have been informed that very many of them have been illegally killed for their horns. If these rhinos disappear entirely, Amboseli would lose much of its attraction. Each animal is worth many thousands of shillings to you, the Masai, and to your Council, if it remains alive; but dead it is worth only a few shillings to the selfish and miserable poachers who killed it. I hope you will take the sternest measures to prevent and stamp out this illegal theft of your assets."

Providentially, the Masai passed by-laws to conserve game in the West Chyulu and Kitengela areas; the former is a game reservoir for Amboseli and the latter for the Nairobi National Park. This form of protection is of paramount importance to the continued life and the varied species found in the two main game areas. Though the Nairobi Park covers the smallest area of any game park in Africa, as Sir Patrick said on that occasion at Amboseli, "it is one of the modern wonders of the world", and entirely dependent on the Athi and Kapiti Plains for pasture to help its grazing of the herds of game. Hence the absolute necessity for a protected game reservoir if this "wonder of the world" on Nairobi's doorstep is to continue.

The Masai having taken over a trust for mankind, the world at large watched the progress of Amboseli under their care in the opening years of this unique idea. Let it now be recorded that they have been successful, with the Government's aid. What they have done at Amboseli, other local authorities are repeating in minor ways in their own areas, reaping the benefit for the betterment of social conditions among their people out of the revenue from permits and licences.

The success of the "Amboseli experiment" prompts me to divert for a few moments and look at the African attitude to wildlife, which so many uninformed sceptics have criticised. Recently, a visitor wrote to the *East African Standard* a lugubrious letter in which he repeated the old story that "the African does not appreciate the pleasantness of unspoilt Nature, the wonder of the unknown does not fascinate him, etc.". The letter was published, though it may have been a tongue-in-cheek effort to remind people of their responsibilities. Incidentally, the National Parks grew out of an anonymous letter sent to the *Standard* many years ago urging the destruction of wild animals. It was written by Mr. Mervyn Cowie in collusion with the then editor, the late Mr. George Kinnear, and provoked such devastating retorts that the colonial Government of the day was goaded into taking protective action. Mervyn Cowie became Director of the newly established National Parks.

The visitor who theorised about what ought to be done by the "unappreciative" African, was answered in no uncertain terms. Here is a specimen, written by Mr. Kesuna Mutisya, quoted because his letter most adequately expresses African thoughts on this explosive subject. He set off by quoting the correspondent's opinions:

"To call a spade a spade, the African's concern is subsistence. He wants to grow maize and raise cattle for his daily food. Mountains and plains, the wonder of the unknown, do not fascinate him. He takes them for granted." And this is how Mr. Mutisya replied:

"How ludicrous! What does he [the correspondent] think about the African business owner, the coffee farmer, the civil servant, painter, doctor, engineer, lawyer, university tutor, Government official, etc? Has none of them any appreciation for Nature? When do they 'grow maize and raise cattle for their daily food'?

"Subsistence living, world-wide and common in Europe, especially in England, is nothing to be scorned. All countries endeavour to eliminate this problem through objective thinking. It is irresponsibility to suggest Africans should be encouraged to continue with what he thinks is typical of them, namely, subsistence living.

"Ironically, it is the Africans now who are involved in the preservation of wildlife in East Africa, without European imposition or remote controlling. We Kenyans, especially, have realised the importance of our wildlife, the boost to our economy through tourism, among other things. More foreign revenue is earned by the Game Parks than any other enterprise.

"If parts of these Game Parks were alienated for smallholding purposes, heavy Government subsidies would be necessary to see the younger smallholders on their feet, bearing in mind the difficult country. Further, taxpayers' money would be needed to consolidate and compartmentalise the remaining areas for the various animal species to be 'zoo-ed'. Dollar-carrying tourists go to East Africa primarily to see our unique method of preservation of game. They would never go to East Africa just to see another zoo like those at home."

The correspondent, it should be explained, had suggested keeping wildlife to areas cordoned off in the form of open zoos, such as Whipsnade, but to mention confining wild animals in zoos is to invite almighty wrath in Kenya.

"Certainly," Mr. Mutisya concluded, "the East African Governments are aware of the need for farming land and have considered this in their town and country planning. Mr.—[the correspondent] need not panic, for the Africans have their projects under control. To ask 'why should the European impose such sublime values on the African who cannot comprehend them?' is a bit extravagant and bigoted. Europeans do not impose on Africans today. It would be silly to do so."

Millions of readers have become familiar with the behaviour and antics of Elsa and her brood. It is true, of course, that wild animals can be, and have been, domesticated; but serious problems can arise when they are "liberated" back to their natural habitat. After a while, some of the "civilised behaviour" rubs off in the *bundu* and they can be a menace if inquisitive humans overstep the mark of curiosity. I recall the Trustees of the National Parks saying they felt proud that the famous denizens of Ol Tukai, such as Gertie and Gladys the friendly rhinos, had been taught to accept man's intrusion into their domain. They acquired such confidence in their tutors that they were willing to display themselves to photographers at a range of only a few yards. Unhappily, Gladys was speared by poachers during the 1961–2 floods—just for a few shillings' worth of rhino horn. The Masai took a serious view of this wanton killing and the four African poachers were taken to court where they were sentenced to three years' imprisonment.

The photogenic and publicity conscious rhinos are renowned for their tameness, but some other animals are not so camera conscious, so you are adjured to stay in your vehicle when visiting the game in the parks.

Spiv was another favourite wild animal star and, as his name implies, was an idle old scoundrel among the lions in the Nairobi National Park. Incidentally, young and old visitors are enthralled by the close contact they have when viewing wild animals in their pens at the Orphanage constructed adjoining the park entrance. Young animals found in distress, or wandering in search of their parents, are placed there and taken care of until they are well and old enough to go back and fend for themselves.

Two of the most famous game park lionesses were Brunette and Blondie, who often teamed up in the same pride. Their best-known exploit was to take post on the Mombasa Road, which skirts the park, effectively preventing traffic moving in either direction and resisting all attempts to shoo them away. At some stage of her life, Brunette lost her tail, believed bitten off by a crocodile. In her declining years, she became weak but was cared for by the pride and played her part as "auntie" to the young cubs.

Blondie, who survived Brunette by two or three years, was one of the most photographed lionesses in Africa and a most handsome animal. She had the reputation of being fast, fickle and promiscuous; also of being a poor, though vain, mother to her cubs, abandoning at least one litter and treating others off-handedly. Several of her offspring survive, including one that is remarkably like her.

Blondie had a habit of leading her cubs on raiding parties out of the park confines. Sometimes they stole cattle, once from the veterinary premises close to a drive-in cinema, holding up the traffic while they dragged the luckless creature across the main road. She also had a marked aversion for bicycles and would attack Park Rangers cycling about the park, not to molest the Rangers but to "kill" their machines.

As you have gathered, Kenya is a photographer's paradise, which accounts for the films constantly being made in the country by the big movie companies. The scenery, the sunshine and the general predictability of the climate combine to produce ideal, and sometimes idyllic, conditions for making films. If you want to avoid misunderstanding and possible unpleasantness, one thing you must never forget is that most Africans are sensitive about being photographed in their traditional dress by tourists. How would you like somebody crashing into your back garden and clicking the shutter at you? So, remembering your manners, you should first ask permission and, if the African concerned does not mind posing for your picture, all's well and good.

Very much more shooting is being done with cameras than with guns; movie films, colour transparencies and snapshots are taking the place of those hunting trophies of yesteryear which used to look down through sightless eyes from their mountings on the walls. In making your pictures, you should be a little wary of the brilliant sunshine and the evening shadows. For your guidance, here is some advice from Mr. John Perry, for some years the *East African Standard*'s chief photographer, who has many brilliant pictures to his credit:

A very wide range of photographic films and materials is available in Kenya, to suit even the most advanced amateur needs.

"The Kill"—lion attacking a wildebeeste in the Nairobi National Park

Lion in the Ngorongoro Crater, Northern Tanzania

At the time of writing, there is no purchase tax on cameras bought in Kenya, and the visitor, therefore, enjoys a complete range of continental and Japanese apparatus from which to choose.

FOR BLACK-AND-WHITE PHOTOGRAPHS

Choose a film with a wide tone and contrast range because bright sun and deep shadow are the normal conditions for Kenya during most of the year. If you can afford one, a portable mini-flash is invaluable. For outdoor portraits it will help to fill in shadows around the eyes caused by the overhead sun, and be kinder to your subjects. It will also be most useful to improve your close-ups of African tribesmen and similar studies.

If you are doing your own processing, "expose for the shadows and develop for the highlights", will be a most useful rule. For the would-be game photographer, remember that animals have a natural camouflage when seen in monotone. Giraffe and lion pictures can be particularly disappointing. Try to photograph these subjects against the skyline.

Sometimes the best animal pictures are made during the early morning or late evening, when game are on the move or looking for prey. Remember to carry a reserve supply of fast film for the failing light; otherwise, you may lose your best pictures of the day. In such cases, it may be well to under-expose slightly and develop for more contrast. Most wild animals tend to be shy of man and a miniature camera fitted with a medium focal length lens will be found most useful. A 135-mm. lens on a miniature reflex camera is, perhaps, ideal. Trying out too long a lens for the first time will often lead to camera-shake; and some, with their complicated reflex-housings, are particularly difficult to operate when shooting from the window of a car.

Beware of those sweeping vistas, i.e. the Great Rift Valley. They are rarely the same when transferred to film. Remember to use some foreground interest, or your picture will look flat and uninteresting.

FOR THE COLOUR PHOTOGRAPHER

He will have fewer problems than his black-and-white counter-part. East African conditions can be ideal. An ultra-violet filter

will be found most useful in the Highlands over 10,000 ft., and on
Mt. Kenya, particularly during the middle of the day. At the
end of the day keep some film available for one of those glorious
East African sunsets—a sight very rewarding on colour film.

If you are at the Coast, be on your guard for false meter read-
ings. Strong highlights reflected from sand and sea can easily
lead to under-exposure and disappointment.

Finally, do take care of your camera when on safari. The Kenya
dust and fine particles of sand can easily jam or wreck a sensitive
shutter. Put your camera back into its gadget bag while travelling.
When in constant use, a polythene wrapper is one of the most
useful protective covers and will allow you to be at the ready for
a picture in a matter of seconds.

From all the foregoing in these chapters, you will be able to
appreciate the courteous retort given by a Kenya police officer to
an American visitor who was restrained from approaching
President Kenyatta over zealously in order to take his photograph.

"Now, sir, you would not do that to the President of the
U.S.A.", the police officer remonstrated.

"Yeah—but the U.S.A. is a big country," the visitor replied.

"Well, we think Kenya is, too, in a rather small way."

CHAPTER XII

Swahili: the Lingua Franca

You can get along tolerably well by speaking English in all the urban areas of Kenya. As education has spread, an ever-increasing number of Africans and Asians have learnt to speak English at primary level in school. Educated people of all races speak and write English fluently, in addition to their own tribal languages or vernaculars.

Yet it is well for the visitor to acquire a smattering of Swahili, while anybody intending to stay for a period of years must certainly be sufficiently proficient to understand, and be understood, in Swahili. Though there are Africans in remote areas who speak only their native tongues, Swahili is the lingua franca of Kenya, as of East Africa and many other African countries.

There has been a considerable agitation, intellectual and nationalist, to make Swahili the official language, spoken in the National Assembly and used in official documents as in Tanzania; but, like Uganda, Kenya has retained English as the official language, though documents are frequently printed in both languages. The Bible and many other classics have been translated into Swahili. The difficulty, which seems unsurmountable, about introducing Swahili as the medium of education is that few textbooks are printed in the language, allowing even for the activities of various publishing houses in Nairobi. Moreover, there are no Swahili equivalents for terms used in the technical language of the space age. To this Philistine, Swahili seems to be not a very precise language for technology, legal matters and careful explanation, but this must obviously depend on how well one can speak it and one's vocabulary—even though the same word is often used for varying shades of meaning.

Dr. Mohamed Hyder, and other redoubtable champions of Swahili, contend that every language is "living" and assimilates words from other origins. None the less, it still sounds odd to hear somebody speaking fluent Swahili, say in a broadcast, suddenly drop in one or two words of English which have no counterpart. The Vice-President, Mr. Moi, adequately summed up the arguments by saying that, although English is an important medium of expression, he felt Swahili is just as important as a unifying factor in the country. Both languages are essential in the development of Kenya, and the country is lucky in having both.

Spoken fluently, Swahili has a distinctively musical cadence, remarkably like Italian. This is due mainly to the "i" on the end of so many words: it is jocularly, though not entirely incorrectly, said that if you do not know the Swahili word for something, take the English word and Italianise it by adding "i". Ticket into *ticketi* is an example; gazette into *gazetti* another.

In pronunciation, consonants come out more or less as in English, with vowels having an Italian value. "G" is always hard, like the "g" in go—never a "j" as in George. "C" is only used in partnership with "h"—"ch" and "th" are identical with their English counterparts. Remember that the accent is universally put on the last but one syllable.

This is a guide to the vowel sounds: "A" as the "ar" of star; "E" as the "e" of met; "I" long as the "e" of me; "O" as the "aw" of law; "U" as the "oo" of moo.

Grammatical Swahili is seldom spoken in the rough-and-tumble conversation of everyday life. It is quite possible, indeed this is the general practice especially among Europeans, to talk intelligibly by stringing together a series of words without much regard to syntax, but there is a precise form about the grammar of Swahili, properly written and spoken. The adjective follows the noun; the numeral follows the adjective; and there is no definite article. Prefixes change from singular to plural; thus *mtu* "a person" becomes *watu* "people", *Mkamba* "a Kamba tribesman", *Wakamba* "the Kamba people".

These are the personal pronouns: I *mimi*, we *sisi*, you *wewe* (pronounced way-way), you *ninyi* (plural), he or she *yeye*, they *wao*.

The numerals: 1 *moja*, 2 *mbili*, 3 *tatu*, 4 *ine* (pronounced eeny), 5 *tano*, 6 *sita*, 7 *saba*, 8 *nane*, 9 *tisa*, 10 *kumi*, 11 *kumi na moja*, 12 *kumi na mbili* and so on to 20 *ishirini*, 21 *ishirini na moja* and so on to 30 *thelathini*, 40 *arobaini*, 50 *hamsini*, 60 *sitini*, 70 *sabaini*, 80 *thamanini*, 90 *tisini*, 100 *mia moja*, 200 *mia mbili* and so on to 1,000 *elfu moja*.

The "m" before a word like *mbili*, which occurs frequently, is pronounced more like *um-bili* than *mer-bili*.

Days in the week begin on Saturday and are numbered to Wednesday, before having their own names, thus: Saturday *Jumamosi*, Sunday *Jumapili*, Monday *Jumatatu*, Tuesday *Jumanne*, Wednesday *Jumatano*, Thursday *Alhamisi*, Friday *Jumaa*. The word *Jumaa* also means week, though the English word is usually used instead.

Remember that the Equator runs across Kenya, so there is relatively little variation throughout the year in the times of sunrise and sunset. Dawn breaks, night falls, with only short twilight periods.

Time-keeping in Swahili is not easy for the uninitiated. Night—*usiku* (the hours of darkness)—and day—*mchana*—are divided equally into periods of 12 hours.

The day is reckoned to begin with dawn at 6 a.m. The succeeding hours are added in Swahili numbering as the day advances, through 12 hours, to 6 p.m. and so on again to 6 o'clock next morning.

To distinguish between a given hour at night and its opposite number by day, the hours in darkness have *usiku* added. The Swahili word for *hour* is *saa*. To give examples of time-keeping, Swahili style against the clock:

At 4 a.m. it is still dark, so this hour is called *saa kumi usiku*—the tenth hour in the darkness reckoning from 6 o'clock the previous evening. Thus, 5 a.m. is *saa kumi na moja usiku* the 11th hour in the darkness; and 6 a.m. becomes *saa kumi na mbili usiku* the 12th hour in the darkness.

By this time, the sun is beginning to rise, so the hours are numbered in succession from 6 o'clock in the morning, dropping the word *usiku*. One hour later it is 7 a.m. which becomes *saa moja*—the first hour; 8 a.m. is *saa mbili*, 9 a.m. *saa tatu* and onwards to 12 noon, which is *saa sita* (six hours past the start-point of 6 a.m.).

Lunch-time, 1 p.m., being seven hours after 6 a.m., is *saa saba*, 2 p.m. (eight hours after) *saa nane*, 3 p.m. *saa tisa* and 4 p.m. *saa kumi* but now, as it is afternoon daylight, there is no *usiku* which, you will remember, is inserted to denote 4 a.m. Neither is there with *saa kumi na moja*—5 p.m.—nor *saa kumi na mbili*—6 p.m.

At this point, having worked right round the 12 hours of the clock, we start off again—7 p.m., being the first hour afterwards, is *saa moja* and so on numerically, with the word *usiku* added, to 12 midnight, which is *saa sita usiku* (again, 6 o'clock plus 6), through the "witching hours" to 4 a.m. (6 o'clock plus 10) *saa kumi usiku*, 5 a.m. *saa kumi na moja usiku* and 6 a.m. *saa kumi na mbili usiku*.

When considering time in relation to other countries, do not forget that Kenya is three hours ahead of G.M.T. and two hours ahead of British Summer Time, now adopted as standard throughout the year in the United Kingdom.

VOCABULARY

To help you on your way with the language, here is a selection of words and phrases in common use:

ENGLISH–SWAHILI

Aeroplane *ndege*

Affair *shauri* (*shauri mungu*, an affair of God, or something beyond human control); *shauri* can also mean argument

Alcohol *tembo, pombe* (generally meaning beer, with whisky, gin, brandy as in English)

All *yote*

Also *na* (also means and)

And *na*

Animal *nyana*

Ant *siafu*

Bad *mbaya*

Basket *kikapu*

Bath *bafu*

Beautiful *mzuri* (good or excellent)

Big *mkubwa*

Bird *ndege*

Book *kitabu*

Bottle *chupa*

Bread *mkate*

Buck *swara*

Bullet *risasi*

Bush country *porini*

Butter *siagi*

Car *gari* (or wagon)

Cat *paka*

Cattle *ngombe* (also *ngombe* a cow)

Cent *centi*

Charcoal *mkaa*

Chicken *kuku*

Chief *chifu*

Child *mtoto*

Cigarette *sigari*

Clock *saa*

Coat *roti*

Coffee *kahawa*

Cold *biridi*

Come *kuja*

Come in *karibu*

Cook *mpishi* (n.) *kupika* (v.)

Day *siku*

Daytime *mchana*

Die *kufa*

Dish *sahani*

Doctor *daktari*

Dog *mbwa*

Door *mlango*

Eat *kula*

Egg *yai* (pl. *mayai*)

Electricity *stima*

Elephant *ndovu*

Enough *bas*

Entirely *kabisa*

European *Mzungu*

Far *mpaka*

Farm *shamba* (field or garden)

Fast *pesi*

Father *baba*

Fierce *kali* (or sharp)

Finish *kwisha*

Fire *moto* (or hot)

Fish *samaki*

Flesh *nyama* (or meat)

Food *chakula*

Free *bure*

Freedom *uhuru* (independence)

Friend *rafiki*
Fruit *matunda*
Gift *bakshish*
Giraffe *twiga*
Glass *bilauri*
Go *kwenda*
God *Mungu*
Good-bye *kwa heri*
Government *serikali*
Government station *boma*
Hello *hodi*
Her *yake*
Here *hapa*
Hippopotamus *kiboko*
His *yake*
Hit *piga*
Horse *farasi*
Hotel *hoteli*
Hour *saa*
House *nyumba*
How many? *ngapi?*
Husband *mume, bwana*
I *mimi*
Ice *barafu*
Immediately *mara-moja, sasa-hevi*
Indian *Muhindi (Hindi)*
Insect *dudu*
Iron *chuma* (clothes iron *pasi*)
Its *yake*
Journey *safari*
Key *ufungu*
Knife *kisu*
Later *bado*
Lavatory *choo*
Leopard *chui*
Letter *barua*
Lion *simba*
Loaf *mkate*
Look after *ku-chunga*
Machine *mtambo*
Maize meal *posho*
Make *tengenesa*
Man *mtu*
Many *mingi*
Master *bwana* (or Mr.)
Matches *kibiriti*
Me *mimi*
Meat *nyama*

Mechanic (expert) *fundi*
Medicine *dawa*
Milk *maziwa*
Money *pesa*
Monkey *kima, myanya*
Mother *mama*
Much *sana*
News *habari*
Newspaper *gazetti*
Night *usiku*
No *hapana*
Noise *kalele*
Note *barua* (message), *noti* (money)
Nothing *hapana kitu*
Now *sasa*
Of *ya*
Oil *mafuta*
Old man *mzee*
Once *mara moja*
Open *kufunga*
Pawpaw *papayi*
People *wananchi* (or *watu*)
Petrol *petroli*
Plate *sahani*
Policeman *askari*
Potatoes *viazi*
Pull together *harambee*
Quick *pesi*
Railway train *gari la moshi*
Rhinoceros *kifaru*
Rice *mchele*
Rifle *bunduki*
River *mtoni*
Room *chumba*
Sharp *kali*
She *yeye*
Sheep *kondoro*
Shilling *shilingi*
Ship *meli*
Shoes *viatu*
Shop *duka*
Shut *funga*
Slowly *pole-pole*
Small *kidogo*
Soap *sabuni*
Stomach *tumbo*
Sugar *sukari*
Sun *jua*

Vocabulary

Sword *panga* (or agricultural implement)
Table *meza*
Take care *angalia*
Tea *chai*
Telephone *simu*
Thank-you *asante*
There *huko*
Thing *kitu*
Ticket *ticketi*
Time *saa*
Tobacco *tumbaku*
Today *leo*
Tomorrow *kesho*
Unity, *umoja*
Us *sisi*
Useless *bure*

Vegetables *mboga*
Voice *sauti*
Water *maji*
We *sisi*
What? *nini?*
When? *saa ngapi?*
Where? *wapi?*
Who? *nani?*
Why? *kwanini?*
Wife *bibi*
With *na*
Woman *mwanamuke* (pl. *wanawake*)
Work *kazi*
Yes *ndiyo* (usual form *diyo*)
Yesterday *jana*
You *wewe*
Zebra *punda milia*

SWAHILI-ENGLISH

Angalia *take care*
Asante *thank you*
Askari *policeman, soldier, watchman*
Baba *father*
Bado *later*
Bafu *bath*
Bakshish *gift*
Barafu *ice*
Barua *letter*
Bas *enough*
Bibi *wife*
Bilauri *glass*
Biridi *cold*
Boma *Government station*
Bunduki *rifle*
Bure *free, useless*
Bwana *Mr., master, husband*
Centi *cent*
Chai *tea*
Chakula *food*
Chifu *chief*
Choo *lavatory*
Chui *leopard*
Chuma *iron*
Chumba *room*
Chupa *bottle*

Daktari *doctor*
Dawa *medicine*
Dudu *insect*
Duka *shop*
Farasi *horse*
Fundi *mechanic (expert)*
Funga *shut*
Gari *car, wagon*
Gari la moshi *railway train*
Gazetti *newspaper*
Habari *news*
Hapa *here*
Hapana *no*
Harambee *pull together*
Hodi *hello (are you there?)*
Hoteli *hotel*
Huko *there*
Jana *yesterday*
Jua *sun*
Kabisa *entirely*
Kahawa *coffee*
Kalele *noise*
Kali *sharp, fierce*
Karibu *yes, come in*
Kazi *work*
Kesho *tomorrow*

151

Kibiriti *matches*
Kiboko *hippopotamus*
Kidogo *small*
Kifaru *rhinoceros*
Kikapu *basket*
Kima *monkey*
Kisu *knife*
Kitabu *book*
Kitu *thing*
Kondoro *sheep*
Ku-chunga *look after*
Kufa *die*
Kufunga *open* (colloquially *fungua*)
Kuja *come*
Kuku *chicken*
Kula *eat*
Kupika *to cook*
Kwaheri *good-bye*
Kwanini? *why?*
Kwenda *go*
Kwisha *finish*
Leo *today*
Mafuta *oil* (also *petrol*)
Maji *water*
Mama *mother*
Mara moja *once, at once*
Matunda *fruit*
Mayai *eggs*
Maziwa *milk*
Mbaya *bad*
Mboga *vegetables*
Mbwa *dog*
Mchana *daytime*
Mchele *rice*
Meli *ship*
Memsaab *Mrs.*
Meza *a table*
Mimi *I, me*
Mingi *many*
Mkaa *charcoal*
Mkate *loaf of bread*
Mkubwa *big*
Mlango *door*
Moto *hot, fire*
Mpaka *far*
Mpishi *a cook*
Mtambo *machine*
Mtoni *river*

Mtoto *child*
Mtu *man, person*
Muhindi *Indian* (colloquially *Hindi*)
Mume *husband*
Mungu *God*
Mwanamuke *woman*
Mzee *old man, elder*
Mzungu *European*
Mzuri *beautiful, good*
Na *also, and, with*
Nani? *who?*
Ndege *aeroplane*
Ndiyo *yes*
Ndovu *elephant*
Ngapi? *how many?*
Ngombe *cow, cattle*
Nini? *what?*
Noti *note* (money)
Nyama *flesh, meat*
Nyana *animal*
Nyumba *house*
Paka *cat*
Panga *sword, agricultural implement*
Papayi *paw-paw*
Pasi *clothes iron*
Pesa *money*
Pesi *quick*
Petroli *petrol*
Piga *hit*
Pole-pole *slowly*
Pombe *alcohol*
Porini *bush country*
Posho *maize meal*
Punda Milia *zebra*
Rafiki *friend*
Risasi *bullet*
Roti *coat*
Saa *clock, hour, time*
Saa ngapi? *when?*
Sabuni *soap*
Safari *journey*
Sahani *dish, plate*
Samaki *fish*
Sana *much, very*
Sasa *now*
Sasa-hevi *immediately*
Sauti *voice*
Serikali *Government*

Vocabulary

Shamba *farm, garden*
Shauri *affair*
Shilingi *shilling*
Siafu *ant*
Siagi *butter*
Sigari *cigarette*
Siku *day*
Simba *lion*
Simu *telephone*
Sisi *us, we*
Stima *electricity*
Sukari *sugar*
Swara *buck*
Tembo *alcohol*
Tengenesa *make, get ready*
Ticketi *ticket*
Tumbaku *tobacco*
Tumbo *stomach*

Twiga *giraffe*
Ufunga *key*
Uhuru *freedom* (independence)
Usiku *night*
Umoja *one-ness, unity*
Viatu *shoes*
Viazi *potatoes*
Wananchi *the people*
Wanawake *women*
Wapi? *where?*
Watu *people*
Wewe *you*
Ya *of*
Yai *egg*
Yake *her, his, its*
Yeye *she*
Yote *all*

To intensify the meaning of any word add *sana* (very, much); thus, *moto sana* (very hot), *pesi sana* (very fast), *mzuri sana* (very good indeed), *mbaya sana* (very bad or wicked).

USEFUL PHRASES

Here are a few useful phrases, which also show how words can be strung together in Swahili, even without verbs, and their meaning can be understood.

I want *nataka.*
I want a car *nataka gari.*
I want something to eat *nataka chakula.*
I want tea (coffee) *nataka chai (kahawa).*
How do you do? (in greeting) *Jambo?* Or this could be *Habari?* (what's your news?). To which the answer is *mzuri* (good), or *mbaya* (bad).
Good-bye *kwa heri.*
I do not like *sipendi.*
I do not want *sitaki.*
I do not understand *sifahamu.*
Close the door *funga mlango.*
Open the door *fungua mlango.*
Wait awhile *ngoja kidogo.*

A little time later *bado kidogo*.
What do you want? *wataka nini?*
Where is the Post Office? *Wapi Posta?*
Where is the hotel? *Wapi hoteli?*
Is the food ready? *Chakula tayari?*
I want a bottle of beer *nataka chupa tembo* . . . large bottle of beer *chupa tembo mkubwa* . . . bottle of cold beer . . . *chupa tembo biridi*. Glass *bilauri*. Generally the name of the brewery is specified instead of using the Swahili word *tembo*.
Where is the newspaper? *Wapi gazetti?*
Be very careful *angalia sana*.
Bring the tea at 7 o'clock *Lete chai saa moja*.
Get the bath ready *tengenesa bafu*.
There is no Swahili word equivalent to "please", but "thank you" is *asante*.

Section Two

SPECIALIST CHAPTERS

CHAPTER XIII

Tourist Attractions and the Game Policy

by the Hon. S. O. AYODO, E.G.H.

MINISTER FOR TOURISM AND WILDLIFE 1965-69

Since Kenya attained independence in 1963, we have witnessed considerable progress in the fields of tourism and the conservation of wildlife. In the past, the indigenous population did not understand or appreciate the importance of wildlife, but the enthusiastic and co-operative support for Government policy in this sphere is evidence enough that this situation does not now prevail.

We fully understand the urgent need for careful conservation for all time. Kenya is eminently suited for development as a holiday resort, but until recently this fact was known and exploited by only a few. The vast fisheries' resources—capable of development in a variety of ways—were practically ignored and even abandoned. Fishing for sport was a luxury enjoyed by only a handful of people.

The Government is pursuing an enlightened policy, fully conscious that in the hands of the present generation lies the responsibility of conservation and exploitation of our natural resources for posterity.

As a basic requirement for lasting success in our conservation policy we have adopted the line of intensive and extensive propaganda, directed mainly at the local population to ensure that the full value of our wildlife, with which Nature has endowed us, and the need to look after it to the best advantage, is firmly and permanently the aim of everybody in the country—not only the people who have chosen to make it their career.

Towards this end we have also established a Wildlife Extension Department, whose responsibility it is to co-ordinate all wildlife educational work in the Republic. The Kenya National Parks also carry out very far-reaching and successful work through the Education Centre which is situated at the National Parks Headquarters in Nairobi. In this work we have received, and continue to receive, most valuable help from many friends from overseas notably America and Europe.

Large numbers of people, both adults and children, have visited the Centre and, as interest mounts, we expect many more visitors. The National Parks intend to open more centres in other parts of the country, principally in the more densely populated areas and near parks and game reserves.

These measures have produced most welcome results. We have increased the number of National Parks from five in 1963 to ten in 1969; a new Game Reserve, Lambwe Valley, has been established; and we have under active discussion the possibility of setting aside even more land for this purpose.

There is popular demand for more hotels and game lodges to be erected, which in turn provide more employment for the local people and markets for the local farmers and dairy-men to sell their produce. The people have accepted the fact that the growth of tourism is a result of certain basic conditions without which not much success will be achieved. Of these, the presence of wildlife is one of the most important factors in our successful expansion.

Attractions for tourists are many and varied in Kenya. I have already referred to wildlife at some length, but we also have magnificent beaches, uncrowded and peaceful, where there already exists accommodation of various types; luxury hotels, family hotels, holiday bandas let on a "do-it-yourself" basis, camping sites and beach cottages. There is still room for development of all types of accommodation and attractions and progress continues to be made steadily in this field.

We turn to the mountains—Kenya, Elgon, Aberdares, Longonot, Kilimambogo—to mention but a few, which are areas of healthy recreation already attracting overseas and local mountaineers and simple climbers alike. There are delightful picnic spots, also, in these areas and others can be found beside beautiful lakes and rivers.

On some of our lakes there are full-scale marinas, and good

hotel accommodation, both of which provide places to stay either for a day or for longer periods. Lake Naivasha is a popular week-end resort for many Nairobi residents as well as overseas visitors. Lakes Baringo, Victoria and Rudolf, which are further away from Nairobi, are also popular with tourists, receiving many visitors every year.

The ocean, lake and mountain rivers are rich in many kinds of fish and interesting birds abound on the banks and shores. Sport fishing in Kenya—deep-sea fishing at the Coast, bass at Lake Naivasha, Nile perch at Lake Rudolf and trout in the rivers—is among the best in the world.

Kenya's people, with their varied cultures, fascinate the visitor and the holiday-maker. Folk-dancing or tribal dancing is both colourful and exciting. Photographers from all over the world have field-days at our *ngomas* (festivals of dancing) and there must be innumerable records on film of these occasions in homes in most countries of the world.

Of great interest to the visitor from the colder countries is the fact that all these attractions are set against a superb climate to suit all requirements; hot and humid, dry and hot, cool and even wet!

In order to exploit all these natural assets, with their vast possibilities for development, the Government has devoted much time and work to careful planning. Organisation is geared to develop the potentials for the benefit of the people of Kenya, striving at the same time to ensure that the visitor receives true value for his money. Foreign investment in welcomed and the investor enjoys conditions guaranteed by the laws of the country.

Hotel development and tour organisation for tourists is under-taken by private enterprise, and to this sector of our business community goes full credit for the immense achievements already gained in Kenya. At the same time, the Government has set up the Tourist Development Corporation through which it invests in the tourist industry itself. This Corporation, together with several foreign investors, has formed a local company—Kenya Safari Lodges and Hotels Limited—which has so far built two game lodges, with a third project, a large hotel at the Coast nearly completed as I write.

The same company has plans to develop more lodges and hotels in the future, for which, with the steadily increasing number of tourists over the last six years, we have need. We expect these numbers to continue to increase as Kenya becomes more and more popular as a holiday centre.

We set aside increasing amounts of money every year for our publicity campaign and more people are now aware that any month in Kenya is a holiday month and that all tourists, whether wealthy or not, are always welcome.

Having referred earlier to our game conservation policy, it is necessary to mention that these policies are decided after facts are made available to us by research workers. Both the National Parks and the Game Department pursue an active research policy, again assisted by overseas friends, and already there exists a nucleus around which a strong game research investigation is being developed. In this way we keep abreast of the latest methods of wildlife management and conservation.

Relatively new is our world leadership in marine parks. Our new Marine Parks at Malindi and Watumu are already proving popular and the day is not too far off when under-water tourism will draw visitors from overseas to enjoy some of the rarest sights and scenes under the sea.

The poacher, of course, is always a threat to continued wildlife existence in Kenya, as he is in other countries. The problem of stamping out poaching is made more difficult because the most persistent offenders are those professionals who make large sums of money from their activities, but we are aware of this danger and alert against it.

We are also on the alert against commercial cropping under any guise, as this would be one of the surest ways of thwarting Kenya's economic progress in one of the most promising fields. Whatever game control work is found necessary must always be carried out by the State, and that only after careful research.

There is still much to be learnt, though much has already been discovered, in the task of effective control alongside improving our tourism industry. We are constantly on the look-out for new ideas but, at the same time, ensuring that strict control is kept on all aspects of hunting and cropping. Only in this way can we preserve this wonderful heritage for posterity.

[Mr. Ayodo was succeeded as Minister for Tourism and Wildlife by Mr. J. Shako in the 1970 Cabinet.]

Elephant giving himself a sand shower

Giraffe and young in Nairobi National Park

CHAPTER XIV

Wildlife and its Conservation

by Dr. D. R. M. STEWART

HEAD OF THE RESEARCH DIVISION OF THE KENYA GAME
DEPARTMENT AND EDITOR OF THE E.A. WILDLIFE JOURNAL

To many people the term "wildlife", in an African context, brings to mind the spectacular large mammals which are such an outstanding feature of the continent's fauna. It is as well to remember, however, that the birds, vegetation and marine life, to mention only three other facets of Kenya's wildlife, are equally remarkable in their way.

The attraction which Kenya holds for so many overseas visitors largely depends upon the rich diversity of its animals, plants and scenery and these, in turn, are the result of the great variety of climate and habitat which are to be found in conditions ranging from snow-capped mountain to tropical coast, and from luxuriant forest to bare desert.

The modern conservation specialist is essentially an ecologist; that is, he is particularly concerned with the interrelationships of plants and animals, or of animals with one another, rather than with a particular animal or plant considered by itself. This chapter lays stress upon the fact that the conservation of, for instance, large mammals is not simply a question of protecting the animals themselves, but is a much more complicated matter involving the protection of habitats and their basic biological resources. Often, there is little point in going to great lengths to protect particular animals unless their habitat is also going to be given effective protection.

A century ago, man took Africa's wildlife largely for granted. To the inhabitants of Kenya, for instance, the wild animals were nothing remarkable, for who was to know that other countries were not similarly endowed? To the visiting sportsmen attracted to East Africa in increasing numbers towards the close of the nineteenth century, the numbers of wild animals seemed almost unlimited. Few gave much thought to the future.

By the end of the century, however, a minority of far-sighted individuals had begun to appreciate that positive measures were required if the country's wildlife was to survive man's impact in the form of increasing hunting and agricultural development. Already, there were signs that the numbers of certain species had been seriously reduced. Among the first steps taken to remedy the situation were the creation of two large game reserves in northern and southern Kenya in 1899, the appointment of the first Game Ranger in 1901 and the formation of a Game Department in 1906.

These early measures, albeit very desirable, were largely aimed at preventing poaching and at controlling sport-hunting by limiting the numbers of animals shot or by affording complete protection to certain of the rarer species. They did not provide for the less obvious, but equally important, need to protect different wildlife habitats and their extremely vulnerable soil, water supplies and vegetation. Nearly half a century was to go by before such measures were taken.

During the first half of the twentieth century, further inroads were made into the most spectacular element of Kenya's wildlife, the large mammals. Distribution maps published in 1963 in the Journal of the East African Natural History Society and National Museum show how, over large areas formerly rich in wild animals, most of the latter had by then been eliminated. These areas included, in particular, western Kenya, where the reason lay in extensive agricultural development, north-west Kenya, where hunting for food had taken an excessive toll of wildlife, and parts of central Kenya, where both these factors played a part.

Where agricultural development was concerned, animals were often destroyed deliberately, either by the farmers themselves or as part of Government policy, but in other instances they simply died out or moved away when their habitat disappeared. Only in sparsely populated country, and in areas such as Masailand where they were a source neither of food nor of conflict with other interests, did wild animals survive in large numbers. Even there, certain species such as elephant, rhino and leopard were, and still are, extensively poached for commercial purposes.

The real villains of the poaching scene are not so much the

poachers themselves but those who tempt them by providing a lucrative market for the poachers' wares. Until fashions change, for example, and leopard coats no longer command prices of thousands of pounds apiece, one must expect poachers and middle-men to continue to go to enormous lengths to obtain the skins. Fortunately, there is some hope at the present time that legal measures will be taken to prohibit the import of such skins into various countries, thus effectively closing the markets. With regard to rhino horn, the deeply ingrained tradition in the East of using this as an aphrodisiac seems unlikely to be changed in a hurry, so that conservationists will continue to be faced with this threat to all rhino populations. The demand for ivory, too, seems unlikely to alter appreciably in the foreseeable future.

The numbers of many animals were thus undoubtedly severely reduced during the latter part of the nineteenth century and the first half of the twentieth, although, since few counts were made in the earlier days, the extent of this reduction cannot be assessed. In the late 1940s, however, this dismal trend at last suffered a reverse with the creation of the first National Parks—areas set aside by the Government for the conservation of wildlife and its habitat, or for the protection of sites of particular archaeological or other interest, and from which all human activity is excluded except under strictly controlled conditions.

First to be created were the Nairobi and Tsavo National Parks in 1948 and the Mountain National Parks (Mt. Kenya and the Aberdare Mountains) in 1949 and 1950. More recently, Meru, Mt. Elgon, Lake Nakuru—the latter created especially because of its outstanding bird life—and the Marine National Park near Malindi have been added to the list, making a countrywide system of outstanding variety and interest.

Ideally a country's network of National Parks aims to include examples of all the habitat types most typical of the country, be they terrestrial, freshwater or marine, and as many as possible of the most spectacular and interesting plants and animals, especially those which are absent or inadequately protected elsewhere. This ideal is well-nigh impossible to achieve, however, although Kenya is far ahead of many countries in this respect.

Despite the aesthetic, scientific and educational advantages of con-servation, no country can afford to set aside large areas for these reasons alone, least of all Kenya, with her expanding population.

Wherever possible, wildlife conservation has to be a paying proposition before governments or local authorities can set aside land for this purpose. Unfortunately, although wildlife is largely responsible for Kenya's rapidly expanding and valuable tourist trade, a major part of the financial benefits of tourism tend to accrue elsewhere than in the wildlife areas which attract the tourists, and an individual National Park seldom shows much profit.

In addition, whatever profit there is from a National Park usually goes into the national coffers rather than to the people of the area concerned. Thus, there is often little incentive for county councils or other local authorities to set aside land for a park, and it is difficult for central governments to persuade them to do so for the benefit of the nation as a whole.

For these reasons, although Kenya's National Parks are extensive and extremely valuable conservation units, they are not, and probably never can be, a fully comprehensive system. In the first place, boundaries have often had to be drawn for reasons other than biological ones; consequently many animals need to migrate out of the parks to find sufficient food or water at certain seasons. In this sense, many of the present parks are incomplete, perhaps because of insufficient information on animal movements and habits when the boundaries were first laid down, or because some of the land needed by the animals during their migrations was being used for other purposes and was not available to the parks.

Occasionally, animal habits can be altered without detriment to the populations concerned; thus there was formerly a well marked elephant migration route between the Aberdare Mountains and Mt. Kenya, across 30 miles of what is now farmland. When the Mountain National Parks were created, it was clear that continued movement of this kind would result in constant problems, so an elephant-proof ditch was constructed along the eastern border of the Aberdares Park. This has successfully prevented the elephants' movements to and from the Aberdares, and there has been no sign of any ill-effects on the elephant populations. In many cases, however, such artificial restriction of movement would be likely to create grave problems of overcrowding and excessive use of vegetation supplies.

Secondly, several important habitat types and species, especially in northern Kenya, are not yet included within a National Park. Among such habitats are the arid, low-lying bush and semi-desert of the North Eastern Province, important coastal forests such as the Sokoke Forest, and the rolling plains of Masailand which are barely represented in Nairobi Park. Species which are inadequately represented in, or completely absent from, National Parks include Grevy's zebra, reticulated giraffe, sable and roan antelope. It may still be possible to create new parks to fill some of these gaps but the amount of land which can be spared for conservation purposes is limited. Fortunately, however, the network of parks is supplemented by other conservation areas which not only increase the numbers of habitat types and species which are effectively conserved, but also help to avoid overcrowding of the parks by spreading the tourist traffic at peak seasons.

These additional areas include National Reserves, County Council Game Reserves, which are created and protected by Council by-laws, and Nature Reserves which are set aside under the Forest Ordinance to protect areas of particular interest or value. The most important of these are the Council Game Reserves, such as the Amboseli, Mara and Samburu–Isiolo Reserves. Despite the political and financial difficulties involved, at least five councils, usually assisted financially by the Central Government or by outside agencies, have been able to create such Reserves and thus to conserve and exploit wildlife through tourism. Such areas are not always so secure legally as National Parks, so that they cannot be regarded as complete alternatives, but they are nevertheless valuable additions to the conservation scene. They have the advantage that they result in direct financial benefit to the people of the area concerned. Perhaps in the future some compromise can be worked out whereby this advantage is retained but under which the areas receive the status and protection of National Parks, so that they are safeguarded for all time.

Despite this encouraging picture, wildlife conservation still faces major problems in Kenya. There is, first, the urgent need to protect the parks and other conservation areas, and their wild animal populations, by creating adequate safeguards in the unprotected areas into which some of these animals migrate, where these areas cannot be added to the park or reserve concerned. Nairobi National Park provides a good example of this problem. The park is seen at its best in the driest periods of the year, especially January–February, because large numbers of animals from the Athi-Kapiti plains move northwards into the park, where there is plenty of permanent water, as the plains dry out. Later on, when rain falls over the plains, the animals move out of the protection of the park again. Were they unable to do this the park's vegetation could not possibly support them all the year round and their numbers would have to be reduced.

In cases such as this, the first step is for the National Parks' or Game Department's research staff to define the area outside the park which the animals require. This is done by marking animals and recording their movements, or by following the changing distribution of animal concentrations from the air and on the ground. Where the park boundaries cannot be readjusted to include the necessary land a compromise then has to be sought between the interests of wildlife and whatever other forms of land-use are being practised. This is not an impossibility; ranching of domestic stock can be carried on in these circumstances, while the numbers of wild animals can be controlled by cropping.

Other major problems of vital interest in parks and reserves mainly concern conservation of the habitat rather than direct protection of the fauna. The latter is usually a minor problem within Kenya's conservation areas thanks to efficient administration and anti-poaching measures. Protection of the habitat is less easy. Two hazards are particularly important. The first of these is fires which, whether they start outside the park and sweep over the boundary, or are carelessly or deliberately lit inside, are extremely difficult to control in a park the size of Tsavo (8,069 sq. miles), for instance.

Firebreaks which are completely effective against burning vegetation blown by high winds at the height of the dry season are extremely expensive and may be very difficult to make in awkward terrain. They cannot, of course, provide protection against fires lit inside them by poachers, honey-hunters, pyromaniacs or careless tourists. Even when fire protection is successful, it leads to its own difficulties; once vegetation has been protected from fire for several years the accumulation of dry matter greatly increases the fire hazard, and any consequent fire is exceedingly hot and does great damage. Hence the policy is not to stop all burning, but to burn selected areas at intervals of several years and at the least damaging time of year. Much more research is nevertheless required before the best burning policy for particular vegetation types and different climatic conditions can be worked out.

The second major danger to the habitat is, surprising as it may seem, caused by the animal inhabitants themselves. The protection afforded by a park, and the increasing difficulties and dangers often faced by wild animals in the surrounding regions, mean that more and more animals concentrate within the park where they are left at peace to multiply without hindrance. Over-populations of animals, with consequent destruction of the vegetation to such an extent that it can no longer support either the animals responsible or other species, may be the result. Formerly, the opinion was widely held that the flora and fauna of a National Park should be left to look after themselves as far as biological changes were concerned; now it is generally appreciated that for the overall good of such an area conservation authorities must be prepared to undertake research and management operations in order to recognise and control such problems as they arise.

Several notable examples of over-population problems have occurred in East Africa. In the Murchison Falls and Queen Elizabeth Parks in Uganda, concentrations of hippo severely overgrazed the grasslands along the banks of the Nile and Lake Albert; this damage to the grass cover in turn resulted in severe erosion of the banks. Reduction of the numbers of hippo led to a marked improvement in the pasture and consequently to an increase in various other animals whose food supply was thus enhanced. Elephants are another species of particular concern where over-population and damage to the habitat are concerned for, in several African countries, trees and other woody vegetation are being destroyed by elephants at an alarming rate. In the Tsavo Park, for instance, large areas of former bush and woodland have been changed to open grassland by the combined effects of elephants and fires.

Although to some extent this has had a beneficial effect in that the numbers of grass-eating plains animals have increased, and although while the rains are adequate the elephants are able to support themselves on the grasses and herbs which have replaced the trees and shrubs, a careful watch has to be kept on what happens in the event of a drought; in addition, the effect of the vegetation changes on browsing, bush-loving animals such as the rhino and lesser kudu have to be studied.

Turning from problems particularly associated with parks and reserves, it is probably true that the majority of difficulties faced by conservation in Kenya concern other categories of land. Except on urban and intensively-farmed land, much of Kenya still possesses very considerable wildlife populations. The land on which this is especially true includes the national forests, the larger private ranches and the vast acreages, occupying a large proportion of Kenya's land surface, where rainfall is low and where more intensive farming is often a difficult and extremely expensive process. At present wildlife is tolerated, but not exploited, in the national forests. On private land the extent to which wild animals survive depends very much on the whim of the individual landowner; the laws allow him, if he wishes, to eliminate any animals whose presence could possibly be construed as being inimical to his own interests. On the other hand, they do not allow him to exploit his wildlife populations to anything like the full extent, so that he has little financial incentive to conserve them.

Only on the third category of land, the communally occupied rangelands, is wildlife exploited in a rational manner although even here its full potential is certainly not realised at present. At present this land is divided up, for wildlife purposes, into a number of Controlled Areas which are in turn split into hunting blocks. Whereas the Kenya National Parks organisation is solely responsible for all National Parks and National Reserves, the Controlled Areas and hunting blocks are the concern of the Game Department, which is responsible for the conservation of wildlife in these areas and its exploitation through tourism, sport-hunting and game-cropping. The Department also advises county councils on the management of Council Game Reserves, and undertakes the control of animals which are causing damage to crops or stock.

Some of the hunting blocks are exclusively reserved for photographic or game viewing purposes. These blocks, therefore, supplement the National Parks and Game Reserves by providing additional space and variety for tourists. The remaining blocks are available for hunters who can book a block for a period such as a fortnight for their exclusive use. Although there is a general trend away from hunting towards photography, there is, nevertheless, still a great demand for hunting facilities in Kenya, and the sport is a significant source of foreign-exchange earnings. Other forms of wildlife utilisation which take place in the Controlled Areas include the capture of live animals and birds for overseas zoos and research institutions, and the cropping of animals for meat and other products. Both these activities are closely controlled by the Game Department.

Fees charged by the Department for hunting or capture licences go to the Central Government, but an additional Controlled Area fee is charged and the revenue from this source goes to the County Council within whose jurisdiction the particular Controlled Area lies. Councils are expected to use this money for some project which will benefit the people who have to put up with the wild animals, since the latter often represent a danger to the people themselves or to their livelihood. In this way it is hoped that both Councils and individuals will be encouraged to appreciate that the wildlife populations outside parks and reserves, as well as within them, constitute an extremely valuable, and perpetually renewable, natural resource.

The continued existence of wildlife outside National Parks and Game Reserves, whether in the Controlled Areas, in national forests or on private land, depends entirely on whether it can continue to co-exist with the other forms of land-use being practised; that is, whether combinations, for instance, of forestry and wildlife conservation, or of ranching and wildlife utilisation through hunting and cropping, are really practicable. Such multiple land-use exists, in fact, but it must be admitted that up to the present the continued existence of wildlife in these areas has been more a matter of chance, or of *laissez-faire*, than because it is paying its way. As other forms of land-use develop, wildlife conservation in these areas must no longer be left to chance; it cannot be too strongly emphasised that the wildlife must be made to pay in order to justify its survival in these circumstances. The difficulties involved in incorporating wildlife into a multiple land-use system allow no other conclusion to be reached.

Protagonists of wildlife conservation may point out it that has been clearly demonstrated that wild animals in reasonable numbers are not inimical to the interests of forestry provided that they can be kept out of young plantations, and that many successful cattle ranchers have been able to retain considerable wildlife populations on their properties. Masai, Samburu and other pastoralists, and their stock, have for many years co-existed with large numbers of wild animals. The revenue derived from these animals through sporting or photographic safaris and the capture of live animals is already considerable and it is probable that the numbers of animals taken in this way could be greatly increased without exceeding their natural increase.

On the debit side, however, there are many problems. First, wild animals may cause a certain amount of direct damage, such as to fences and water-supplies. Cattle and some wild animals such as zebra undoubtedly compete with each other for grazing.

Wild animals are implicated in the spread of various stock diseases, especially those borne by ticks, although their part in this respect is often exaggerated and will become less important as methods of disease prevention in stock are improved. Secondly, where game-cropping is concerned, it is by no means easy to harvest wild animals. They are difficult and expensive to kill or capture by virtue of the very fact that they are wild; their seasonal movements often take them into difficult terrain and make it impossible to keep up a regular supply to markets, and there is prejudice against eating wild animal meat in many quarters, to name but some of the problems.

In addition, Kenya's laws do not allow the sale of game meat except under special permit and the sale of other animal products is restricted; thus the individual farmer or rancher lacks an incentive to conserve and harvest the wild animals on his land. The amendment of these laws, which is necessary to allow greater utilisation of wildlife and hence to provide an incentive towards conservation, has to be approached with caution because of the opportunities it might offer for abuse.

Despite these difficulties, some progress has been made in harvesting wild animals. Profitable markets have been shown to exist both locally and overseas for meat, skins and other products, and cropping schemes have been under way for several years in Kenya and elsewhere. Nevertheless, great strides must still be made in the framing and implementation of new laws, in market research, in techniques of cropping and processing wild animals, and in alleviating conflicts between wildlife and other forms of land-use, if this kind of utilisation is to become sufficiently important to justify and encourage wildlife conservation on Kenya's rangelands.

The use of free-ranging wild animals in this way suggests other possibilities. Research workers have clearly demonstrated how, as might be expected, wild species are generally better adapted to the conditions in which they have evolved than are the domestic animals which have been introduced into these conditions. Able to use a wider variety of foodplants, capable of going without free water for long periods, more resistant to disease, faster growing and producing a carcase with a higher proportion of lean meat, many wild animals are the equal of, or superior to, cattle and other stock especially in the harsh conditions of low-rainfall areas. Thus it seems illogical that man has not made better use of the indigenous wild animals of Africa, and has concentrated on trying to adapt exotic domestic species to African conditions. Long overdue attempts to rear African animals in conditions of partial or complete domestication are still in their infancy and face many problems, but they have begun in Kenya and elsewhere and the day may come when farmers in the areas least suitable for cattle, sheep or goats find it more profitable to rear eland, impala and gazelles.

To many people, the materialistic approach which this chapter adopts towards wildlife conservation in areas other than parks and reserves may seem distasteful. Nevertheless, it must be repeated that, unless conservation can be made profitable, through more intensive sport hunting, cropping of wild herds and ranching of enclosed or semi-domesticated herds, to the landowners and others who must put up with its difficulties and disadvantages, it will fail. It is both illogical and unreasonable to expect the majority of people to conserve wildlife on grounds of sentiment alone.

One final and all important aspect of wildlife conservation is the need for education. The great majority of the country's population does not realise the incomparable asset Kenya possesses in her wildlife, since so many people have lacked the opportunity to compare the country's good fortune in this respect with the deplorable consequences of man's destructiveness elsewhere in the world. Steps have been taken by the Government and by a number of wildlife societies and other groups to put forward this point of view, especially to school-children, and already an encouraging awakening of interest is apparent. Wildlife clubs have been formed in a number of schools, and effective wildlife conservation may thus in future spring from public opinion and pressure rather than have to be imposed and encouraged by the Government and a minority of enthusiasts.

WHERE TO FIND THE GAME

Visitors to Kenya may wish to know in which park or reserve they are most likely to see particular animals.

The larger carnivores, such as lion, leopard and cheetah, are widespread but lion are particularly easy to see in the Nairobi Park and the Masai Mara Game Reserve, where they are sometimes found in prides numbering 30 or more. Cheetah are also often seen in these two areas. Leopard are never easy to see, but one is probably more likely to come across them in the Amboseli and Mara Game Reserves than elsewhere.

Elephant and rhino are also widespread; Tsavo National Park is particularly well known for both these species but they are also often encountered in the Amboseli and Mara Reserves in southern Kenya, and the Samburu-Isiolo Reserve and Meru National Park in the north. Both are also frequently seen at Treetops in the Aberdares National Park. Meru is the only area in Kenya where the white or square-lipped rhino is found, a small herd having been introduced there from South Africa a few years ago. Elephant are not found in Nairobi Park, but the black rhino population now numbers 25–30, additional animals having been moved into the Park in recent years.

The open, grassy plains of Nairobi Park, Amboseli and the Mara are the best places to see the gregarious plains animals such as common zebra, hartebeest (kongoni), wildebeest, Grant's and Thomson's gazelles and the Masai giraffe. Another such species, the topi, is common in the Mara Reserve. Plains areas throughout most of Kenya also contain eland and warthog. The woodland and bush of Tsavo Park, on the other hand, contain oryx, lesser kudu, gerenuk and dik-dik, while the arid bush and plains of northern Parks and Reserves such as Samburu-Isiolo and Meru are the habitat of Grevy's zebra and reticulated giraffe; oryx are again common here. Bushbuck, impala and buffalo occur over much of Kenya in wooded habitats.

Rivers and lakes in most of the parks and reserves contain hippo and crocodiles. Waterbuck are also closely associated with water; the defassa waterbuck occupies the western half of Kenya while the common waterbuck is found in the east.

A number of the other most spectacular large animals in Kenya are less easy to see. Bongo and giant forest hog occur in the

Aberdares and Mount Kenya Parks but are unlikely to be seen except from Treetops at night, and then only by the particularly fortunate visitor. The Shimba Hills National Reserve is the only protected area in which sable antelope are found, and likewise the Mara is the only Reserve containing roan antelope.

The distribution maps mentioned earlier in this chapter contain more detailed information regarding forty of Kenya's principal mammals; the publication containing these maps is available at the National Museum.

CHAPTER XV

National Parks

by the Director, PEREZ OLINDO

Kenya was the first country in East Africa to establish a system of National Parks and National Reserves. Soon after the end of the Second World War a number of areas were set aside for the "preservation" of wildlife and objects of historical, archaeological, geological and other scientific interest.

After some twenty-four years of very progressive existence, the network of National Parks and equivalent areas has expanded and the approach to wildlife "conservation" has been and continues to be refined, not only to cover the preservation aspect, but also many other branches of wildlife conservation in its widest sense. This new approach includes Wildlife Research, an intensive programme of Wildlife Education and, an inclusion within the Organisation's terms of reference, the control of Marine environments.

The first area to be proclaimed was the now famous Nairobi National Park, only a few minutes drive from the centre of Kenya's capital city of Nairobi. The establishment of this park in June 1945 followed a long period of endeavour by various people after an active Government-sponsored "bounty system" whereby active programmes were financed officially to reduce the then vermin which "threatened the very existence of the farming community". The few far-sighted pioneers maintained that there was need to protect Kenya's valuable wildlife and, further, that this wildlife constituted an important factor in the development of tourism.

In those early days, it must be appreciated that any reference to tourism as an important factor in the economic development of Kenya was mainly an ideal held by a minority of enthusiasts. Today, tourism has earned its way, through stiff competition with agriculture and light industry, to become the first single earner of foreign exchange at a time when the surface of this activity has hardly been touched. The potential for development is here, and in recognition of this, the Government has established the Kenya Tourist Development Corporation, with provisions to establish, operate and participate in heavy holdings of or related to the tourist activity.

It was not until 1963, just before Kenya became an independent State, that the Internal Self Government Cabinet issued a definite policy, in the form of a Manifesto, for the first time in the history of the country. The Manifesto, which is quoted hereunder, has been fully implemented, and the international community continues to give Kenya not only moral support, but support also by way of monetary donations for scientific research, wildlife education, water for wild animals and other capital development.

THE MANIFESTO

CONSERVATION OF NATURAL RESOURCES:

The natural resources of this country—its wildlife which offers such an attraction to visitors from all over the world, the beautiful places in which these animals live, the mighty forests which guard the water catchment areas so vital to the survival of man and beast—are a priceless heritage for the future.

The Government of Kenya, fully realising the value of its natural resources, pledges itself to conserve for posterity with all means at its disposal.

We are confident of the co-operation of other governments of East Africa in this important task, but, at present, we are unable, unaided, to provide the specialist staff and money which are necessary. We therefore invite other nations, and lovers of nature throughout the world, to assist us in honouring this solemn pledge.

[signed]

[Jomo Kenyatta]

in his capacity then as leader of Government.

The intention expressed by the Government of Kenya, "pledges itself to conserve for posterity with all means at its disposal", has been religiously followed, so much so that it did not take long after the attainment of full independent status for

Kenya to prove to the world that the prediction of some observers that the wild animals would be turned into ready meat was both ill conceived and inaccurate.

The second prediction which has been proved wrong stipulated that the National Parks, National Reserves, Game Reserves would all be turned into *shambas* (Swahili for "gardens" or "farms"). The number of these parks, etc. was doubled by 1968, after some four years under an African Administration. In a span of some 18 months, between 1966 and 1968, seven areas were declared parks—Meru National Park, Mt. Elgon National Park, Ol Doinyo Sabuk National Park, two Marine National Parks and two Marine National Reserves, and the areas of Lake Nakuru National Park, the Aberdares and Mt. Kenya National Parks were substantially increased.

On the occasion of the setting up of the Marine Parks and Reserves, Kenya achieved what many oceanic countries are hoping for, and trusting that the outward-facing policies of the Trustees of these parks will be continued in the future, she will definitely also soon reach a stage where her views in conservation circles within the international community will carry due weight and recognition.

This status is not easy to achieve, and Kenya must be advised that the road she has to traverse to realise this goal is very steep, long and difficult. Achieving a status is much easier than living up to the expectations of the office, and it seems, from prevailing trends, that the foundation upon which Kenya is building her wildlife conservation policies is sound. It is hoped, therefore, that Kenya will become more active in internationally orientated programmes in the field of conservation.

It is now an established fact that if an attempt was made to disregard the rôle of wildlife in the economic development of Kenya, a vacuum would develop to the extent where no Government would sustain it without shaking the very foundations on which we are building. To be able to maintain rising standards acceptable first to her targets and objectives, Kenya has accepted the fact that her recruitment policy for Park and Game Department personnel must be realistic and ensure specific technical training. This is a very expensive exercise and is one more field in which Kenya is seeking the help and encouragement of private individuals, organisations and public institutions.

Mt. Kilimanjaro from Amboseli

Elephants in the Tana River—North-Eastern Province

The original two Game Reserves which must be recognised as the first good move towards the system that has eventually developed, were, in effect, undefined and without definite legal boundaries. One of the Reserves just about covered the whole of North Kenya, and the second the South—stretching to the Tanzania border.

To the north, some of the spectacular mountain ranges and deserts of what was referred to then as the Northern Frontier Province, were included. These extensive areas were also settled by the indigenous African peoples, and those pioneers made one glaring mistake of considering these peoples as the greater part of a natural habitat. Little did they understand, or even suspect, that within a few generations what they knew about Africans would be completely transformed to an unbelievable degree. Today, these peoples are part and parcel of the international community playing an active and beneficial rôle towards tackling and solving human and other technical problems, and now actively making an effort to take a leading rôle in environmental conservation of the world. I will now venture a prediction that, sooner than is expected, they will achieve this goal. The circumstances surrounding this prediction are obscure as yet, but are sure.

When the Masai, for example, were included in the Southern Game Reserve, the consideration that wild animals were to share the use of this domain with the people and their cattle, on the basis of undefined priorities in the sharing of grazing and water resources, was left in a state of trust and hope. The limitations of the habitat in the form of carrying capacities of given areas was not realised, or to be more precise, was not known. With low human population and high wild animal densities, the widespread mistake of "unlimited resources" was also made here. Fortunately, realisation returned before it was too late.

We must, therefore, confirm from experience that the co-existence between man and beast, on an equal footing, has not worked, and it must be accepted that even in Kenya the arrangement turned out to be entirely untenable. The key to the failure was not how many animals the Masai could kill, but rather how the habitat was utilised. The passage of time revealed the true picture, and confirmed that the trend leading to the possible eradication of wild animals was real. A better approach emerged whereby these animals were accorded certain places for their exclusive protection, under the wise consideration that the competition between livestock and wild animals for grazing and water was bound to increase, with the inevitable result that the wild animals would have to give way.

As originally conceived, Game Reserves, National Parks and National Reserves remain areas in which hunting is legally prohibited, and today, unlike the early days, no other activities are excluded, especially within the parks, and measures are being taken to ensure not only that the future security of these areas is ensured, but that their basic justification, for a variety of reasons, is understood and appreciated by as many of our people as possible. The Wildlife Education which was started in 1963, by the assistance of the African Wildlife Leadership Foundation, has been so successful that the facilities that were established at the beginning of 1965 became many times too small to meet the demand. An expanded and definitely improved approach is being implemented. Kenya is sharing experiences with neighbours in Eastern Africa, and does not hesitate to caution and point to mistakes that have been made so that they may be avoided in a continent where it is accepted that the optimum use of resources must become a way of life, and not only academic theories or national symbols.

Today, there are specific areas allocated for the total protection of wildlife, proclaimed by statute as National Parks, and administered by a Board of Trustees. Until recently, the operations of this Board have been largely in accordance with an International Convention held in London in 1933 to which the British Government and its dependencies were subscribers. Currently, the African Convention for the Conservation of Nature and Natural Resources provides the guide-lines for operation. This is an O.A.U.-sponsored document and was signed by a large number of Independent African States in Algiers in 1968. This new convention is interlaced with the latest theories, ideals and approaches of Modern Conservation.

Its useful application is yet to be tested. However, it excludes from the Kenya National Parks Trustees' terms of reference the jurisidiction over geological, prehistoric, historical and archaeological sites, and Kenya has implemented this provision by handing over these responsibilities to the Trustees of the National Museums of Kenya. Details of other provisions of the Convention are shortly to be released, but it will, in a number of cases, be necessary to amend the present legislation to incorporate the changes.

In the National Parks, it remains the duty of the National Parks Service to prevent, as far as possible, any unnecessary destruction of fauna and flora and to safeguard the entire environment for the benefit of present and future generations, with due provision of reasonable facilities for people to see and enjoy the national Parks. It is possible that development of public accommodation and such other facilities will be located on the periphery of these sanctuaries.

Against this background, each of the National Parks is described more precisely.

NAIROBI NATIONAL PARK

East Africa is both beautiful and unique—the expanse of the rolling plains dotted, and many times well stocked, with a large diversity of wildlife species, stands out as a must on the itinerary of any holidaymaker. To make this possible, Kenya and other East African countries are developing accommodation facilities to meet the requirements of any taste, and also to suit humble purses.

The fame of outstanding sanctuaries, like the Nairobi National Park, is international, and in many parts of the world our larger animals, the lion, rhino and buffalo, are quickly becoming household words. When we speak of going on safari, the world community understands and expects plenty of excitement and a fair amount of adventure. Usually no one wants to think of danger, but I feel we should remember that the animals one finds in our National Parks and Game Reserves, although they have learnt to tolerate the presence of a large number of cars, remain basically wild and capable of inflicting critical harm to anyone exposing themselves excessively from their cars. The rule of thumb remains very brief—mutual respect.

Nairobi Park is only 44 sq. miles in area and, while it has taken, and continues to take, the lead in popularity with some 200,000 visitors per annum, I must state that newer parks, such as the Lake Nakuru National Park with its millions of colourful flamingos, and the Marine National Parks, covered with an array of beautiful coral beds and bright tropical fish, some of the best silver-sanded beaches in the world and a pleasantly warm/hot climate all year round, are beginning to prove worthy competitors. We accept that a certain amount of orderly competition is healthy to any system charged with the responsibility of catering for the general public. In the final analysis, the consumer, or rather the visitor, benefits.

In the early days, people clamoured for *simba* (lion) and any party failing to see the King of Beasts reigning over his wild domain became disappointed and quickly concluded that the entire safari was not worth while. Today, while the visitor looks for and expects to see the mighty lion, he realises also that this is but one species within the overall environment which is shared by many other wild animals. An awareness is developing that without the plains species, the lion, cheetah, etc. would soon vanish, and that an interrelated complex would no longer exist. It is this complex, with all the forces of Nature at work, and with as little human interference as possible, that they want to see.

Reference to the "forces of Nature" does not appeal for preservation as against the broader concept of conservation. This clarification appears to be necessary. With the Nairobi Park's close proximity to a high human population density, it was decided some time ago that where a common boundary with the city of Nairobi existed, it was necessary to erect a "game proof" fence to ensure the safety of human beings. This decision did not mean that the animals were completely fenced in, and the entire southern boundary remains open to facilitate free annual migration of these animals. Along the entire length of this boundary is a permanent river which, during the dry season, attracts large concentrations of animals.

We have both herbivorous and carnivorous animals in this park and, whenever one group moves, it is followed by the other. Within the carnivores exist the important scavenger element, to whom credit must be given for keeping these areas clean.

It is gratifying to record that through legislation, and an intensive programme of wildlife education, Kenya has completely eliminated the undesirable human element within the National Parks.

Three visual habitats dominate the scenery. There is the forest area which covers the higher ground, to be found in the western section of the park and very close to the Kenya National Parks'

Headquarters. A very large part of the park is covered by open plains, and the remainder by a riverine type of habitat. In each of these zones one finds different animals adapted to living there. On the plains, the lions tend to sleep for most of the day, and their close relative, the cheetah, now disregards even large concentrations of cars, and goes about his hunting to the delight of the camera-carrying visitors.

In planning a visit, one wishes to know what animals one may expect to see. For Nairobi Park it is easier to tabulate what should not be expected, than to detail what might be seen. No fruitful outcome should be expected if we are looking for the oryx, kudu and elephant, otherwise we guarantee our visitors pleasant viewing all the year round.

LAKE NAKURU NATIONAL PARK

This park lies some 100 miles to the north-west of Nairobi in the famous Rift Valley. It is an ornithologist's paradise and, possibly, also a great challenge to the biologist. It is not known precisely how many different habitats can be found within the park, but it is known, through identification, that at least 389 different species of birds live in these 52 square miles of water, bush and forest. The flamingos, both Greater and Lesser, predominate and many visitors are tempted to forget that these are but one of the hundreds of resident species of Nakuru.

While tourism grows and services are continually being improved, we cannot leave aside the fact that Kenya is basically an agricultural country, and Nakuru town is the headquarters of the farming community; so while visiting this area you may wish to see a different aspect of our life.

Consistent with the 1963 pledge, the Government has spent large sums of money on upgrading hundreds of miles of road leading to, and inside, parks to an all-weather standard. In the case of the main links between the large towns, tarmac has taken over, and the era of virtually closing the country for a number of months on account of the rain is rapidly becoming a relic of the past.

TSAVO NATIONAL PARK

Tsavo remains the stronghold of the large and dangerous wild animals—the elephant being the most predominant. This species has become so predominant and the increasing numbers in and around the Tsavo Park have caused so much concern that a high-powered research project has been established. This investigation will embrace many aspects of the greater Tsavo ecosystem. The park is open for the general public to see what work is being done, and what problems face the Kenya National Parks.

Apart from the foregoing, Tsavo may be briefly described as the largest (some 8,024 sq. miles), the driest, and yet the most scenic of Kenya's National Parks. Almost all species of both large and small mammals are to be found here. Accommodation is plentiful, and is of international standard. Also available are self-service lodges, one student hostel and a number of camping grounds for the use of the public.

From the early days, poaching was viewed as the biggest problem facing the National Parks. With the help of the "Friends of Kenya National Parks" and the Government, anti-poaching units have been established and remain operational on a round-the-clock basis throughout the year. Modern equipment, including SSB radio, four-wheel drive vehicles and light aircraft is used to maintain constant contact and provide an effective operation. The Game Department is beginning to utilise similar methods and it is possible that this threat to the survival of wildlife will be eliminated.

The main problem, now, is the availability of trained personnel and, in this respect, it is hoped we will be assisted once again by our friends all over the world.

In other areas we manage Mountain Parks, including the Aberdares National Park, Mt. Kenya National Park, Marsabit National Reserve and Mt. Elgon National Park.

A new horizon has been tackled, and two Marine Parks and two Marine Reserves have been established. It may be said that Kenya is on the right road towards sound wildlife management and we certainly invite comment and discussion to meet this end. We hope our readers will find the opportunity to visit a system for which we are truly proud.

CHAPTER XVI

Birds—and Where to Find Them

by JOHN G. WILLIAMS

DIRECTOR OF ZOOLOGICAL EXPLORATIONS LTD.
AND FORMERLY CURATOR OF ORNITHOLOGY AT
THE NATIONAL MUSEUM, NAIROBI

Kenya possesses one of the richest and most varied avifaunas in the world. At present 1,036 species of birds are known to occur in the country, compared with approximately 440 recorded from the British Isles, and well below 800 known from North America. But what makes the bird life of Kenya even more remarkable is the accessibility of the principal bird habitats and the ease with which birds may be studied here. A person with some little knowledge of birds can count on seeing between 600 and 800 species during a four or five weeks' visit, depending on the season, weather conditions and areas visited.

The National Museum in Nairobi offers outstanding facilities to visitors who may be interested in birds. In addition to an exhibition series of mounted East African birds, the Museum houses a research collection of African birds' skins of world renown and an extensive library of books on East African ornithology. These are available for reference and study by any interested visitor.

A great deal remains to be learnt about the birds of Kenya and many forested hills and mountain ranges in the remoter parts of the country are still ornithologically unexplored—a challenge to the more serious naturalist who visits Kenya.

Examples of such areas are Mt. Kulal, the Nyambenis (Jombeni) range, and the Matthews range and its northern outliers the Ndoto mountains, and Mt. Nyiru. In northern Turkana—a region of super-abundant bird life—little field-work has been done in the extreme north and more than one forested mountain top awaits the arrival of its first naturalist!

To aid visitors with perhaps limited time in the country I have detailed some of the better bird haunts near the main centres, and listed localities in which certain interesting species are most likely to be encountered.

BIRD HAUNTS NEAR THE MAIN CENTRES

The various localities enumerated are all within an easy day's run by car from a main centre.

FROM NAIROBI

1. *Nairobi National Park.* The local park which includes a number of different habitats—open plains, acacia woodland, riverine scrub and dry highlands forest—has an abundant avifauna, but the number of species to be observed in any one day varies according to weather conditions and season. Among those constantly recorded are such interesting birds as all six species of East African Vultures, Secretary Bird, Hartlaub's Turaco, Bateleur Eagle, Black-breasted Harrier Eagle, Reichenow's Helmeted Guinea-fowl, Yellow-throated Spurfowl, Crowned Lapwing, Yellow-throated Sandgrouse and Temminck's Courser. Although the park is only some 40 sq. miles in extent, more species of birds have been recorded there during the past decade than have ever been recorded in the British Isles!

2. *Lake Magadi.* Permission must be obtained from the Magadi Soda Company to enter their concession area and to visit the hot springs at the southern end of the lake. A sturdy vehicle in good repair is recommended for this trip and plenty of water must be carried. The road from Nairobi to Magadi traverses a variety of country, from the high grasslands of the Ngong Hills at 7,000 ft. to semi-desert bush country below 2,000 ft. at Lake Magadi.

April and May are the best months in which to visit Magadi as then all the many dry country birds will be nesting—that gem among the sunbirds, the Black-bellied Beautiful Sunbird, is common below 5,000 ft.—and large numbers of migrant Arctic-breeding waders will be seen on the southern end of the lake. Among the weavers which nest in this general region are Vitelline, Masked, Black-necked, Chestnut and Grey-capped Social Weavers; the tiny Mouse-coloured Penduline Tit occurs near the Olorgesailie Prehistoric Site (passed *en route*); on open, flat plains with sparse acacia bush look for the Masai Double-banded Courser and Heuglin's Courser; in areas of thicker bush the Rufous-crested Bustard is not uncommon. The special bird at the lake is the Chestnut-banded or Magadi Plover. As Magadi is an alkaline lake there are not many waterfowl, except for the red-billed Cape Wigeon which is a resident.

3. *Ngong Hills Circular Tour.* This is a recommended afternoon trip. Many interesting birds of prey may be observed, including Augur Buzzards, Secretary Bird, various Vultures, Lanner Falcon and East African Goshawk. The Yellow-throated Long-claw, which will remind American visitors of their own well-known Meadow Lark, is common after good rains. When the orange-flowered Leonotis is in blossom it attracts Yellow-bellied, Variable, Malachite, Scarlet-chested and Golden-winged Sunbirds. In the thickets on the Ngong boma side of the hill look for the Kenya Robin-Chat and the Kilimanjaro Stonechat.

4. *The Karura and Langata Forests, Nairobi.* The Karura Forest off the Kiambu road, and the Langata Forest off the Ngong road, are both good birding areas within easy reach of the centre of the city. In the former such rarities as the Crowned Hawk-Eagle, Ayres' Hawk-Eagle and the Cuckoo Falcon are residents. Other birds of prey which breed in the forests are White-backed and Hooded Vultures, Little Sparrow Hawk, East African Goshawk and Black Sparrow Hawk. Several species of bulbuls and Ruppell's Robin-Chat give the lie to the story that African birds have no song. Along the stream in the Karura Forest look for the Mountain Wagtail. The emerald green and scarlet Narina Trogon occurs in both forests.

5. *Lukenia Hill and the Athi Plains near Athi River.* This is privately owned land and permission must be obtained from the local farmers before birding on their properties. On Lukenia there is always the chance of seeing Verreaux's Eagle, one of our finest and rarest birds of prey. The Egyptian Vulture also nests during some years on the cliffs, and at least one pair of Lanner Falcons has its home there. On the plains look for Kori, White-bellied and Hartlaub's Bustards; several rare larks also occur in this area including the Kenya Short-tailed Lark and the Athi Short-toed Lark. Flocks of migrant Caspian Plovers winter on these short-grass plains and the Yellow-throated Sandgrouse nests there in colonies during September and October.

6. *Makueni, Machakos District.* This is an interesting bush area with non-permanent water courses edged with acacias and large fig trees. Bird life is abundant: one of the commonest species from October to April is a winter visitor, the Thrush-Nightingale or Sprosser, and it is also a good locality for the White-throated Robin or Irania. Wahlberg's Eagle and the Shikra are fairly common birds of prey.

7. *Katamayo Forest.* Details on how to reach the Katamayo River Forest may be had from the Chief Fish Warden at the Kenya Game Department as this is a trout-fishing area. It is the most easily reached highland rain forest near Nairobi, where one can have the pleasure of seeing giant tree ferns and colobus monkeys in addition to many interesting birds. Along the river look for the Giant Kingfisher and the Black River Duck: in the undergrowth watch for the yellow-breasted White-spotted Bush Robin and in the trees the beautiful Bar-tailed Trogon.

8. *Thika and the Fourteen Falls.* The river above the Fourteen Falls is exactly what an African river should look like, with dense over-hanging riverine forest, crocodile-infested pools, acres of water lettuce and abundant bird life. In the quiet lagoons and backwaters above the falls, look for the rare and elusive Peters' Finfoot. Two other good birding localities near Thika are the forested hill Donyo Sabuk, the home of many interesting birds of prey, including the African Harrier Hawk, and the thorn-bush country and marsh bordering the Yatta furrow, one of the few places where the Grey-headed Silverbill is common and where the Yellow-crowned Bishop nests.

FROM MOMBASA

1. *The Shimba Hills.* Forest patches of varying size alternate with open plains to provide a habitat for many interesting birds. In the forest the African Broadbill is not uncommon and other birds likely to be encountered are Red-necked Spur-fowl, Lizard Buzzard, Trumpeter and Silvery-cheeked Hornbills, Fischer's Turaco and the Green Barbet: flocks of Black-bellied Starlings and Violet-backed Starlings are in evidence in fruiting trees. The Flappet Lark is common on the plains. The Green-headed Oriole has been recorded recently in the Shimba Hills forest.

2. *Port Reitz Creek.* While not in the same class as a wading-

birds haunt as Mida Creek to the north, Port Reitz has many interesting species. The Terek Sandpiper is sometimes numerous on spring migration, and Peters' Finfoot inhabits the remoter mangrove swamps. In fig trees bordering the creek, look for Wakefield's Green Pigeon.

3. *Tern Island, south of Wasin Island, off Shimoni.* This island can be reached easily by small boat or fisherman's canoe. Between July and October it is the breeding-place of a large colony of terns, mainly Roseate and Sooty Terns. The rare grey and white plumage phase of the Little Egret also occurs on the island.

4. *Kilifi.* The area between the Kilifi boma and village and the sea is an exceptional place to study spring migration, from the second half of March and during April. Among the uncommon migrant species the Lesser Cuckoo is sometimes quite plentiful. The old, dead coral of the inshore reefs at Kilifi is a favoured haunt of the Woolly-necked Stork. The Bat-eating Buzzard is often seen at dusk in the vicinity of baobab trees.

FROM NAKURU

1. *Lake Nakuru.* Whenever the bulk of the African population of Lesser Flamingos is concentrated on Lake Nakuru this locality affords one of the greatest bird spectacles in the world. Other wading and water birds occur in great abundance and Maccoa Ducks are to be seen along the edges of the sedge beds which extend in places into the lake. Along the muddy margins look for the Painted Snipe which is a resident here.

2. *Lake Elmenteita.* Permission must be obtained from the landowners before proceeding to the lake shore. This is the chief locality of the Greater Flamingo in eastern Africa, the species nesting spasmodically on rocky islets in the lake. When not occupied by the flamingos the islets are the breeding ground of colonies of Grey-headed Gulls, Sacred Ibis and other birds.

3. *Lake Baringo.* In addition to water birds—there are colonies of Goliath Herons nesting on the islands in the lake—there is an abundance of bird life in the acacia woodland which borders the lake edge. The Sudan Beautiful Sunbird is common and in full plumage from June to September. Verreaux's Eagles nest on near-by cliffs, which are also the home of the Long-tailed Bristle-crowned Starling and Hemprich's Hornbill.

4. *Ol Bolossat Lake*. This freshwater lake is a great haunt of many species of resident and migrant waterfowl; Garganey Teal are often common there in the spring. It is the breeding-place of a colony of Squacco Herons and Night Herons. The few remaining forest patches near Ol Bolossat and Ol Joro Orok are the best area to search for the rare Mt. Kenya Green Ibis.

FROM KISUMU

1. *The shores of Lake Victoria near Kisumu*. There is an abundance of bird life all along the shores of the lake and many kinds of weaver-birds, including the brightly golden-yellow Orange Weaver. The long-tailed Red-breasted Sunbird is also common along the shore and in gardens.

2. *The Kakamega and Kaimosi Forests*. This is one of the best bird localities in Kenya, where many West African types of forest birds occur. Among them are Petit's Cuckoo-Shrike, the Blue-headed Bee-Eater, the Grey-chinned, Orange-tufted and Green-throated Sunbirds, Thick-billed Honey-Guide, the Red-headed Malimbe, Stuhlmann's Starling and the Yellow-spotted and Yellow-billed Barbets. Several species of turacos are common, including the fine Great Blue Turaco.

FROM KITALE

1. *The Mt. Elgon forest track above Endebess and the Endebess Bluff*. The Bluff is the nesting place of several species of swifts including the Mottled Swift and perhaps the rare Scarce Swift. Along the forest track look for Doherty's Bush Shrike in the undergrowth and Red-headed Parrots in the podocarpus trees.

2. *The Forest Department nursery in Kitale township*. This is a good place for a number of interesting birds, including Ross's and White-headed Turacos Honey-guides and Double-toothed Barbets.

3. *Kapenguria and the Cherengani Mountains forests*. This is the best locality in Kenya for the uncommon Rufous-breasted Sparrow Hawk. Another rare bird of prey is the Lammergeyer which is sometimes seen from "Flat-top" in the Cherenganis. Look for the Black-winged Oriole in the forest tree-tops and the Spotted Creeper in the acacia woodland.

4. *The Kongelai Escarpment and West Pokot Country*. This extremely rich bird locality lies immediately north of Kapenguria. The Stone Partridge occurs on the rocky outcrops at the base of the Escarpment. Over two hundred species of birds have been seen in this area in a single day.

FROM MALINDI

1. *Mida Creek*. The tidal flats of Mida Creek near Gedi are a paradise of shore-birds, especially during late March and in April when great flocks of arctic-breeding sandpipers and plovers pass through on their way north. Among these are parties of Terek Sandpipers, flocks of hundreds of Curlew Sandpipers and Little Stints breeding plumaged Grey Plovers with chequered backs and black bellies, Great Sand Plovers and Mongolian Sand Plovers. Terns are sometimes common and those which may be seen include Caspian, Little, White-cheeked, Lesser Crested and Swift Terns. Two other birds of note, usually to be encountered at Mida Creek are the Reef Heron and the black-and-white Crab Plover a wader which has the remarkable habit, for a shore-bird, of nesting at the end of a burrow.

2. *The Sokoke-Arabuku Forest*. This forest lies immediately inland between Kilifi and Gedi and is the home of one of our rarest birds, the recently described Morden's Owlet. This tiny owl, only 5½ inches long, may be located on moonlight nights by its call, an un-owl-like, metallic tink, tink, which is reminiscent of a tinker-bird's notes. Other special birds to look for in this locality are the Sokoke Pipit, Sokoke Akalat, Clarke's Weaver— in flocks in the tops of Brachystegia trees—and the very local and uncommon Southern Banded Harrier Eagle.

3. *The Great Heronry of Garsen*. See vol. XXIII, no. 4, of the *East Africa Natural History Society's Journal*, June 1959, on details of how to reach the Garsen Heronry which is in use between May and September. Among the interesting species breeding in this colony are Black Heron, Open-bill Stork, African Spoonbill, Yellow-billed and Great White Egret and Sacred and Glossy Ibis.

FROM NANYUKI

1. *Isiolo and the Samburu Game Reserve*. The abundance of birds in this area is almost bewildering. Pygmy Falcons are common,

sitting on the tops of trees and bushes and looking like shrikes: and the grey-plumaged East African Chanting Goshawk and Gabar Goshawk are also plentiful. One of the special birds to note is Donaldson-Smith's Sparrow-Weaver, a species which has increased during recent years and which is now common in Isiolo township.

2. *Naro Moru Track to the high moorlands of Mt. Kenya.* At the top edge of the forest look for the very rare Abyssinian Long-eared Owl. Sunbirds are abundant, the Tacazze, Malachite, Golden-winged and Double-collared in the leonotis beds, and the long-tailed Scarlet-tufted Malachite Sunbird among the proteas and giant lobelias on the moorland.

3. *The Aberdares National Park.* That finest of Kenya francolins, Jackson's Francolin, is common in the forest and is seen in numbers on the track after rain. The tame, robin-like (in habits) Mountain Chat is common on the moorlands.

FROM NAIVASHA

1. *Lake Naivasha and Crescent Island.* I have observed 147 different species of birds on Crescent "Island" in a single day: African Marsh Harriers are nearly always to be seen and many species of waterfowl—Spur-winged Geese are common—nest in the extensive papyrus swamps. Both the Goliath Heron and the Saddle-billed Stork are often seen. Crescent Island is private property and permission must be obtained before going there.

2. *Hell's Gate.* The vast cliffs and precipices of the Hell's Gate gorge are the breeding place of many Ruppell's Griffon Vultures and a few Egyptian Vultures. Verreaux's Eagle also occurs and a pair of Lammergeyers nest on the first main vulture cliff. White-winged Cliff Chats, Red-winged Starlings and a multitude of Nyanza and Mottled Swifts also make the cliffs their home.

3. *The South Kinangop plateau.* This is mainly farming country with intersections of the original moorland. The spectacular Long-tailed Widow-bird is common and in breeding dress from November to June. During seasons of good rains Semini's Swamp on the Kinangop is a paradise of water birds and is one of the few places where the Black-necked Grebe is found. It is also a favourite winter haunt of all the harriers.

FROM VOI

1. *The Tsavo National Park.* Again, this is an outstanding region for bird life, being especially rich during seasons when heavy rains have fallen. The beautiful Golden-breasted Starling is found locally throughout the scrub country, but is usually shy, except at Kilaguni Lodge, where it nests in tree-holes on the compound. Among birds of prey look for the Brown Harrier Eagle, the Ovampo Sparrow-hawk and the African Hawk-Eagle. The Bat-eating Buzzard occurs at Voi and at the Mazima Springs in the park. Sunbirds include the Tsavo, Somali Scarlet-chested and Purple-banded.

2. *The Teita Hills.* A number of endemic birds occur in the small patches of forest remaining on the Teita Hills. These include the richly coloured Heller's Thrush and the Teita White-eye.

WHERE TO FIND BIRDS OF SPECIAL INTEREST

MASAI OSTRICH: Nairobi National Park.

SOMALI OSTRICH: Isiolo area; along the Isiolo–Garissa road; along the Isiolo–Marsabit road.

AFRICAN GREAT-CRESTED GREBE: Lake Naivasha.

DARTER: Amboseli Reserve.

WHITE AND PINK-BACKED PELICANS: Lake Naivasha; Ferguson's Gulf, Lake Rudolf.

GOLIATH HERON: Lakes Naivasha and Baringo. Nesting colonies on islands in Lake Baringo.

HAMMERKOP: dams in Nairobi National Park; Amboseli Reserve; shores of Lake Victoria at Kisumu.

WOOLLY-NECKED STORK: along the Kenya coast on old, raised coral reefs.

OPEN-BILL: swamps near Kisumu.

SADDLE-BILL STORK: Amboseli Reserve.

SACRED IBIS: Lake Naivasha.

GREEN IBIS: upper edge of mountain forest on Naro Moru track, western Mt. Kenya.

GLOSSY IBIS: Lake Naivasha.

AFRICAN SPOONBILL: Lake Magadi, at south end near hot springs.

GREATER FLAMINGO: Lake Elmenteita: also in small numbers on other alkaline lakes in the Rift Valley.

LESSER FLAMINGO: Lakes Nakuru, Elmenteita and Magadi: also at Ferguson's Gulf, Lake Rudolf.

MACCOA DUCK: Lake Naivasha: occurs also on Lakes Nakuru and Elmenteita when these lakes are "full".

WHITE-BACKED DUCK: Lake Naivasha; Amboseli Reserve.

BLACK RIVER DUCK: mountain streams on the Aberdares and Mt. Kenya.

189

CAPE WIGEON: Lakes Elmenteita, Nakuru, Magadi and at Ferguson's Gulf, Lake Rudolf. Occurs on alkaline, not fresh water.

PYGMY GOOSE: Lake Victoria, near Kisumu; dams in coastal districts of Kenya, including inland from Malindi.

SPUR-WINGED GOOSE: Lake Naivasha, especially on Crescent Island.

SECRETARY BIRD: Nairobi National Park; farm-lands of the Rift Valley Province.

LAPPET-FACED VULTURE: Nairobi National Park; Amboseli Reserve.

LANNER FALCON: Hell's Gate gorge, near Naivasha; Lukenia Hill, Athi River.

TEITA FALCON: this very rare bird has been seen perched on dead trees near the Amboseli Reserve camp.

GREY KESTREL: the Kitale–Mt. Elgon area; usually along streams where there are acacia trees.

PYGMY FALCON: appearance very shrike-like; perches on top of trees and bushes; common in the arid bush country immediately north of Archer's Post, Northern Frontier Province.

CUCKOO FALCON: Karura Forest, Nairobi.

SWALLOW-TAILED KITE: spasmodic anywhere in Northern Frontier Province; in some years breeds in colonies in acacia trees in the Lodwar District, Turkana, April–June.

BAT-EATING BUZZARD: Malindi township; Voi (at railway station where it attacks the bats as they leave their roosts at dusk); and at Mzima Springs, Tsavo National Park.

VERREAUX'S EAGLE: Lukenia Hill, Athi River; Hell's Gate gorge near Naivasha; cliffs in the Lake Elmenteita area.

AYRES' HAWK-EAGLE: Karura Forest, Nairobi; forest on Donyo Sabuk, Thika area.

MARTIAL EAGLE: locally in thorn-bush country in Tsavo National Park; and in the Northern Frontier Province.

CROWNED HAWK-EAGLE: a forest eagle which occurs in Karura and Langata forests, Nairobi; coastal forests, including the Shimba Hills; and the Kakamega Forest in Western Kenya.

GRASSHOPPER BUZZARD: visitor to the Tsavo National Park between November and April.

BATELEUR EAGLE: seen usually in flight: Tsavo National Park; Amboseli Reserve; and the North-Eastern Province.

LAMMERGEYER: Hell's Gate gorge near Naivasha, where a pair nests on the first Griffon Vulture breeding cliff; cliffs on northern face of Cherengani Mountains, above Kapenguria.

RUFOUS SPARROW HAWK: not uncommon in the forests of the Cherengani Mountains near Kapenguria; forests along the road through the Aberdare National Park.

AFRICAN MARSH HARRIER: Lake Naivasha; swamps and dams on the South Kinangop plateau.

MONTANE FRANCOLIN: alpine moorland, usually just above the forest, on Mt. Kenya and the Aberdare Mountains.

JACKSON'S FRANCOLIN: along forest roads and tracks on Mt. Kenya and the Aberdare Mountains.

Lesser Flamingos on Lake Nakuru

Mt. Kenya Safari Club, with Lesser Flamingos and a pair of East African Crowned Cranes (right)

Birds—and Where to Find Them

STONE PARTRIDGE: stony hills in North-Eastern Province: common just north of Isiolo; also common on the Kongelai Escarpment, West Pokot.

KENYA CRESTED GUINEA-FOWL: the Sokoke Forest, inland from Kilifi; seen commonly on roads and paths immediately after rain.

VULTURINE GUINEA-FOWL: Common locally in the Tsavo National Park, especially in the Voi area; along the Isiolo–Jombeni track; in the Samburu Game Reserve, and along the Tana River near Garissa.

KAFFIR RAIL: Amboseli Reserve.

PURPLE GALLINULE: papyrus beds at Lake Naivasha.

FINFOOT: on the Athi and Chania rivers near Thika; perhaps most frequent immediately above the Fourteen Falls. Also high up Port Reitz creek at Mombasa, and at Mzima Springs, Tsavo National Park.

EAST AFRICAN CROWNED CRANE: South Kinangop plateau; throughout the Rift Valley district near dams and lakes; Nairobi National Park; the Amboseili Reserve.

KORI BUSTARD: Nairobi National Park; widespread species.

HEUGLIN'S BUSTARD: the black lava desert country north of Marsabit, North-Eastern Frontier Province, along the old Moyale track.

HARTLAUB'S BUSTARD: the Athi plains.

WATER THICKNEE: common along the Tana River from Garissa eastwards: mainly nocturnal in habits.

JACANA: Lake Naivasha.

CHESTNUT-BANDED SAND PLOVER: Lake Magadi, common at the southern end of the lake around the hot springs area.

SPUR-WINGED PLOVER: very common at Ferguson's Gulf, Lake Rudolf; also occurs, alongside the closely related Blacksmith Plover, at Lakes Naivasha, Elmenteita and Nakuru.

BLACKHEAD PLOVER: a mainly nocturnal bird to be seen during the day resting in the shade of acacia trees; common throughout the Turkana area; also at Isiolo (where it frequents the air-strip after dark); Lake Baringo; and locally in the Tsavo National Park.

LONG-TOED LAPWING: a plover with the habits of a Jacana or Lily-trotter: uncommon at Amboseli Reserve.

CRAB PLOVER: Mida Creek, near Gedi, Kenya coast; coastal areas north of Malindi.

QUAIL PLOVER: extreme northern parts of Turkana and the Ilemi Triangle; recorded recently from grassy plains near Natapal waterhole (Kapatadie), and in the Tsavo National Park East.

PAINTED SNIPE: often to be flushed among the sedges which grow around Lakes Elmenteita and Nakuru.

MADAGASCAR PRATINCOLE: a migrant which passes along the coast—often common in the Malindi area—during August.

SKIMMER: common at Ferguson's Gulf, Lake Rudolf, where it sometimes breeds: most nesting takes place on the black lava sand beaches of Central Island.

YELLOW-THROATED SANDGROUSE: Athi and Kapeti plains.

WHITE-WINGED DOVE: along the Daua Parma River at Mandera, Kenya–Somalia border.

o

THICK-BILLED CUCKOO: Sokoke Forest inland from Kilifi and Gedi, Kenya coast.

EMERALD CUCKOO: this species, one of the most beautiful birds in the world, is not uncommon in the Karura and Langata Forests near Nairobi. It is a tree-tops bird, best located by its distinctive call—"tee,ooo—tooo, deee".

SCHALOW'S TURACO: riverine forest in the Narok and Mara River areas.

FISCHER'S TURACO: the coastal forests of Kenya, most frequent south of Mombasa: one specially good locality is the Shimba Hills forest patches, another the forest on Marima Hill on the Tanzanian border.

HARTLAUB'S TURACO: forests around Nairobi; Molo.

WHITE-CRESTED TURACO: wooded areas near Kitale; the Kacheliba Escarpment, north of Kapenguria, West Pokot.

GREAT BLUE TURACO: Kakamega Forest and the forest along the Yala River and at Kaimosi, Western Kenya.

RED-HEADED PARROT: forests on Mt. Kenya, the Aberdares and the western highlands of Kenya; common in the Mt. Elgon forests above Endebess.

ORANGE-BELLIED PARROT: country where there are many baobab trees growing, between Kibwezi and Mtito Andei.

ABYSSINIAN ROLLER: in northern Turkana, along the road to Lodwar: nearly always in the vicinity of large termite hills, in which it nests.

GIANT KINGFISHER: streams on Mt. Kenya and the Aberdares.

MALACHITE KINGFISHER: the margins of Lake Naivasha.

CARMINE BEE-EATER: common on the Kenya coast from October to April, when it moves north to its breeding grounds.

CINNAMON-CHESTED BEE-EATER: forests in Kenya Highlands; common in Karura Forest, Nairobi.

SOMALI BEE-EATER: Isiolo and Archer's Post and northwards; Garissa on Tana River.

WHITE-FRONTED BEE-EATER: main road from Nairobi to Naivasha in low bush below base of Escarpment.

BLUE-HEADED BEE-EATER: Kakamega Forest, Western Kenya, where it occurs in tiny natural glades inside the forest.

JACKSON'S HORNBILL: common in acacias along dry water courses around Lodwar, Turkana.

GROUND HORNBILL: Nyeri and Nanyuki; the Rift Valley farming area, especially near Lake Elmenteita.

AFRICAN HOOPOE: Crescent Island, Lake Naivasha.

GREEN WOOD-HOOPOE: in the belts of yellow-barked acacia trees around Lake Naivasha.

ABYSSINIAN SCIMITAR-BILL: the dry bush country of the Tsavo National Park, especially near Mtito Andei and Voi.

ABYSSINIAN LONG-EARED OWL: at the top edge of the forest on the Naro Moru track, western Mt. Kenya.

VERREAUX'S EAGLE OWL: Amboseli Reserve.

NARINA TROGON: Karura Forest, Nairobi.

BAR-TAILED TROGON: Katamayo Forest, near Limuru.

DOUBLE-TOOTHED BARBET: Kitale, where it frequents fruiting fig trees inside the town; Kongelai Escarpment, West Pokot.

Birds—and Where to Find Them

YELLOW-SPOTTED BARBET: fruiting fig trees in Kakamega Forest, Western Kenya.

RED AND YELLOW BARBET: along the road through arid thorn bush country between Nairobi and Magadi.

GREATER OR BLACK-THROATED HONEY-GUIDE: bush in the Thika area and near Fourteen Falls, Thika. Listen for the call note "weet-ear, weet-ear".

FINE-BANDED WOODPECKER: forests on the Aberdares and Mt. Kenya.

GREY WOODPECKER: Lake Naivasha (in acacia trees); the Nairobi National Park.

BOEHM'S SPINETAIL SWIFT: around small hills and baobab trees near Mtito Andei.

AFRICAN BROADBILL: Ololua Forest, Ngong, Nairobi.

SHORT-TAILED LARK: stony Athi plains near Lukenia Hill, Athi River.

MASKED LARK: along the Isiolo-Jombeni track through acacia scrub on black cotton soil: not to be attempted during rains! Also at Marsabit.

MALINDI PIPIT: airfield at Garsen, Kenya coast.

GOLDEN PIPIT: near Mtito Andei; in bush country near Garissa.

ROSY-BREASTED LONG-CLAW: short grass plains in the Mara River area.

BLUE FLYCATCHER: Kapenguria, Cherengani Mountains, Western Kenya.

ABYSSINIAN GROUND THRUSH: among scrub at upper edge of forest, Naro Moru track, Mt. Kenya.

HEUGLIN'S RED-BREASTED WHEATEAR: on slopes of small rocky hills along the track between Lodwar and Lokitaung, northern Turkana.

BLUE-SHOULDERED ROBIN-CHAT: Kakamega Forest: sings at dusk.

WHITE-STARRED BUSH ROBIN: throughout highland forest; Katamayo River Forest, near Limuru.

WHITE-WINGED APALIS: in riverine forest along Tana, 20 miles upstream from Garsen: in tree-tops in mixed bird parties.

YELLOW-VENTED EREMOMELA: common in Archer's Post area, North-Eastern Province.

BLACK-FACED RUFOUS WARBLER: in undergrowth of Kakamega Forest.

PETIT'S CUCKOO SHRIKE: the Kakamega Forest, Western Kenya.

CURLY-CRESTED HELMET-SHRIKE: bush country at the bottom of the Kongelai Escarpment, West Pokot.

CHESTNUT-FRONTED SHRIKE: the Sokoke Forest inland from Kilifi.

YELLOW-BILLED SHRIKE: riverine acacia woodland along the Swam River at Kacheliba, West Pokot.

BLACK-HEADED GONOLEK: Euphorbia hedges planted around huts in the Kisumu area.

DOHERTY'S BUSH-SHRIKE: in undergrowth of conifer plantations on lower slopes of Mt. Elgon, above Endebess.

ROSY-PATCHED SHRIKE: areas where small isolated bushes are growing at Amboseli Reserve.

AFRICAN PENDULINE TIT: bush at the base of the Mua Hills, Athi River.

MOUSE-COLOURED PENDULINE TIT: dry bush country on the Nairobi–Magadi road.

BLACK-WINGED ORIOLE: forest around Kapenguria, West Pokot.

FAN-TAILED RAVEN: around the Somali bomas near Isiolo.

GOLDEN-BREASTED STARLING: common in the arid bush country along the Tana in the Garissa area; Tsavo National Park.

193

SLENDER-BILLED CHESTNUT-WING STARLING: alpine zone of Mt. Kenya and the Aberdare Mountains; Thomson's Falls.

BRISTLE-CROWNED STARLING: cliffs and craters at Marsabit, North-Eastern Province; Lake Baringo.

SHELLEY'S STARLING: the Garissa area, but spasmodic in its appearances.

MALACHITE SUNBIRD: much attracted to flowering patches of the orange leonotis on the South Kinangop plateau.

SCARLET-TUFTED MALACHITE SUNBIRD: the protea and lobelia zones on Mt. Kenya, above 11,000 ft.

TACAZZE SUNBIRD: South Kinangop.

RED-CHESTED SUNBIRD: near the edge of the lake and in gardens at Kisumu.

GOLDEN-WINGED SUNBIRD: alongside the Malachite Sunbird in leonotis patches on South Kinangop.

PYGMY SUNBIRD: patches of *Salvadora persica* bush along the dry river beds in northern Turkana, most frequent between Lodwar and Ferguson's Gulf. Appears in September and leaves again in April.

GREY-CHINNED SUNBIRD: the Kakamega Forest, where it often visits flowering Nandi Flame trees.

GREEN HYLIA: in dense undergrowth in Kakamega Forest.

SPOTTED CREEPER: open woodlands around Kapenguria, West Pokot.

WHITE-HEADED BUFFALO WEAVER: Tsavo National Park and at the Amboseli Reserve; Isiolo.

DONALDSON-SMITH'S SPARROW-WEAVER: Isiolo township.

BLACK-CAPPED SOCIAL WEAVER: near Archer's Post, North-Eastern Province.

CLARKE'S WEAVER: the Sokoke Forest inland from Kilifi.

YELLOW-BACKED AND GOLDEN-BACKED WEAVERS: papyrus beds along the edge of Lake Victoria near Kisumu.

GOLDEN PALM WEAVER: common along the Kenya coast, including Mombasa town.

TAVETA GOLDEN WEAVER: Amboseli Reserve.

BROWN-CAPPED WEAVER: Karura Forest, Nairobi.

RED-HEADED MALIMBE: Kakamega Forest.

BLACK-WINGED RED BISHOP: areas of cultivation around Kisumu.

MARSH WIDOW-BIRD: in marshes along the Eldoret–Tororo road.

LONG-TAILED WIDOW-BIRD: the South Kinangop plateau; open country between Nyeri and Nanyuki.

JACKSON'S WIDOW-BIRD: rough pasture near the Kabete Veterinary Research Station, Nairobi.

GREY-HEADED SILVER-BILL: Masai watering point near Olorgesailie, on the Nairobi–Magadi road.

RED-HEADED BLUE-BILL: common, but little seen, in the undergrowth of the Kakamega Forest, Western Kenya.

PARASITIC WEAVER: rough pasture land near the Kabete Veterinary Lab., Kabete, Nairobi.

PETERS' TWIN-SPOT: coastal scrub near Kilifi.

STEEL-BLUE WHYDAH AND FISCHER'S WHYDAH: Masai watering point near Olorgesailie, on the Nairobi–Magadi road.

CHAPTER XVII

Butterflies and Mimics

by Lieut.-Col. H. F. STONEHAM, O.B.E., F.Z.S., F.R.E.S.

WHO FOUNDED THE STONEHAM MUSEUM, AT KITALE, TURNED
OVER BY THE TRUSTEES, AFTER HIS DEATH, TO THE NATIONAL
MUSEUM TO BECOME ITS WESTERN KENYA BRANCH

Overseas visitors to tropical countries interested in the fauna are usually attracted largely by the birds and butterflies, the latter excelling in numbers, variety and beauty those that are to be seen in the colder climates of the north. There is no region on earth that can show such richness as the Tropics. However, the visitor can only hope to see but a small fraction of the 100,000 tropical species known to occur.

Although the magnificent bird-wing butterflies of Asia and the resplendent Morpho butterflies of South America are not present, nevertheless some of the most interesting butterflies in the world are found in suitable African localities. The great variety and number of forms is ever a fascination and charm that, to some of us, never fails. It has been said with truth that man, with all his modern inventions, cannot create anything so exquisite as the wing of a butterfly.

The finest butterflies are normally dwellers in the forests, and it is to the forests at the lower elevations that the visitor must go if he wishes to see them. Unfortunately, many are no longer as abundant as they were some 40 or 50 years ago. The advance of civilisation and modern developments, the destruction of forests and the spread of cultivation have, without doubt, decimated many of the lovely species that used to be common and a delight to see.

Africa is divided into several faunal zones or regions in which species may occur but not elsewhere. In Kenya the Great Rift Valley roughly separates the West African zone, which extends to Western Kenya, from the South-East zone which is located from

Eastern Kenya to Natal. Where a species inhabits both, it may be represented by distinct racial forms in each.

Perhaps the butterfly that will first attract the attention of the visitor will be the Citrus Swallowtail, which is common throughout Africa from the Sahara to the Cape. It can easily be recognised as it sips nectar from flowers in gardens, fluttering its wings while it does so, like many members of the Papilio family to which it belongs. The wings above are blackish with conspicuous yellow markings forming a transverse row of more or less conjoined spots on the forewings and a narrow median bar on the hindwings. There are also two red and black eyespots on each hindwing, but there are no tails.

The caterpillars feed on orange trees as well as certain wild plants. The butterflies are often exceedingly confiding and can be approached quite closely when feeding, and sometimes even be picked from the flower heads with the fingers.

The African Swallowtails form an important group, some of which are widely distributed and not uncommon. On the other hand many of them are confined to forest areas, and may be exceedingly rare. In the drier coastal parts of Kenya, and in Uganda, large numbers congregate, in company with other species, such as the "Whites" and "Blues", on damp sand or mud to imbibe the moisture. After rain in the dry season they come to puddles on the roads or to other damp spots.

In Kenya we have 23 species and many varieties or forms. The King Swallowtail is a fine mimetic tailless species that is to be found both sides of the Rift Valley. It has black wings with pale yellowish-white spots, and normally two orange-yellow basal streaks on the forewings and a large creamy-yellow basal area on the hindwings. It is such a magnificent flier that it is well-nigh impossible to catch it on the wing unless it descends to some flower heads.

The Merope Swallowtail has been described as the most amazing butterfly in the world because of its numerous forms, many of which are mimetic.

Before proceeding with more details about Kenya butterflies it will help if something is said about that remarkable phenomenon known as "mimicry". Many butterflies and moths at rest with wings closed bear a strong resemblance to dead or discoloured leaves, lichens, etc., and some caterpillars simulate dead twigs.

Butterflies and Mimics

There are insects of other Orders, known as stick-insects or leaf-insects on account of their resemblances to their surroundings. These adaptations are for protection.

About 100 years ago, the distinguished naturalist, H. W. Bates, working in Brazil, observed that among his captures of certain conspicuously coloured butterflies were others which resembled them very closely in form, colour and markings, but, on account of the venation, belonged to a totally different family. These similar butterflies Bates termed "mimics". He also noticed that the former were rarely attacked by birds, and he attributed this fact to their being distasteful.

Therefore, he considered that the bright coloration was in reality a warning to possible predators that they were not palatable. Birds would learn to associate such colours with disagreeable flavours and so would not attack them or eat them, and the brighter and more conspicuous the pattern the greater the protection achieved.

The "mimics" have, by means of natural selection over millions of years, been able to change the pattern and coloration of their wings so as to resemble the distasteful "models" and thus obtain similar immunity from attacks by birds. This is what scientists term "Batesian Mimicry". It has since been found to be a wide-spread phenomenon among butterflies of the world and is well exemplified in Africa.

There is, also, a second kind of "mimicry". In this, one conspicuously marked distasteful species resembles another similarly marked distasteful species. For a time this was an unsolved problem. A German scientist, Fritz Muller, supposed that young birds had to learn by experience which butterflies were distasteful and which were not, and therefore it was of advantage to have as few warning patterns as possible.

This theory is known as "Mullerian mimicry". Tropical Africa is possibly richer in "mimetic" butterflies than Asia. The chief "models" in the Ethiopian Region belong to the two families *Danaidae* and *Acraeidae*.

The Merope Swallowtail, already mentioned, is a very remarkable butterfly, for the females are not like the males at all (except the island forms in Madagascar and Comoro) but exhibit wonderful "mimetic" similarities to distasteful species of entirely different families. The male is a splendid and majestic swallowtail with cream-coloured wings, margined with black broadly on the forewings but narrowly on the hindwings.

This species has a wide distribution from Sierra Leone to Ethiopia and to South Africa. Some ten distinct local races have been named, those found east of the Rift Valley being normally different from western forms. The hindwings are furnished with long conspicuous tails, and the flight is very graceful.

The most interesting feature of this butterfly is the large number of its distinct female forms, quite unlike the males, and about fifty of them have been named and described. Some of these resemble very closely distasteful butterflies belonging to different families. All are tailless with the exception of some found in Ethiopia. The commonest is black and white and appears to be a "mimic" of the Danaid, popularly called the Black Friar. Another has brown wings with black-and-white apices. This may be a "mimic" of the almost ubiquitous Golden Danaid. A third has blue-black forewings, spotted with white or cream and a large creamy basal area on the hindwings. This mimics the various spotted Ballerinas.

It is not possible in the present article to detail all the many forms of this most interesting butterfly or to describe the many differences. To do so would require very considerable space, and in any case would not help the visitor to distinguish them on the wing. However, a female Merope "mimic" sipping on a flower head can usually be known from its "model" because the former normally flutters the wings while the latter does not.

Of other Swallowtail butterflies that the visitor is likely to see, if the season be right, mention may be made of the Noble Swallowtail, a large ochre-yellow tailed species with brown apex and margins to the forewings and with brown tails and marginal spots on the hindwings. The females are distinguished by having an extra discal row of spots on both wings. The markings are usually darker in the rainy season form.

The Swallowtail named *Constantinus* also has black and yellow markings and is to be seen in suitable localities on the coast. Visitors sometimes confuse it with the common Citrus Swallowtail, but because the yellow markings are more restricted and the hindwings are tailed it should be easy to distinguish. Mackinnon's Swallowtail, which is closely related, is usually larger and almost all black with a transverse row of small yellow spots across each wing. An extreme all-black form without yellow spots occurs on Mt. Elgon, and has been named Elgonia.

A common and variable species, the Green Swallowtail, is found from the West Coast to the Indian Ocean. The normal coloration is black with a broad transverse vivid green band spread across the wings. The undersides of the hindwings are largely silvery-white. The tails are very brittle and frequently break off when the butterfly flutters about in the net. So, to secure perfect specimens they must be killed as soon as captured.

There are several blue-banded Swallowtails in East Africa, but unless one has long series from different localities it will be difficult for the visitor to separate them correctly. Of the forms that will be observed two distinct groups may be noticed, one black with narrow blue band and the other black with broad blue band. The former has a transverse median band which is metallic blue in the male but metallic green in the female. The race occurring east of the Great Rift Valley differs from that in Western Kenya. In the latter species the metallic blue band is much broader and is metallic green in the female.

In Western Kenya is found a fine Swallowtail with a wing span of four and a half inches or more, carrying long tails on the hind-wings from fourteen to twenty millimetres in length. This is Lormier's Swallowtail. The general coloration is black with a transverse row of large yellow spots, and on the hind-wing a yellow median band of varying width. All wings have large submarginal spots. In addition there are two conspicuous red and blue eyespots. It is a stately flier and is a splendid sight as it floats gracefully high up amongst the forest trees.

An allied species is found on the Kenya Coast. They are much alike, but the latter has much wider yellow pattern. It has been named *Ophidicephalus.*

Another group is represented by several small species, the females of which are usually considered to be "mimics" of the common distasteful Ballerinas which they resemble. None of them carry tails. The forewings of the males are normally black with a row of white or yellowish-white spots from the apex to the inner margin and a broad band on the hindwings. The dissimilar females have white-spotted borders and spots in and below the cell of the forewings. The basal area on the hindwings is yellowish. The Cynorta Swallowtail, found uncommonly in Western Kenya, has some very interesting female forms some of which are "mimetic".

The so-called Kite Swallowtails are represented by small tail-less swift-flying butterflies, the commonest of which is the Angolan Swallowtail. The white wings have black markings in which are numerous white spots. Two races are to be found in Kenya, the typical being distributed from the coastal zone to Nairobi, and the West African race abounds in Western Kenya.

The Leonidas Swallowtail is another widespread species which bears a superficial resemblance to the Common Striped Danaid. The black or blackish wings have light-blue, greenish or bluish-white markings covering much of the surface in stripes or rows. It is distributed over a wide area in Africa, and there are several varietal forms.

Omitting several groups of East African Swallowtails, the last to be mentioned are sometimes popularly known as Swordtails because the tails are long, narrow and tapering instead of the tips being widened as in typical Swallowtails. In general appearance the wing pattern consists of transverse stripes and spots which are greenish-white on a blackish ground colour.

Two, the Anthena Swallowtail and the Policenes Swallowtail, occur in Western Kenya. The latter may be easily distinguished by the green bars in the cell of the forewing being straight and not curved. In the coastal areas others are to be seen, some of which are rare. Both *Porthaon* and *Colonna* are common, and Kirby's Swallowtail locally so.

The Emperor Butterflies or Charaxes are well represented in East Africa. They are mostly large and powerful insects, some with bright and conspicuous coloration. The females are often very different from the males both in wing markings and in habits. Like their ally, the Purple Emperor butterfly in England, they are not lovers of flowers, but are attracted to carrion and and other evil-smelling baits. The caterpillars are smooth and slug-like in appearance, with horns on their heads. It will not be possible to enumerate here all the many species.

In the Western Kenya forested country some of the finer West African Emperors abound, whereas those seen in the environs of Nairobi and in the coastal zone show affinities to the southern faunal groups. Most Emperor butterflies exhibit two short tails on each hindwing. These are "target marks" and are not infrequently snipped off by attacking lizards and other enemies. When an Emperor butterfly alights it quickly turns round so that the head is downward and the tails uppermost. This is a safeguard, the predator attacking the tails instead of the head.

Probably the finest of this group in Kenya is the splendid King Emperor, which above has a blue-black ground colour and yellow markings. Below it is prettily marked with an intricate pattern of white and brown lines. All black specimens are sometimes met with. Its flight is rapid and powerful, making capture on the wing not easy. The Tawny or Golden Emperor is usually the commonest, and sometimes numbers may be seen chasing each other round the tree-tops. Above the coloration is a rich tawny, bordered by a broad blue-black unspotted marginal band on the hindwings. Below there is a lacework pattern with silvery-white markings.

In the Western Kenya forested areas several species occur in which the males are brilliantly iridescent deep blue while the females are stone-grey with black-and-white apices. The largest bears the name of the renowned Persian monarch, Tiridates. Beneath, the wings are warm olive-brown with darker markings. Another, Numenes, is similar above in both sexes but smaller. But beneath there is a distinguishing fine transverse black line edged with white.

Near Nairobi Cithaeron is often common. It has a broad white area on the hindwing which is margined with light blue. The female is very different, having a curved white transverse band across both wings.

The North African Emperor butterfly is also found in southern Europe where it has been called the Pasha. Above, the wings are unicolorous blackish-brown, bordered by a dark yellow marginal band, and on the hindwings suffused by bluish or greyish-green towards the hind angle. The underside is very prettily marked, much like the King Emperor, with white and brown lines. It frequents the more open savannah country. The Roman Emperor is closely related to it, but the very dark sepia wings are crossed transversely by a white band which is broken up into spots towards the apex.

Another large species is the Fulvescent Emperor, with dark fulvescent brown upper surface and light yellow at the base. It closely resembles the Varanes Emperor, but that has the basal areas milky-white and more brightly pigmented borders. Besides those Emperors mentioned there are several small ones which space will only allow passing reference. Many have very distinct female forms.

The White butterflies of the family *Pieridae* are very numerous indeed. In Western Kenya alone, no fewer than 61 species have been recognised. Included are (besides the many common whites) groups of splendid Ornamental-Tips, with metallic colours at the apices of the forewings, Clouded Yellows, Grass Yellows and the fine Dryads. Among the last, the Forest Dryad is, with perhaps the exception of some of the females of the related Cleodora, the largest of the African Whites.

In this extensive family seasonal migration is a well-known phenomenon. Every year, principally in the earlier months, white butterflies may be seen migrating for weeks on end. In favourable seasons such vast numbers appear that they have earned the popular names of tropical or butterfly "snow storms". The dry months of 1926 were an outstanding period when the countless millions of white butterflies passing day after day literally dazzled the eyes to watch them.

The Golden, Striped and Beautiful Danaides, the Friars or Nuns, and the graceful Ballerinas, are among some of the most abundant butterflies in Kenya; mostly of medium size and, with certain exceptions, not brightly coloured. They are considered to be distasteful and for this reason to serve as "models" for various "mimetic" species belonging to other families.

The Golden Danaid is widespread throughout the greater part of Africa and adjacent islands, and also occurs in South Europe, South Asia and South America. Several well-marked forms are known, the typical being golden brown with broad black apices to the forewings. This black area is crossed by a subapical band of four or more white spots.

A very similar form lacks the black-and-white apices on the forewings, and was considered to be a distinct species before the life-histories were known. The two forms fly together (except in West Africa) and interbreed. Varieties of both forms may be seen with the hindwings white instead of golden-brown.

The Striped Danaid, typically found in Eastern Asia, is represented in Kenya by a very closely allied race. The colour of the wings is generally dull blackish, striped and spotted with light blue-green markings. It is a regular annual migrant in Western Kenya during the early part of the year before the rains commence.

The Beautiful Danaid is a more local butterfly, its black wings beautifully marked with light ochre, creamy white in the basal areas and white spots. It prefers the open savannah country and likes the marshy land near rivers. A dark variety occurs commonly in the forested areas which resembles the typical form but the light ochreous markings are obscured by chestnut-brown.

A large and conspicuous Danaid, with black forewings and sepia hindwings, both marked with white, is known as the Black Friar, or the Nun. The race found along the coast from Somalia to Natal differs from that in Western Kenya in having the sepia border of the hindwings narrower.

Other Danaids are found in the forests, some being abundant, but most are of dull coloration. In wooded glades or in shady gardens the various Ballerinas may be watched. There are several species, all resembling each other, with blue-black forewings spotted with white or buff, and a broad ochre or pale-yellow band on each hindwing. These butterflies have a graceful dancing flight, and numbers of them often perform together, chasing one another among the flowers and undergrowth, or floating about under shady trees, presenting a delightful and fascinating sight to the watcher.

To the immense Nymphalid family belong such familiar European butterflies as the Tortoiseshells, Admirals, Fritillaries, Peacock and Painted Lady. Practically none of these is to be found in Kenya. Several species seen in our gardens will call to mind those of the northern regions. To this family belong some of the most majestic of African butterflies, but many of them are restricted normally to the forested areas. Some do come to gardens that are situated near to wooded localities and present a charming sight as they bask in the sun and raise and lower their wings at intervals in the characteristic manner of butterflies of this family.

One butterfly that is to be seen almost everywhere is stone-grey, adorned with numerous white black-ringed spots arranged in three transverse rows. It is not a high flier but likes to sit with wings spread on the bare earth such as pathways, and when alarmed it flies away close to the ground. It is sometimes called the Ground Butterfly.

Another group of Nymphalids consists mainly of black-and-white butterflies with patterns recalling the White Admirals in England. Their method of flight suggests skimming or floating with but few beats of the wings which are kept horizontal and not flapped like those of most butterflies. The commonest and the one that the visitor is most likely to notice is *Agatha*, which is sometimes very abundant. Many closely allied species are not rare in woods and forest glades, but they are so similar that it is by no means easy to separate them specifically in the field.

The *Hypolimnas* genus contains some of the real gems of Africa, but, again, most of them are only to be found in the tropical forests at lower elevations, where they sail about among the forest trees with majestic flight displaying their splendid colours in the sunshine. Many of them belong to the West African faunal region, and are not found in Eastern Kenya.

The first is distinguished by having the central area of the hindwings violet-blue and white and small submarginal white spots; the forewings having a white subapical transverse band and a large median expanse of blue. It was named *Salmacis* by Drury nearly 200 years ago, and since then more forms from various parts of Africa have received varietal names.

Another very fine butterfly of this genus which occurs in the Western Kenya forest country is *Dinarcha*. The colour is a deep velvety black ornamented with white discal spots on the forewings and a large ochre-yellow basal area on the hindwings and small submarginal dots. The apices of the forewings are falcate and the flight is very graceful.

Passing over many interesting butterflies on account of limited space, the Diadem butterfly must receive brief notice, because it has several notable characteristics and is usually common. The sexes are quite dissimilar. Whereas the wings of the male are blackish, with a large mirror-like area on each hindwing, and two similar areas on each forewing, the females are brown and resemble the Golden Danaid and some of its forms, of which they are doubtless "mimics". The white oval markings on the wings of the males are surrounded by iridescent violet-blue, which changes as the wings are moved to catch the light at different angles.

The Diadem is not restricted to forested localities. It is a migrant and in 1917 large numbers were seen migrating west, 500 miles off the West African coast! It has established itself in America.

Another fine group of Kenya butterflies, closely agreeing with the foregoing in neuration, is *Salamis*. The forewings are falcated and the hindwings lobed at the anal angle. The largest and finest is the Mother of Pearl Butterfly. Above, the wings are whitish with a Mother of Pearl gloss, reflecting green in the females and pink in the males. Beneath, the wings are shining silvery-white. On the upper side the apex is black and there are several conspicuous eyespots.

Sometimes these butterflies have occurred in such large numbers in Western Kenya that the forest roads have been obscured by the hundreds of insects on wing so that it has not been possible to motor, except at a very slow speed. There is also a smaller species which is very similar but has broader black borders to the wings and the white ground colour is not so glossy.

A third, named *Temora*, is a beautiful dark blue, though the sombre females are violet-brown. It is not present in Eastern Kenya. Another, called *Cacta*, has dark-brown upperside with pretty pink and violet reflections and a broad orange-yellow transverse band separating the brown base from the black margin. Beneath, the wings closely represent dead leaves, so that when the butterflies are at rest they are extremely difficult to locate. They exhibit a wide range of variation with scarcely two undersides similar, being brown, grey or dusky, with white or other markings.

Probably the butterflies that a visitor will notice principally in our gardens will be some of the many pretty *Precis*, because not only are they attracted to flowers, but are usually abundant. They are of especial interest, too, on account of the very different seasonal colorations and markings displayed by some of them. To this genus belongs the senator, or Commodore. It is of medium size with strongly undulated margins to all wings. During the hot dry season the upperside of the wings is deep blue and blackish, ornamented with bright-red spots forming an almost continuous transverse discal bar on both. Beneath is dull drab.

On very warm days the Senator flies little but seeks shade under eaves of houses and huts, or indoors. This form is followed during the rainy months by butterflies that look entirely different, all wings having a light reddish ground colour with only a few black markings, and dark marginal borders in which are crescent-shaped bluish spots. In those localities where the dry and wet seasons are not markedly differentiated, intermediate forms may be met with, some of which are extremely interesting and show characteristics of both generations.

Another common garden butterfly has been named *Sophia*. It is one of the smallest of this group, and several forms of it are known, the typical one being light ochre-brown with a broad pale median band across each forewing. Specimens with the light areas white are quite common while others more or less black are known. They have been named *Albida* and *Nigeria* respectively.

There are so many butterflies in this genus that it will not be possible to mention more owing to lack of space. For the same reason, no reference can be made to the "Blues", "Coppers", "Browns" or "Skippers" in which our fauna is very rich, or to African moths which are abundant.

About 12 miles east of Kitale in Western Kenya there is a museum with large collections of African animals, birds and insects. Founded in 1926, it was incorporated as a public museum ten years later. The most comprehensive section is that of entomology. Herein are long series of East African butterflies and moths, as well as many from other African territories for comparative study.

The museum forms a link in the chain of museums across East Africa from Mombasa to Uganda. It is open to the public daily. Students and members are granted special facilities to examine the study collections and make use of the museum reference library with its thousands of volumes and scientific publications.

Those visitors to Kenya who wish to know more of its fine lepidoptera, only a few of which has it been possible to mention, should not fail to inspect the wide collection in the museum.

[At the time when this contribution was being revised for the present edition, the Stoneham Trustees were planning the erection of a building on a one-acre site given in Kitale, to which it is intended to move the museum.]

206

CHAPTER XVIII

Flowers and Gardens

by H. B. SHARPE

LATE OF NDARAGWA, NGOBIT, WHO DESIGNED AND
LAID OUT THE GARDENS OF SAGANA LODGE,
KENYA'S WEDDING GIFT TO
QUEEN ELIZABETH AND THE DUKE OF EDINBURGH

Kenya is a land of flowers and gardens, and is one in which there are many lovely indigenous flowering trees, shrubs and plants: the red-flowering kaffir booms, the pink Cape chestnut, the white moringa, the yellow and orange aloes and the blue pentas of the plains, and many more, all give a show for a time; it is the addition of the exotics that really keep us going with beauty. Take the Flamboyant with its great trusses of scarlet flowers ornamenting and shading the streets of coastal towns; it is of great importance, but in Madagascar, its home country, it is of less importance. The Jacaranda, with its wonderful blue plumes of flower, is of supreme importance, whereas in South America it may still be lovely but is only one among the forest of trees. The Nandi Flame of Kenya, when covered with its great red trusses of flowers, is a wonderful sight wherever it may be. It is just one of the sights of Kenya, but transport it to the gardens of Madagascar or South America and it immediately becomes a lovely exotic.

Kenya is a land of varying climates, ranging from the coast, through the desert brush-covered lowlands with isolated mountains looming up purple in the distance, isolated ranges of them beyond far-spreading plains which may be coloured green or gold or pinkish grey, according to the season—and remember there are two seasons in the year. There is distant, rolling downland country and far away sharp-cut mountain ranges with snowclad Mt. Kenya queen of it all. No wonder there is such a wealth of floral beauty. It has been brought from all over the tropical and temperate world. There is, and has been for many years past, a

P

constant stream of plants and seeds coming in and going out from England, Hawaii, America, Singapore, Japan, India and Australia. In Nairobi alone there can be seen plants from all these countries growing happily. There is no mailing list with Antarctica yet!

Flying over Nairobi, one realises it is a city of trees and gardens, and arriving in the city this immediately becomes a reality. Look where you will, there is colour everywhere with flowering trees, shrubs and climbers. Nairobi's wide avenues are lined with trees and palms and hedges and banks and pyramids of glorious coloured Bougainvilleas; the colour schemes are carefully worked out and they are always blooming, though at certain seasons more than others, a sight never to be forgotten. And the flowering trees, blue jacarandas, yellow cassias, pink oleanders, hibiscus and others all tone in with the Bougainvilleas. I would defy anyone anywhere to find a clash of colours.

All of this present beauty originated under the direction of Mr. Peter Greensmith when he was the Nairobi Parks Superintendent (he has since retired and set up in private practice as a horticultural consultant). The Queen made him an M.B.E. which will surely be followed by something else one day, and the Almighty must have taken him into partnership because Peter is always creating something new. He turns a bulldozer on to the work and the clearings are levelled and quickly become green lawns, beds of flowers, groups of young trees bursting into bloom and of sweeping drives bordered with Bougainvilleas. Of course, there will be a clump of something new and lovely, which he has but lately got from Hawaii or Singapore. It never stops, for the process has been continued by his successor and the Parks' staff after the same imaginative manner.

Take the Bougainvillea which originated from the Andes in South America and was named after a French navigator of the sixteenth century. There were probably only the magenta, pink and red types. They quickly spread over the tropics and Asia and were soon known in India and Malaya. Soon there were some of orange and red shades originating in India and Malaya. They were fairly easy to propagate and so they spread through the tropics and as far as favoured parts of the Riviera. Now there are hundreds of different colours and types of foliage and growth. Then seedlings were grown which were found to have hybridised. Mr. Greensmith has grown thousands of them but only used the best. Outstanding ones are increased quickly by tip shoot cuttings grown in electrical heaters.

There are about half a dozen folk devoted to the cult of the Bougainvillea. It is now the chief plant used throughout our public and private gardens within the country. Every little township has a splash of Bougainvilleas in its square or gardens. All this began through Mr. Greensmith's drive and initiative. There is one thing you should do and that is get an invitation to visit the wonderful Bougainvillea nurseries at City Park. From what I have written, it is obvious that most of the brightness of our gardens and parks is given by the Bougainvilleas, which all originally stemmed from possibly not more than twelve species.

Before telling you about some of the rarer plants in our finer gardens, I will tell you about the Queen's Garden at Sagana. When I was asked, towards the end of 1949, to lay out the grounds at Princess Elizabeth's lodge at Sagana, I went to see the place, and was a little despondent at the task confronting me. There was nothing but trees, trees everywhere, natural forest, most of it very thick, sloping down in front, and behind it, forest plantations of exotic gums.

Early in January 1950, I reported my doubts to the then Governor (Sir Philip Mitchell) who, I understood, had given an order that no trees were to be cut down. He told me he had naturally given that order, as otherwise trees would have been cut and mutilated wholesale, but he knew I was not a murderer of trees, and was good enough to give me a free hand. Nevertheless, a closer scrutiny only increased my fears. The amount of murdering of lovely trees to be done—whole plantations of them, glades of them—was upsetting, to say the least. Most of the natural forest growing up to and on the very steep bluff on which the house was being built would have to go.

There were trees, some of them very lovely, even overhanging the building, growing out of the terrace, almost in the house itself, and the steep bank down to the river had to be dealt with. It obviously could not be made into a lawn. The saving factor was the dense tangled thicket down by the river, with handsome trees growing up through it. The river could be heard but hardly seen, owing to the density of the overhanging vegetation. The lower half of the hill across the river was covered with primeval forest, mainly of Cape chestnuts and crotons, and above it a plantation of blue gums cut crudely and harshly across the skyline.

It was obvious that those trees, lovely though they were, overhanging the house and growing out of the terrace and immediately in front of it down to the river, must be removed. It was also certain that, by degrees, the hard line of gums on the opposite skyline would have to go, and also it was necessary to cut a large chunk into the plantation between the road and the house.

That meant a tactful approach to the Forest Department and the man in charge of the building. When I broke the news to the latter he looked dismayed. "If you knew", he said, "the hours I have spent in planning the house to fit between these two trees, you would understand how I feel about it." But when I pointed out that half the roots of the beautiful chestnut overhanging the house had already been cut away, and that the first storm would probably bring it crashing down on the building, he at once agreed and made a very good job of it.

The Forestry officials, too, were very co-operative and helpful. They jibbed at removing the hard line on the hill, but we compromised on that by cutting two V-shaped gaps in it. As the trees disappeared one by one, the view to the river opened out, and a vista looking away to the Aberdare Mountains appeared as if by magic. Ground down near the river was cleared of its tangled undergrowth, and only the trees were left. Some of these, too, had to go. Often a group of three or four trees may be almost perfect, but after hardening one's heart and cutting out three, one finds that the fourth is infinitely more beautiful by itself.

This had to happen in many cases at the Royal lodge. Even some of the silver-stemmed albizzias down on the bottom flat were sacrificed in order to enhance the beauty of the remaining ones. Single branches of some trees had to be removed, and others may still have to be sacrificed to allow for a view of the snows of Mt. Kenya itself.

Meanwhile, other young trees of value, for either their foliage or flowers, were being planted either as individuals or in groups. It seemed advisable to plant the approach side of the house, where the blue gum plantation had been, with the hardier plants, some of them indigenous, and generally speaking, of stronger colouring —oranges, yellows, reds and browns. For this purpose tecomaria, tecoma, streptosolen, poinsettia, abutilon, the brown bauhinia and such-like shrubs were used.

Also, one very dry bank was planted with a mixture of local aloes, and above it are specimen Bougainvilleas and succulents hanging down the banks. On either side of the entrance gate three pyramid cypresses have been planted, and it is pleasant to recollect their Italian symbolism of health, wealth and happiness. The fence itself on either side of the gate has been covered with the climbers, cherry red bignonia-charere and blue ipomoea leari.

By the side of the drive from the road to the gate the same flowering shrubs, together with white and mauve bauhinias, were planted, and the space between them was grassed. Behind them are alternate pink Cape chestnuts and blue jacarandas, and they again have been backed by indigenous foliage trees and conifers.

The edges of the red murram drive leading to the front door and round the pear-shaped bed have all been edged with a strong-growing dark green succulent, a mesembryanthemum species, and behind it are clumps of the silver-leaved succulent dudleya and bright-coloured geraniums.

For the time being, and until these fill the space, bright annuals have been used. The bed encircled by the drive contains many bright-flowered shrubs, salvias, hibiscus, cestrums, streptosolen, callistemons and others.

On the right of the drive, near the housekeeper's cottage, there are large clumps of the white sweet-scented moonflower and other sweet-smelling shrubs. At each side of the top of the steps leading down to the front door are two grey vases with the silver-leaved dudleya in them. Running round the house side of the curve of the drive is a hedge of lavender and at each side of the steps are planted rosemary and the scented southernwood, which I always knew as a child as ladslove. Below that is a bank of verbena in blue, mauve and purple shades, sloping down to a little green lawn which runs to the walls of the house. Here there is a display of white sweet-smelling philadelphus.

On either side of the front door are two more grey vases in which grow the cerise-flowered orchid, *Epidendron radicans*. This same motive of the verbena bank and the lawn below it is carried round to the eastern side of the house with the little lawns on two levels, with the retaining banks between them; one is covered with pink ivy geranium and blue lobelia, and the lower one with a geranium species and a low shrubby jasmine.

On the house wall itself, below the living-room, the self-clinging *Ficus repens* has been planted, and on the lower terrace wall are honeysuckle and pink (Dainty Bess) and red (Poulsen) roses. Near the bedroom are bushes of deliciously scented Yesterday, Today and Tomorrow (*Brunfelsia Hopeana*).

To the left of the terrace there is an enormous fig tree which is always the haunt of all kinds of fruit-eating birds, and, just before the Queen, as Princess Elizabeth, paid her first visit, I noticed that two golden orioles, plumed in glorious yellow with black heads, were already in residence.

Below and stretching away into the natural forest and down the steep bluff to the river, the ground is carpeted with purple- and mauve-flowered mesembryanthemums. Beyond them, under the trees on the steep slope, are masses of blue agapanthus, periwinkle and other pastel-shaded flowers, which give a hazy effect beneath the trees. A path bordered by zephyranthes, cyrtanthus and other bulbs with demurely coloured flowers descends to the lawn, which is shaded by the big albizzia trees.

The river runs along one side of the lawn, but long wide beds with bright colours have again been used, and large masses of cannas, together with irises, arum lilies, Shasta daisies, Madonna and other true lilies, tigridias, echiums and other flowering shrubs, encircle some of it.

The river bank itself, in some places, has been grassed to the water's edge. In others there are clumps of arums and other water-loving plants. Here and there, on both banks, are specimens of the wild banana plant. The varying shades of green in their great long leaves, especially in the sunlight, are a joy in themselves. It is sad that the life of this plant is so short. After two years' growth it produces a long purple drooping flower spike, consisting of quantities of flowers which turn into little atrophied bananas, the seeds of which fall to the ground to become plants in place of the parent which has died. Incidentally, the banana is a plant, not a tree.

The lawns are composed of the local Kikuyu grass (*Paspalum clandestinum*), not one from Uganda as some accounts have stated. The opposite bank of the river, which has been cleared enough to allow comfortable fishing, comprises the natural forest growths.

It would be boring to catalogue everything in this garden, but it may be remarked that the garden cost nothing to make and every plant was given generously and joyfully by owners of gardens (starting at Government, now State, House) and nurseries in Kenya. Nothing was bought.

Of course a great deal may still be done to improve the many parts of the grounds, but it seems to me it would be well-nigh impossible to make the lovely stretch of lawn overshadowed by spacious trees and almost encircled by the silver sparkling river a more perfect setting for the two podocarpus trees which Her Royal Highness, as she was then, and His Royal Highness the Duke of Edinburgh planted there on the morning of their arrival at the lodge.

Most of the garden rarities are in private gardens. There are a few in hotel grounds. The Mawingo, which is now the Mount Kenya Safari Club, is one, and was originally a private house. It contains a very old walled rose garden, some fine Michelia trees, a sweet-scented American magnolia, a fine Beaumontia creeper with enormous white cups of flowers, and a huge, very sweet-scented giant honeysuckle. Its flowers scent the whole courtyard. It is a place to visit if you can possibly manage it.

The Outspan Hotel at Nyeri has a garden which was properly designed and contains some nice palms and flowering trees and shrubs to enhance the wonderful view of Mt. Kenya. Blue jacarandas have been used in abundance. The Tea Hotel at Kericho has quite nice gardens, but tea somehow dominates the whole atmosphere. Thinking back, I cannot remember one striking thing in the gardens beyond some good roses. There are pleasant memories of the food, however!

The Gloriosa lily, which is a true lily (lilies are not common in Kenya), is found everywhere from the Coast up to 8,000 ft.; it is very lovely and somewhat exclusive. It does not grow in gardens much, but scrambles over other vegetation, sometimes reaching up to 12 ft. and displaying its striking red and yellow flowers. I have seen a lovely buff-flowered self-coloured one at the Coast.

Ndaragwa is a private garden. Water is one of its main attractions. There are two large pools—one sweeping across to the rocks of wild Africa on its far side. Aquatic plants have been used extensively: water lilies at times grow to become a nuisance and spoil the reflections of the waterside flowers in the pools. Cannas are particularly used for this effect, and so is the Gunnera with its enormous rhubarb-like leaves, some 10 ft. across. It comes from the upper reaches of the Amazon River. It will grow in the wetter, cooler parts of Kenya and forms enormous crowns of leaves under which one is able to walk.

Of the exotic trees used to great effect are the beautiful cypress of Kashmir with its lovely blue-grey weeping foliage: there are but two or three in Kenya, and now cypresses are not allowed to be imported into the country on account of spreading disease. It can be grown from cuttings but it is not easy. Another lovely tree is the Japanese Pagoda tree (Cryptomeria), which grows to a big tree in Japan. There are two different strains in this garden; one is very slow-growing but covered to the ground with foliage of a very pleasing reddish-brown colour—it is over twenty years old and only about 20 ft. high.

A number of Australian and New Zealand plants do very well, including the bottle brushes, with varying shades of red racemes, and the leptospermum, with red, pink and white flowers. The Choisya, Mexican Orange, does quite well with its white, scented flowers. Then one of the queens of the garden is *Luculia Gratissima* which is magnificent and covers itself with deliciously scented almond-pink flowers. It is in several gardens but it is nowhere common and is difficult to establish.

After Bougainvilleas, the oleanders and hibiscuses take pride of place, especially in our public gardens; they are grown as shrubs, bushes and as standards very effectively. The Ceanothus, known as Californian lilac, in its many varieties in varying shades of blue should be used more than it is. Possibly it is suited more to private than to public gardens, for its flowers are so delicate and unassuming, not like some of the Bougainvilleas which almost shout at one.

The Bauhinias, the Camel's Foot, are named after Charles II's gardener, the Abbé Bauhin. There are many varieties found all over Africa from south to north: it has flowers of all colours, from yellow and reddish-brown to white, pink and lilac, and some of them somewhat orchid-like in flower. They are useful in private and public gardens, and some of them adorn the waysides through the forests.

Unfortunately, most of the brightest flowers, particularly those of flowering trees and shrubs, lack scent and the Brunfelsia, commonly called "Yesterday, Today and Tomorrow" on account of its flowers which open blue and fade through mauve to white, is an exception to the rule: its deliciously scented flowers perfume the air all round them. This shrub is very much one of the "musts" in Kenya gardens. The scent is strong enough to use the plant in public gardens.

Ceratostigma is a very vivid blue plumbago of which there is a wild one growing in some of the northern mountains of Kenya and Ethiopia. There are less vivid blue ones found all over Africa in dry river valleys down to the Cape the flowers being a bit sticky and almost white. Where Miss Willmott the famous landscape gardner after whom it was named got her wonderful blue one from I do not know. It is known in gardens all over the world. There is also a lovely one from the Himalayas.

The brooms of which there are many must be mentioned. The White Portugal is one of the best and the Common Yellow with its large panicles of bright yellow flowers is always worthy of a place.

Fuchsias came from Central America and down as far as the Straits of Magellan except for four species, one a tree, and one a minute climber, which come from New Zealand. Of the hundreds there are now in circulation most of them originated from *F. Magellanica* and *Speciosa*. In most countries they are great house and verandah plants and it is the same in Kenya except in a very few favoured spots. I imagine the fuchsia gives most pleasure to more people than any other plants in Nairobi.

Among climbers, the honeysuckles and jasmines hold a special position on account of the delicious scent of their flowers. *Jasminum Polyanthus* is a king of plants with its pink-tinted buds opening to its intoxicating scented white flowers. Veronicas and cacti add charm and variety to the gardens, and cypresses, thuyas and the various Norfolk Island pines, sculptured by Nature in curious designs, add interest and beauty to the general picture of Nairobi gardens.

CHAPTER XIX

On Safari with a Professional Hunter

by SYDNEY DOWNEY

WHO BEGAN PROFESSIONAL HUNTING IN 1930, IS A
MEMBER OF THE COMMITTEE OF THE EAST AFRICAN
PROFESSIONAL HUNTERS ASSOCIATION, HONORARY GAME
RANGER AND PARKS OFFICER

Not so many years ago the question was frequently asked—what is a Professional Hunter? Indeed—due to my interest in matters pertaining to wild animals, this was almost my first question, when I arrived in Nairobi in the mid-twenties. All I could learn was that a Professional Hunter was a "mystery" man, who just disappeared with his safari—reappearing some two or three months later. He did not say where he had been—and no one asked—but if he could be persuaded to talk, he would tell of distant areas—fabulous for the wildlife which could be seen there—and also of near escapes from elephants, lions and buffaloes. Scanty as was this information, it made me keen to experience such an exciting and adventurous occupation.

It is believed that the profession came into being around the turn of the century when the late Lord Delamere hired a white man to assist him on his hunting expedition (hence the original term "white hunter"). By the advent of the First World War, the numbers of hunting trips had increased considerably, due in part to an expedition led by the President of the U.S.A., Theodore Roosevelt. This expedition, which was guided by R. J. Cunninghame and L. J. Tarlton, received world-wide publicity. With the cessation of hostilities, professional hunters—all of whom had been engaged in active service—returned to their work. The profession flourished until the world slump set in, in 1929, when employment became so irregular that some were obliged to abandon their chosen interest, and to seek their fortunes in other fields.

In 1934, an Association of Professional Hunters was formed with

about 15 members. The late Philip Percival was elected President
—an office which he held, to the lasting benefit of his colleagues,
until his retirement in 1956. Now, in 1969, this office is efficiently
held by Antony Dyer.

Membership has risen beyond all expectations to 87 full mem-
bers, the majority of whom are kept busy during the season.
Close co-operation is the spirit of the Association, with Game
Departments, National Parks and the East African Wildlife
Society, where dedicated men work—not for glory or reward—
but for the benefit of the wild animals in their charge.

The next question which may be asked is "What qualifications
must a professional hunter possess?" First and foremost he must
have an outstanding knowledge of African game—the widely
differing habits of each species—where, and how to find it. He
must know a good trophy head, too.

He must be proficient in the use of firearms. Here, let it be
said, he should be a better shot at close range than at distance
since, often, it is by no means easy to shoot quickly and accurately
at a charging animal which threatens the safety of the party. To
illustrate this point, I recall the reply of a well-known hunter, who,
when asked what sort of a shot he was, answered, "I'm good at
10 yards"—a reply which caused some surprise.

The following up of dangerous wounded game into the thickest
cover is also the professional hunter's obligation, as is the need to
do his utmost to put an animal out of its suffering in the shortest
space of time. He must respect wild animals—they are often far
wiser than man. Knowledge of skinning and the preliminary
taxidermy work in the field must also be included in his training.
All trophies should be in first-class condition (and this is no
simple matter) when handed over to the taxidermist who will do
the final work of mounting heads and dressing skins. Messrs.
Rowland Ward and Mr. P. Zimmerman of Nairobi, and
Jonas Bros. in the U.S.A. are acclaimed throughout the world for
their skill in this work.

A safari camp must be well organised. It can and should be
kept as tidy as an average home. Last but not least, a professional
hunter must be a good companion, tactful and understanding
and able to entertain.

What does the future hold for the profession? Obviously, one
part of the answer to this question lies in the ability of all people

to recognise the economic value of wildlife. Further, they must learn to care for wild animals for their own sake. If this can be accomplished, I believe that there will be a bright future for hunting with gun and camera, and that, as the older members drop out, the job can be carried on by younger men, in all confidence.

Undoubtedly, some game areas will cease to exist as such, due to human interests, but this may be balanced by organised culling from the overflow from parks and reserves.

In early times, a safari could only be undertaken with porters, assisted by horses, mules, donkeys or camels, where the country was free of tsetse-fly. These porters would carry a load of 60 lbs., and the number would be likely to vary between 50 and 250 according to the size and duration of the safari. Travelling by this means was, of necessity, very slow, often taking two or three weeks before the first hunting camp was reached. Messrs. Newland and Tarlton were the pioneer outfitters. I am told by an old settler, who first came to Kenya in 1910, that safaris travelling in a westerly direction from their starting-point, Nairobi, would camp for the first night on his farm, in Karen, a march of about 12 miles.

Nowadays, the other extreme has been reached and there are fewer areas (other than mountain forests) where four-wheel-drive hunting cars cannot, or as in some cases, may not go. Light aircraft, also, are extensively used to fly parties to the photo-graphic or shooting areas, since the theme of today is to save time. A safari in, say, 1910 could have taken 12 months to accomplish a trip which the four-wheel-drive vehicle has now made possible in one month. Some of the original feeling of adventure may be lost, but time is saved.

The best times of the year for game safaris in Kenya and Northern Tanzania are from January to March and again from August to October.

The average duration of a present-day safari would be about five weeks for hunting, or about three weeks for photography, and it may here be of interest to note that the proportion of photographic to hunting safaris is increasing steadily.

Outfitting firms (registered with the East African Professional Hunters Association) which undertake hunting and/or photo-graphic expeditions are, in alphabetical order:

Allen Safaris, P.O. Box 174, Nanyuki.

Andrew Holmberg Tours & Safaris Ltd., P.O. Box 30382, Nairobi.

Big Game Safaris Ltd., P.O. Box 12754, Nairobi.

David Ommanney Safaris, P.O. Box 15006, Nairobi.

Hunters (Africa) Ltd., P.O. Box 12450, Nairobi.

Hunters & Guides Ltd., P.O. Box 399, Nairobi.

John Alexander Safaris Ltd., P.O. Box 20127, Nairobi.

Ken Stewart Safaris, P.O. Box 3073, Nairobi.

Kenya Safaris Ltd., P.O. Box 20026, Nairobi.

Ker, Downey & Selby Safaris Ltd., P.O. Box 1822, Nairobi.

J. Kingsley-Heath Safaris Ltd., P.O. Box 2983, Nairobi.

Lawrence-Brown Safaris (T) Ltd., P.O. Box 3624, Nairobi.

Malindi Tours & Safaris Ltd., P.O. Box 52, Malindi.

Monty Brown Safaris, P.O. Box 182, Malindi.

Mount Elgon Safaris, P.O. Box 7190, Nairobi.

Tanzania Wildlife Safaris Ltd., P.O. Box 602, Arusha, Tanzania.

Tsavo Safaris Ltd., P.O. Box 4191, Nairobi.

Uganda Wildlife Development Ltd., P.O. Box 1764, Kampala, Uganda.

Oasis Ltd., P.O. Box 3331, Addis Ababa, Ethiopia.

Safari South (1968) (Pty) Ltd., P.O. Box 40, Maun, Botswana.

Some of the firms listed above have standardised charges—as follows: A safari lasting 30 days for—

1 client and 1 professional hunter K.£1,900
2 clients (1 shooting) and 1 hunter K.£2,215
2 clients (both shooting) and 1 hunter K.£2,320

These approximate rates are, of course, *pro rata* and quotations can be given for a party of any number. Ten to 15 African servants, all necessities for camping in what is usually an unexpected degree of comfort, a four-wheel-drive hunting car, and a five-ton truck, are included in the charges. Luxuries, such as refrigerators, Dunlopillo mattresses, etc., are standard equipment, while a late addition to some outfitters' lists is a radio-telephone.

Personal items, game licences, controlled area fees (safaris must now hire a hunting block in many parts of the country) are separate charges, and the distance to be travelled to obtain the required bag may also slightly affect the cost. Sometimes, it may be necessary due to season, or some other reason, to hunt an elephant in North Kenya, and a Sable or Kudu in Southern Tanzania—and this could mean travelling 800–1,000 miles between areas.

A schedule of costs for Kenya game licences (subject to variations from time to time) is given below:

Full licence   K.£50
14-day licence   K.£25
Bird licence   K.£3
Controlled area fee variable for each animal shot.
(Only two shooting members permitted in each controlled area at one time.)

Special licences must also be obtained for the rarer species or those which have commercial value. These are over and above the cost of the full licence. For these licences, charges in Kenya range from K.£75 for a first elephant (K.£125 for the second) to K.£1 for a blue monkey!

For photography, a comparatively small fee is charged for entry into National Parks, African Game Reserves, etc., except where films are to be used for commercial purposes—in which cases the fee is decidedly higher. Space does not permit details of costs of all special game licences, and entry in National Parks and game reserves for the three East African countries, but this information can be readily obtained from the offices of the Game Wardens, National Parks, and safari outfitters.

A word about firearms. The choice of firearms must, of course, be a matter for the individual. One man may only feel confident with the heaviest rifle he can handle; while, in the hands of another, a medium bore does the job. W. D. M.—(Karamoja Bell) one of the most famous hunters of all time—killed some thousands of elephants with a light bore rifle (·275). His accuracy was probably unequalled, certainly unexcelled, and he could find the brain of an elephant from any angle. An error of an inch or two could have resulted in a wounded and dangerous animal, but he never made that error. On the other hand, the early elephant hunters in Africa (1840–80), Gordon Cumming, Cotton Oswell, Baldwin, Selous and Baker, used among others a double four-bore, i.e. a smooth bore gun firing a bullet weighing a quarter of a pound! No comparisons can be made here, of course, in view of the tremendous

advance in firearm and ammunition construction since that time.
It only proved the preference for the heavy bore. Selous on one
occasion referred to his light bore ·450!

For those who feel any doubts of their marksmanship, a rifle
considered to be on the heavy side for the particular hunt is
generally a wise precaution. The use of the relatively heavier rifle
is insisted on by the Game Departments, and rightly so, since,
in inexpert hands, a light rifle can cause much wounding, with
consequent suffering, and sometimes danger to the local inhabitants.

Until recently the great majority of professional hunters pre-
ferred the heavy double-barrelled rifle of ·450 bore, and upwards,
but now there is a considerable increase in the number of heavy
"singles" used—the ·458 Winchester being among the most
popular. It is not the intention to do more than give a selection
of the many firearms which have been used so successfully on
African game.

The list which appears below merely mentions a few which are
regularly used.

BORE	MANUFACTURER
D/B ·500/465	Holland and Holland
„ ·470	Any well-known British gun maker
„ ·450	
S/B ·270	Winchester
„ ·300	
„ ·30–06	
„ ·375	Winchester
„ ·458	
„ ·300	Weatherby
„ ·378	
„ 7 mm.	Mauser
„ 8 × 60S	
D/B 12 bore shotgun	
„ 16 „ „	Any well-known gun maker
„ 20 „ „	

Dealers in Nairobi carry stocks of many of the firearms mentioned above, together with a full range of ammunition.

The number of purely "camera" safaris is today increasing
steadily. While the late Martin Johnson was not the first to
bring cinematography of big game into the limelight, his work

undoubtedly caused others to realise for the first time what an enthralling sport this could be. Today the work of Armand and Michaela Denis and the availability of modern, easily handled equipment have done much to build up this interest—one outfitting firm in Nairobi alone records 20 per cent of business as purely photographic. While the emphasis is still on hunting with the rifle, the safari which does not bring a camera is rare indeed.

Again the choice of photographic equipment must be left to the individual, though, as a rough guide for keen photographers, the cines most commonly used on safari are manufactured by Bolex, Bell and Howell, and Kodak—while for stills the Leica and Contax are, perhaps, the best known. A wide range of cameras are available in East Africa, as are almost all types of film.

What is the normal routine for a safari? This, of course, depends largely on the type of game to be hunted, because some animals are more easily found during the early and late hours, while others can be seen throughout the day. The general custom is to start the day early, even before daylight has set in, with breakfast and departure for the hunting areas with the first light. If elephant are to be hunted, it will invariably mean a day trip, with only a short time off for lunch, on the trail. With some other types of hunting and (for reasons of light) more particularly when photography is the main object, the party is likely to return to camp before midday. Lunch—a time off for keeping up with diaries, etc.—then out again, returning at dusk. Hot baths or showers are next—a chat round the campfire with a sundowner, dinner and then bed, which, after about 16 hours of constant activity and fresh air will seem most welcome.

An actual experience or two may be of interest but, before giving these, it should be emphasised that by far the greater number of safaris are completed without any real danger, though some must be expected every now and again. Since these occasions are the rarer, I will describe some incidents, as I remember them.

Skipping the preliminaries, I will start at the point where, after a week of searching, a fine lion was seen to emerge from a dense thicket and enter a near-by patch of long grass in which he sat down, disappearing completely from our sight. A careful stalk was made, which brought my client and two gunbearers with me to a low mound situated some 50 yards from the point where the lion had last been seen. With, at best, no more than half an hour of good light remaining, a plan had to be put into operation at once. Whispering to my client to be ready to shoot, I shouted, and the lion was instantly on his feet. For a second or two he stared at us in astonishment and then, with huge bounds, he raced for the thicket. As he entered, a belated shot rang out, followed by a growl—proving a hit—and we found ourselves faced with the sort of situation which no one looks forward to—a wounded lion in thick bush intermingled with wait-a-bit thorn and, just to make it more difficult, the setting sun in our eyes.

While we considered the situation, the lion which could see without being seen, commenced growling savagely. We had to get that sun out of our eyes so, instructing the gunbearers to remain out of range on the plain, my client and I circled the thicket, and crept in, step by step, in the direction in which the lion could be constantly heard. Soon we were so near that—strain my eyes as I would—it seemed incredible to me that I could not see him. Then I noticed a low bank, covered with matted growth, in front of us. The lion must be lying beneath that. With rifles ready at our shoulders, and safety catches off, we crept to within 10 ft. of the bank. Now or never—so, stepping quickly forward, we thrust our guns over the bank, and almost on to the lion. Two shots and he was finished instantly.

Now for a photographic experience. There are those who believe that, since modern photography is mostly done from a car (a regulation in National Parks), it is seldom difficult and never dangerous. This is a fallacy. It is difficult because so many conditions are required to be perfect. It is dangerous because one always wants to go as close as one can and then go five yards closer! I know of a number of occasions where buffalo and rhino, and even elephants, have battered a car, to the bewilderment of the occupants; and lions have sometimes forced the photographer into a hurried and undignified retreat.

Some years ago, my safari was crossing the great open Serengeti plains in Tanzania when I noticed a white object lying some 300 yards off to our right. Stopping to use the glasses, I identified the object as a dead Grant's Gazelle, its white belly turned towards us. Over the body, a round cat-like head peered at us. "Cheetah," I thought, and, hoping for some good film, I turned the hunting car off the track. When 30 yds. distant, no animal was visible except the Gazelle. Where had the other animal disappeared? It could not have run away, unseen.

Behind the carcase was a large hole, and this offered a possible hiding place. With some disappointment and believing that, after all, I had only seen a hyena, I drove closer, warning my client that he might get a picture, as it bolted. Our astonishment knew no bounds when a leopard—rarely seen on open plains—burst from the hole in a cloud of dust, and charged the car within a dozen feet. I had just been reading a book entitled *Leopard in my Lap* and I remember thinking that this title would accurately describe my very next experience unless we withdrew immediately. This we did without delay and, as I looked back, the leopard again took up his position in the hole, and not one of us felt like arguing who was master of that situation!

There can be very few people who, having once undertaken a safari in the game areas of East Africa, have not been thrilled by the experience. Every day something new happens—excitement, surprises and, of course, occasional disappointments, though these are invariably offset by that bit of good luck which comes later.

I feel sure that I utter the sentiments of all professional hunters when I say that not one of us would have changed our life for any other. There have been hard moments for us all, but the thrill of safari, the love of wild animals and the enjoyment of good company have been our most worthwhile reward.

Addresses for Reference

The East African Professional Hunters Assn., Box 528, Nairobi.
The Game Warden, Box 241, Nairobi.
Ministry of Lands and Surveys, Game Division, Box 1994, Dar es Salaam, Tanzania.
The Game Warden, Box 4, Entebbe, Uganda.
The Director, Kenya National Parks, Box 2076, Nairobi.
The Director, Tanzania National Parks, Box 3134, Arusha, Tanzania.
The Director, Uganda National Parks, Box 3530, Kampala, Uganda.
East African Wildlife Society, Box 20110, Nairobi.

Professional Photographers

Alan Root, Box 3747, Nairobi.
Simon Trevor, Box 24767, Nairobi.
Norman Myers, Box 8197, Nairobi.
R. I. M. Campbell, Box 24779, Nairobi.

Taxidermists

Rowland Ward (East Africa) Ltd., Box 991, Nairobi.
Rowland Ward Ltd., 64/65 Grosvenor Street, Mayfair, London, WIX. OEN.
Jonas Bros. Inc., 1037 Broadway, Denver 3, Colorado, U.S.A.
Jonas Bros. Studios Inc., 135 North High Street, Mount Vernon, New York.
Jonas Bros. of Seattle Inc., 1507 12th Avenue, Seattle, Washington 98122.
Louis Paul Jonas Studios, Churchtown, Hallowville Road, R.D.2, Hudson, New York.
Zimmermann Ltd., Box 2127, Nairobi.

Suggested Books for Further Reading

Innumerable books have been written about Kenya: fiction and non-fiction, adventure stories and official reports. Those given below might be found helpful to readers interested in particular subjects. The list lays no claim to being exhaustive or selective. Names of publishing houses are included but not prices, which vary from country to country.

BIRDS: *Treasure of Kenya*, by the Rt. Hon. Malcolm MacDonald (Collins); *A First Guide to South African Birds*, by Leonard Gill (Maskew Miller Ltd., Cape Town); *Birds of Eastern and North-Eastern Africa*, by C. W. Mackworth Praed and Capt. C. H. B. Grant (Longmans, Green); *A Field Guide to the Birds of East Africa*, by John G. Williams (Collins); *A Bird Watcher in Kenya*, by V. D. van Someren (Oliver and Boyd).

FLOWERS AND GARDENS: *Some Wild Flowers of Kenya*, by Lady Muriel Jex-Blake (Longmans, Green); *Gardening in East Africa*, by Dr. A. J. Jex-Blake (Longmans, Green); *Kenya's Trees and Flowering Shrubs*, by Ivan R. Dale and P. J. Greenway (Kenya Government and Hatchards).

HISTORY: Early Travellers in East Africa Series, abridged editions of East African Travel Classics, Krapf, New, Thomson, Gregory, Speke, Baker, Burton (E.A. Literature Bureau); *We Built a Country*, by J. F. Lipscomb (Faber and Faber); *Lugard*, Vol. I, by Margery Perham (Collins) and the *Lugard Diaries*, Perham Edition (Faber and Faber); *White Man's Country, Lord Delamare and the Making of Kenya*, 2 vols., by Elspeth Huxley (Chatto and Windus); *Races of Africa*, by C. G. Seligman (Oxford University Press); *Fort Jesus and the Portuguese in Mombasa*, by C. R. Boxer and Carlos de Azevedo (Hollis and Carter); *An Introduction to the History of East Africa*, by Z. A. Marsh and G. Kingsnorth (Cambridge University Press); *East Africa and its Invaders*, by Professor R. Coupland (O.U.P.); *The Exploitation of East Africa*, by Professor R. Coupland (O.U.P.); *No Easy Way* by Elspeth Huxley (*East African Standard*). *Livingstone's Africa, Yesterday and Today*, by the Rt. Hon. James Griffiths (The Epworth Press); *Freedom and After*, by the Hon. T. J. Mboya, E.G.H., M.P. (André Deutsch); *Kenya's Opportunity*, by Lord Altrincham (Faber and Faber).

GENERAL: *Facing Mt. Kenya*, (Secker and Warburg), *Suffering without Bitterness* by H.E. the President of Kenya, Jomo Kenyatta, C.G.H., M.P. (E.A. Publishing House and Heinemann); *Red Strangers, The Flame Trees of Thika* (Chatto and Windus) and other books by Elspeth Huxley; *Race and Politics in Kenya*, a correspondence, by Elspeth Huxley and Margery Perham (Faber and Faber); *African Afterthoughts*, by Sir Philip Mitchell (Hutchinson); *Nairobi, Master Plan for a Colonial Capital* (H.M.S.O.); *Report of the Royal Commission on Land and Population in East Africa* (H.M.S.O., 1955); *Annual Report of the*

Suggested Books for Further Reading

Colony (from 1946 onwards, H.M.S.O.); *Kenya Diary, 1902–6*, by Col. R. Meinertzhagen (Oliver and Boyd); *Out of Africa*, by Baroness Karen von Blixen (Chatto and Windus); *So Rough a Wind*, by Sir Michael Blundell (Weidenfeld and Nicolson); *A Knot of Roots*, by the Earl of Portsmouth (Geoffrey Bles).

WILD ANIMALS: Joy Adamson's books about Elsa the Lioness and her Cubs (Collins), also *The Spotted Sphinx* (Collins); *Animals of East Africa*, by C. T. Astley Mabery (Howard Timmins); *Big Game Shooting in Africa*, by Major H. C. Maydon (Seeley Service and Co.); *Serengeti Shall Not Die*, by Bernard and Michael Grzimek (Hamish Hamilton); *Between the Sunlight and the Thunder*, by Noel Simon (Collins); *The Animals of East Africa, an Introduction*, by C. A. Spinage (Collins); *Fly Vulture*, by Mervyn Cowie (Harrap); *No Room in the Ark*, by Alan Moorehead (Cassell); *Life with Daktari*, by Suzanne Hart (Geoffrey Bles and Collins); *Leopard in my Lap* (W. H. Allen and Sphere) and other books by Michaela Denis.

Index

Index

Index